A

# ROVER

*January 1885 Rover*

*1889/90 Rational Rover*

*J K Starley IV & younger son*

# A HISTORY OF
# ROVER CYCLES

John Pinkerton
Derek Roberts

Additional chapter by Tony Hadland
Foreword by Andrew Millward

Published in 1998 by Dorothy Pinkerton, 522 Holly Lane, Erdington, Birmingham B24 9LY.


**British Library Cataloguing-in-Publication Data**
A catalogue record for this book is available from the British Library.

ISBN 09507431 9 4

Printed by
Quorum Technical Services Ltd, Cheltenham

Other Books by the Authors
John Pinkerton
    At Your Service - A look at Carrier Cycles
    Guide to The Pinkerton Cycle Collection
and with Tony Hadland
    It's in the Bag! - A history in outline of portable cycles in the UK
and with Derek Roberts
    Sunbeam Cycles Vol I, Vol II and Vol III - the Story from the Catalogues

Derek Roberts
    The Invention of Bicycles and Motorcycles
    This Veteran Business
    Cycling History - Myths and Queries
    Pierre Michaux and His Sons (translation)

*J. K. Starley*


**"The Rover has set the fashion to the world."**
*The Cyclist*

*1890 Rover and 1998 Land Rover APB.*
*Meriden, centre of England, and 10 miles from Coventry,*
*the birthplace of Rover Cycles.*

# CONTENTS

# FOREWORD

It was an honour to be asked to write the foreword for this book for two reasons. Firstly I have considerable admiration and respect for the two authors as researchers and writers as well as their wider contribution to cycling and the veteran-cycle movement. Secondly I know that this is a work that has been a long time in gestation and has been long awaited by a large number of people who have heard about it. Indeed as a relatively new member of the Veteran-Cycle Club I heard that a book on Rover cycles was being considered by the authors during the time I took part in the Rover Centenary Ride (sponsored by Rover and Pirelli) over the weekend of 27th and 28th September 1985. This involved a 100-mile ride from Peterborough to Birmingham with members of the Veteran-Cycle Club, Rover car enthusiasts and interested individuals all taking part.

For those who are sceptical of the value of looking into cycles and their history it is worth noting that one of the interested individuals on that 1985 ride was Mike Burrows, the inventor of the Lotus Super-Bike. He later credited his single-blade fork design to a Victorian machine he had seen on that ride in the Bartleet collection of cycles during a stop over at the Museum of British Road Transport in Coventry. Looking at the evolution of cycles which is charted in this book one cannot fail to recognise the ingenuity and inventiveness of the pioneers of the modern cycle. The "Ordinary" bicycle and the tricycle ultimately gave way to the rear-driven chain-driven "safety" of which the Rover design was to set the "fashion to the world". However, as the book shows, this transition was gradual and the authors chart this process in absorbing detail.

The veteran-cycle enthusiast will find a considerable wealth of material which will assist many a restoration project, and help to identify unknown components and models of a particular machine. It should not be forgotten that the material for this book has had to be gathered from a range of diverse sources and this owes a great deal to the tenacity of the authors in assembling the collection of catalogues prior to writing the book. As one involved with archives I cannot help but emphasise the need to support archival projects which preserve and gather original source material for the benefit of future generations of researchers.

The authors have not taken an uncritical approach to the use of catalogues, and other sources of information, such as patent abridgements, inform the main text. In the authors' comments the general reader can appreciate a number of themes which transcend the interests of veteran-cycle enthusiasts. One cannot help noticing what an important part was played by the family firm in the cycle industry; the Starley family provided a number of important contributions to cycle design through two generations. There is also in the story of the Rover bicycle further confirmation that initial innovative success does not automatically translate into long-term dominance of an industry; this was Rover's experience in respect of cycle production. However, the book does remind us that cycles formed the basis of the Rover company which today is a major part of the UK motor industry.

As someone who has studied the economic and business aspects of the cycle trade in the period up to 1939 I hope that there are no objections to my making some general observations which may place the development of Rover cycles over 40 years into this context. It should come as no surprise that an innovative company such as Rover in the 1890s would have entered motor-car production, but economic logic also played its part. Once the design of the bicycle began to stabilise, others could equally reap the benefits through specialisation and improved production methods. The pressure of international competition, which became apparent by the 1890s, and the declining interest in the high-priced and high-quality machines after the mid-1890s "Society Boom" was over, contributed to lower margins on cycles and made their production less remunerative. Many of the innovations shown in this book, such as Rover's introduction of lighter machines, variable gears, frame configurations and even chainless machines were really the company's response to the changed market conditions. Eventually Rover ceased cycle manufacture and, when interest in making cycles revived some years later, the company relied on bought-in machines. Nearly 40 years after the innovative "safety" bicycle had been introduced Rover had long ceased to set the fashion to the world in the cycle industry. When Rover finally abandoned cycle manufacture altogether (something which many other pioneer companies such as Humber, Singer and Swift also did) they did so only a few years in advance of the appearance of a mass market in cycles which emerged in the 1930s from working-class buyers. It was left to other companies to capitalise on this new market, such as Hercules in Birmingham and Raleigh in Nottingham. However, Rover's subsequent success in the sphere of motoring means that today the association with cars has now supplanted the cycle in the public mind, but the link with cycles is not over. As the authors point out the name "Rover" has been recently resurrected for a new range of ATBs.

This book will fit well alongside the authors' earlier work on Sunbeam Cycles and will provide a useful starting point, if not a model, for analysis of other companies. I hope that you find this a useful book, a book which I have no hesitation in recommending to you.


Andrew Millward
Originator and Secretary of The National Cycle Archive
    Modern Record Centre, University of Warwick
Chairman of Cycle Touring and Countryside Commission

*Above: New Light Rover Safety c1888.*
*Below: c 1895, three Rovers, riders and their charges.*

## Rover tricycle 1884 chain guard transfer

On the chain-guard of Ron Miller's Rover tricycle, found in Canada c1989, were remnants of a transfer.

Catherine Strung (Ontario) produced a pencil drawing interpretation of it, and with the help of Nicholas Oddy (Edinburgh) the illustration opposite was developed.

Extensive research has not shown any evidence that it was registered as a trade mark or design.

# Preface

As in most of our other books, much of the material in this volume has been obtained from the firm's catalogues, although we have supplemented that information whenever possible. Catalogues are valuable for showing what a firm was offering for sale to the public but they cannot cover all the ground; they sometimes omit machines and they sometimes present "new" models that have been on sale for months before the catalogues are published.

This work is divided into six parts. The first deals generally with the affairs of John Kemp Starley and the firm. The second deals with the firm's production of bicycles and tricycles from 1878 to 1884. The third deals with the safety bicycles built from 1885 to 1899. The fourth deals separately with each range of bicycles from 1900 and miscellaneous items such as gears, brakes, accessories etc. The fifth deals with all other cycles built from 1885 onwards. The sixth and final part deals with the Land Rover cycles introduced in the 1990s, and has been written by Tony Hadland.

*****************************

The design of the first Rover safety bicycle will be familiar to many. It has frequently appeared in articles and books, notably in H.W. Bartleet's *Bartleet's Bicycle Book,* on plate 29. But the first version (Fig. 1), which was used in the 1885 Starley and Sutton catalogue and in an advertisement in *The CTC Gazette* for April 1885, shows some differences from the well-known one. This photograph, which was found among Bartleet's papers, was probably of the 1885 show model.

*****************************

We do not claim that this is a definitive work, and we hope that anyone who can add to the information contained in it or correct any mistake will do so.

**John Pinkerton**            **Derek Roberts**

November 1998

# PART 1 - GENERAL

## Rover Cycles

John Kemp Starley was born in December 1854. He was the son of John Starley, elder brother of the famous James Starley whose peers honoured him with the title Father of the Cycle Industry (sometimes misquoted as the Father of the Bicycle). When John Kemp was 17 he followed his uncle to Coventry and worked with him for some time. It is generally accepted that he was employed by Starley Brothers, and there is little doubt that his last wage-earning days were with Haynes and Jefferis (who produced the *Ariel*, *Swiftsure* and *Tangent* bicycles and the *Coventry Lever* and *Rotary* tricycles). He left that firm in 1877 or 1878 and set up in business on his own in the latter year. In 1879 he formed a partnership with William Sutton, a Coventry haberdasher who was an enthusiastic cyclist and willing to risk his money in what seemed a growing industry. The firm of Starley and Sutton built a variety of bicycles and tricycles. Accurate information on the early years is difficult to obtain; the earliest catalogue we have found is for 1884. Contemporary references to the firm and its products are few, and do not always agree. According to H.B. Light, of the Technical Services Department of the Rover Company, Sutton left the firm in 1886 and was killed soon afterwards in a trap accident. After a short period of solo trading John formed J.K. Starley and Co. Ltd, with himself as managing director, in September 1888. By that time the *Rover* safety bicycle was firmly established as the bicycle that had, in the words of the weekly paper *The Cyclist,* set the fashion to the world. Not that that verdict was accepted by Starley's rivals – especially by those who were building cross-frame bicycles.

*Fig. 1 The Original Rover*

13

The Rover Cycle Co. was formed in 1896. We have not been able to establish the month, but a handwritten copy of details taken from a notebook by Mr Greenway, Secretary (presumably Rover), said "In June 1896 the business was converted into a public liability company entitled The Rover Cycle Co. Ltd with Sir Frederick D. Dixon Hartland as Chairman." This June date is included in an undated publication "A Selection of Memorable Dates in the History of the Rover Company". No author is given but it seems probable that it was prepared by H. B. Light (the Rover historian) or his staff before "The Rover Story" was published in *Rover News* in 26 monthly chapters from January 1961 to March 1963. The new company filed its return on 5 November 1896, when the £150,000 in £1 shares was taken up.

In 1898 the factory (known as the Meteor Works) moved from West Orchard, Coventry, to purpose-built premises in Queen Victoria Road, Coventry. Starley had not fallen victim to the expansion fever during the Society Boom of the mid and late nineties, and his was one of the few firms to escape unscathed. He offered to mount a cycle corps of 250 soldiers for the Boer War but his offer was refused. On 29 October 1901 John Kemp Starley, founder and managing director of the company, died suddenly leaving a widow and nine children. In an obituary in *The CTC Gazette* Ernest Shipton described him as one of nature's gentlemen and questioned whether he possessed a single enemy. "He was gentle and unassuming to a degree, and the welfare of those dependent upon him was always one of his first considerations. A good and ardent sportsman, he yet was studious and thoughtful in temperament, and he held strong but sympathetically broad religious views in which . . . 'justification by works loomed large'." He published his own bible in which the New Testament preceded the Old, arguing that as the gospels and epistles were the messages to the Christian church they should be read first. Copies of what is sometimes called the Starley Bible are now rare.

On Starley's death Harry Smith took over as managing director and held that office until he retired on health grounds in 1923; Frank Ward was appointed secretary to the company and retired from the board in 1953 after completing 64 years' unbroken service. When Starley died the Rover Cycle Co. was manufacturing cycles only, and had a reputation for first-class workmanship. The *Rover* racing bicycles were used then and later by some of the foremost cyclists on road and track - men such as W.J. Bailey, Leon Meredith, Vic Johnson, Platt-Betts and A.L. Reed. In the 1908 season the *Imperial Rover Racer* won all the principal handicaps, scratch races and championships; at the Olympic Games held in London every solo-bicycle race decided was won on a Rover. In 1909, for the fifth year in succession, the *Rover* bicycle secured the 100-kilometres title at the Copenhagen world's championships - a distinction claimed for no other bicycle. Rovers held the 1000-miles road record, the North Road 24-hours record, the Brighton-and-back record and the $1/4$-mile standing-start world record. In 1910 W.J. Bailey won the world's championship in Brussels and the Grand Prix de Paris - on his *Rover*.

In 1902 the company introduced the Imperial Rover motorcycle, and on 25 October 1905 the company name became the Rover Co. Ltd. In June 1912 a separate company, the New Rover Cycle Co. Ltd, was formed to control the manufacture of cycles and motorcycles. But in 1904 the first Rover motorcar had been produced, and by the 1920s car production had increased so much that the manufacture of cycles became much less important. In December 1923 the New Rover Cycle Co. Ltd became part of the Rover Co. Ltd.

At a company meeting on 26 February 1925 it was resolved that existing stocks should be completed and that manufacture of cycles and motorcycles should then be ended, as the firm was unable to trade profitably. There had been a post-war boom which had ended abruptly in the winter of 1920-21. Government spending was slashed, taxes rose steeply, Europe was in political turmoil and its exchanges in chaos. Unemployment rose sharply to over two million. The mines and railways, run efficiently during the war by government, were handed back to incompetent private owners. A lockout in the mines heralded a general lowering of working-class standards of living that led to the general strike of 1926. There was little spare money around for the purchase of high-class cycles, except of course among those whose incomes were little affected by a collapsing economy.

The *Rover* bicycle had set the fashion to the world but like its designer it did not reach its fiftieth birthday.

Mr. John Kemp Starley, the introducer of the "Rover" Bicycle, the pioneer of the present-day cycle, and "Rover Cob" - the first of its kind.

# Trade-marks and badges

This section appears before the detailed descriptions of the cycles as it may help owners to date their models.

The Rover (and previous) trade-marks varied during the period of cycle production. We may not be able to show all that were used but here are the versions we do have; as ever we should be pleased to receive any further information.

1884 *Rover* Tricycle. The badge clearly states The Meteor but both catalogue and remnants of transfer on the chainguard indicate *Rover*.

1884
Rover Tricycle
Chain-guard transfer.

1885 (late) *Rover Safety*.

1888  *Rover*  [J K Starley & Co. late Starley & Sutton].

1894 Detail from 1894 *Cyclist Year Book*. One badge of this pattern has been seen with the word Limited in small type at the right-hand end of the line below J K Starley & Co.

16

1896  *Rover* [Rover Cycle Co. Ltd. 1896 cat.].

1899  *Imperial* and *Meteor* (above).

1901

In 1903 the *Imperial Rover* had been surmounted by a crown which was apparently based on the royal crown of England rather than the imperial crown of state.

The firm's name changed to The Rover Co. Ltd on 25 October 1905.

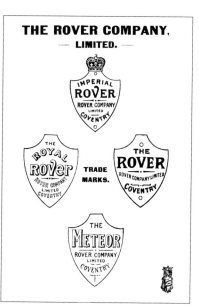

In 1906 the *Royal Rover* badge was shown in the catalogue. This was the first time it appeared, although the *Royal* range had been introduced in 1904. Whether the 1904 and 1905 *Royals* bore the plain Rover badge, or whether the *Royal* badge was in use but not shown in the catalogue, is as yet unknown.

The 1909 catalogue illustrated the *Imperial*, *Royal* and *Rover* badges with the word **THE** above ROVER COMPANY LIMITED.

1911 A new badge appeared on the catalogue but may not have been used on the cycles.

1912. The badge was changed again on the catalogue.

18

1912. At the June AGM the name was changed to The New Rover Cycle Co. Ltd. This appeared in transfer form (copies in Pinkerton Cycle Collection Archive) but to date no metal badge has been found.

In 1923 (December AGM) the name reverted to The Rover Co. Ltd.

After this date Rover sold machines manufactured by someone else. At least four of these still exist but they use at least two different badges (shown here).

1925 The catalogue showed a badge which differs from any metal badge found.

The March 1925 *CTC Gazette* Rover advertisement used the Viking's head. A standing Viking motor car mascot was introduced in 1913 and replaced by the Viking head only in 1928.

Some additional trade marks, which were registered but do not appear to have been much used, are shown in Appendix 3.

# PART 2 - BICYCLES AND TRICYCLES

## 1878 - 1884

The first products of Starley and Sutton were the *Meteor* bicycle and the *Meteor*, *Compressus* and *Tom Tit* tricycles. The *Meteor* tricycle was hailed by the cycling press as revolutionary. A few years later *The Tricyclist* said, "It will be remembered by those of our readers who have had a lengthy experience of tricycling that Messrs Starley and Sutton were the first firm to introduce the well-known *Meteor* pattern of tricycle which, although now almost entirely superseded by the balance-geared machines, was, at the time of its introduction, a fair march ahead of any of its contempories." As will be seen in Fig. 2, the *Meteor* had a "hayfork" frame. The model tested by the staff of *The Cyclist* had a 27" tube running back from the centre of a semicircular tube, the ends of which dropped perpendicularly to near the ground. Those ends supported bearings in which was housed a double-crank pedal-rod, adjustable for a couple of inches by nuts and bolts. In the downward bends of the tubes were projecting pins that formed axles for 40" wheels with crescent rims, 7/8" rubber tyres and "a full number of strong, well-fitted spokes on the 'safety direct' principle". The right-hand wheel was chain-driven, the machine being geared-up to 50". (This right-hand drive was unusual, most single-drivers having the nearside wheel driven. This is still common practice, adopted to counteract the tendency of a tricycle to veer to the left under the influence of the road camber). The rack-and-pinion steering was operated by the right-hand handle and the brake was operated by or from the left one. In the illustration it is clear that a brake on the 22" steering-wheel was applied by pushing the handle forward; the machine tested apparently had a different system. There was a straight upright rod from the frame and a handle projected

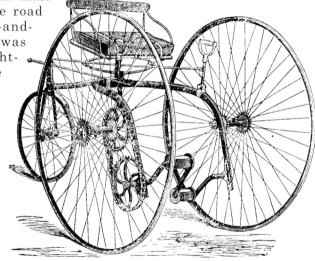

*Fig. 2   The Meteor*

forward at right angles. A few inches below that there was a lever that was connected to the brake-rod. The tricycle weighed from 60 to 70 pounds and cost £16 16s. It is ironical that nowadays this type of machine with a hayfork frame is usually called Cheylesmore-pattern, after the version produced by the Coventry Machinists' Co. Starley's contempororaries knew where credit was due.

The *Compressus* and *Tom Tit* tricycles throw an interesting light on the close co-operation among the Starley family. John Marshall Starley, with his brothers James and William, ran the firm of Starley Brothers, who used Psycho as a trade-mark - their father James was in overall charge. On 16 November 1878 John Marshall Starley and John Kemp Starley were granted patent 4657 which covered a front-steering quadricycle, a front-driving tricycle, detachable wheels, and folding and seating arrangements. Starley Brothers apparently never used the patent; Starley and Sutton almost immediately produced first the *Compressus* and then the *Tom Tit*. (The inevitable question is whether James Starley senior inspired the patent. He always claimed to have invented the *Coventry Lever* tricycle, and no-one has ever queried his claim; his monument in Coventry testifies to it. Yet the patent for that tricycle was granted to his son James and his nephew John Kemp. Did he perhaps work out what was needed for the new tricycle and then tell the young men to add the finishing touches and apply for a patent? Bearing in mind what his contemporaries thought of his achievements this seems highly probable.)

Two of the drawings in the patent application are shown in Fig. 3. As was pointed out in *The Cyclist* for 20 February 1901, "if it was not the first time that a small driving-wheel geared-up by a chain and worked by ordinary bicycle cranks and pedals was patented, it was very near it, and, unlike a number of drawings which repose in the Patent Ofice, it was practically used immediately the patent was taken out, and has been in use ever since, as, of course, to all intents and purposes, it is precisely the same as the drive on a modern bicycle, although only a single fork was used at first." This device of using a single stay with a stub axle seems to have been first used by James Starley and copied by a few makers. It was resuscitated towards the end of the twentieth century by a few makers, notably by Mike Burrows in his racing bicycles and recumbent tricycles.

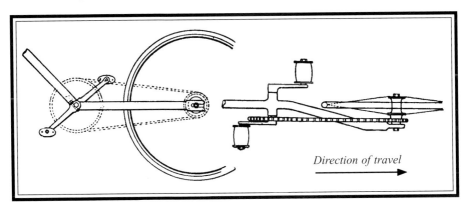

*Direction of travel*

*Fig. 3*

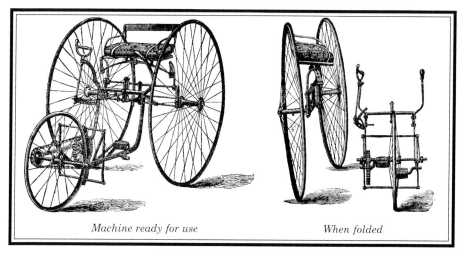

Machine ready for use                    When folded

Fig. 4   The Compressus

The first *Compressus,* (see Fig. 4) was a failure. The space-saving idea was good but it was handicapped by cumbersome framework and large (48") rear wheels. Another fault was that the steering-handle was so close to the spokes that the little finger of the right hand was in constant danger of being badly damaged. *Cycling* reviewed the tricycle in June 1879 - there is no mention of a road-test - and reported favourably but gave few details. The weight was probably over 70 pounds.

The *Tom Tit,* introduced shortly after the *Compressus,* was simpler and smaller, with 18" rear wheels and a 24" driving-wheel geared-up to 48". As in the *Compressus* the driving-gear was detachable; but the frame was rigid. In 1901 *The Cyclist* said that it was "unquestionably the lightest and fastest tricycle of the day, as it was between 20 and 40 lb lighter than any other machine of that era. Its one objection was its tricky steering . . . effected by a pinion and rack, the pinion being turned by a small twisting handle which put a great strain on the wrist on uneven roads, and it was impossible to let the steering go for the fraction of a second, as if one did the machine instantly described a circle . . . Had the *Tom Tit* been fitted with proper design of steering it would have been an even greater success than it was."

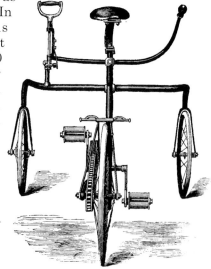

Fig. 5   *Tom Tit introduced about 1880*

22

In June 1880 *Cycling* reviewed the *Compressus* No. 2; the writer said that one in his service was a great favourite. As can be seen, the design had been simplified and the wheels seem to have been reduced to about 40". The weight solo was 65 pounds. There is a tantalising remark that both No. 1 and No. 2 could be obtained as sociables but not a word on how they were driven. What is now clear is that they must have been failures, for they do not appear to have been referred to in the cycling press or the annual reviews of the cycles available. At the 1882 Stanley Show Starley and Sutton had no exhibit, but BSA's *Compressible* tricycle received favourable comment. There was apparently still a need for saving space.

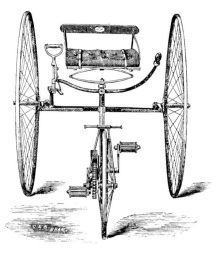

*Fig. 6   Compressus No. 2*

Henry Sturmey's 1879 *Indispensable Bicyclist's Handbook and Guide to Bicycling* listed three bicycles made by Starley and Sutton: the *Meteor Safety,* the *Meteor No. 2* and the *Racer*. The first was so named because it had Starley's "safety" wheels. These were ordinary direct-spoked wheels but the each flange had holes drilled through it at right angles. These holes were fitted with plugs, and the spoke-holes were drilled to pass through the plugs. The threads for the spokes were only in the plugs, the idea being that should the spoke snap at the thread and a part remain in the hub, the broken portion was easily removed by unscrewing the projecting broken end. The specification of the *Meteor Safety* was as follows:

> "⁷/₈" and ³/₄" red rubber tyres on steel crescent rims, detachable cranks, rubber dust-proof pedals, Starley's detachable bearings, Starley's reciprocating head, bone handles, steel backbone, bolted sliding-spring, suspension saddle, Starley's thumb-brake and leg-guard."

The reciprocating head had the usual centres replaced by half balls working in sockets, the upper one adjusted by a set-screw. This was screwed to the front side of a circular metal plug pivoted to a socket at the top of the head. The plug had an 8" handle which rested on the right-hand side of the handlebar. When the handle was swung round to the left-hand side of the bar the upper socket was brought from the front of the head to the back, a distance of about 2"; that made a difference of 5" or 6" in the bicycle's rake and added greatly to the rider's safety when descending hills.

STARLEY'S RECIPROCATING HEAD.

*Fig. 7*

The detachable bearings were described by Sturmey as follows: "Starley's Frictionless Rollers are to my mind a long way in advance of anything of the kind ever introduced before. The axle is provided with a wide steel collar turned upon it, and the case also has the centre diameter much less than at the sides. The rollers used are of two kinds and sixteen are employed for each bearing. The first are long and narrow and have ends nearly twice the diameter of their central shaft, thus resembling Sibert's 'dumb-bell' flat-sided rollers. These run (on the axle itself) on their ends and they touch the outer box, though not the collar on the axle, with their central shafts, and between them are placed shorter rollers of the ordinary shape, which touch the inner surfaces of both axle-collar and case. By this method the friction of the rollers against each other is not only done away with (the ends of the longer rollers being just kept from contact with each other by the insertion of the shorter ones) but the motion imparted to each roller by the axle is actually passed on to the next for the intermediate one, and, besides this, by using such a large diameter of roller to work upon the axle, the friction there is reduced to about one half." A reviewer in *The Cyclist* said that no visible wear could be detected after 3000 miles.

Sturmey described Starley's Thumb Lever Brake as follows: "In this the lever is placed as usual in front of the head, and the top provided with a vertical slot, whilst a straight bar is fixed in front of the handle, working in a long horizontal socket secured to it and provided at the handle end with a thumb-piece, and at the other with an arm or crank working in the slot before-mentioned. By pushing the thumb-piece forward the arm applies the brake. It is neater, and vastly superior to the common thumb, and by contact with the handle much of the strain does not reach the thumb." The *Meteor Safety* was obtainable in 2" steps from 44" to 58", prices rising from £13 by 10s a time to £16 10s; it weighed 42 pounds. Special finishes were all-bright for £1 and plated for £6; Starley's frictionless roller-bearings cost £7.

The *Meteor No. 2* had $7/8$" and $5/8$" red rubber tyres, crescent rims, direct wheel spokes, steel hubs, detachable cranks, dust-proof rubber pedals, open head, bone handles, steel backbone, bolted sliding-spring, suspension saddle, saw step, Starley's thumb-brake and leg-guard. The same sizes were obtainable but prices ran from £12 10s to £16; extras were all-bright for £1 and roller bearings for £2. Sturmey said that the *Meteor Safety* was a new introduction with numerous novelties, well and strongly made with a good finish; the *No. 2* was equal to the *No. 1* (i.e. the *Safety*) but without the improvements; it weighed 38 pounds.

The *Racer* had $3/4$" and $5/8$" red rubber tyres, crescent rims, direct spokes, solid steel hubs, slotted detachable cranks, Starley oscillating pedals, Starley's frictionless roller bearings to front, cones to back, hollow forks, open head, bone handles, steel backbone and bolted sliding-spring. The same sizes were again available but prices ranged from £14 10s for a 44" to £18 for a 58"; it weighed 28 pounds. The oscillating pedals were constructed with two roughened footplates pivoted centrally on each side of the pedal-barrel; they were fitted with two pins on each side which united the two faces and caused them to work together, while four springs pressed against the pins to keep them in position. This arrangement provided a little play that allowed for the natural twist of the foot when describing the driving-circle and so lessened the friction a little.

In the 1880 *Indispensable* the *Racer* had disappeared and the *Meteor Safety* had become the *Meteor No. 1* with the following specification:

"⁷/₈" and ³/₄" red rubber, crescent rims, 60 12-gauge spokes to front wheel, Starley's safety hubs with 6" dish, detachable cranks, plain rubber pedals, parallel bearings to front and long cones to back wheel, iron bayonet forks, open head, double-lever spoon-brake, 1 ³/₄" steel backbone, bolted shackle-spring, suspension saddle and saw step; it weighed 40 pounds."

Prices ranged from £13 for a 46" to £15 10s for a 56". Extras were hollow forks at 15s, ball-bearings at £1, Starley's frictionless rollers at 42s and new handles (not described) at 10s and 15s.

The *Meteor No. 2* had much the same specification but with a Humber head and a bolted sliding-spring; weight and prices were the same. (It will be noticed that, as before, only one weight was given for each model, although it seems unlikely that a 44" would have weighed the same as a 56"!)

In his introduction to the Coventry section of his 1881 *Indispensable* Sturmey wrote, "Messrs Starley and Sutton are the only firm who have left the ranks

*Fig. 8 Meteor No. 1*

of the bicycle makers, they having their hands more than full with the tricycular branch of the wheel trade." How long this concentration on tricycles lasted we have not been able to discover. Neither Sturmey nor H.H. Griffin listed the *Meteor* among the bicycles of 1882 but it seems likely that both *No. 1* and *No. 2* returned in 1883, for in the 1884 *Meteor* catalogue the description of the *No. 2* said, "This Bicycle (the best value in the world) is now so thoroughly well-known and appreciated, that it needs little comment. Stock patterns are now constructed upon the interchangeable system." The specification of the *Meteor No. 2* was:

"Direct spokes in gun-metal hubs, adjustable double ball-bearings to front and adjustable cones to back, $7/8$" red moulded front tyre, $3/4$" ditto back, japanned black and yellow or black and red."

Only 48", 50", 52", 54" and 56" were made, and the price was £12. Extras were all-bright (except rims) £1, bright parts nickel-plated (excluding rims) £1 5s, nickel-plating all over (except rims) 50s, and ball-bearings to back wheel £1. Lining in enamel was 5s, in gold 10s.

Few details of the *No. 1* were given; it was fitted with patent adjustable ball-bearings to both wheels, and prices ranged from £16 for a 48" to £19 for a 60". The finish was black; lining in enamel cost 7s 6d, in gold 15s. Presumably a customer could have asked for burnishing or plating (except, of course, of the rims).

The *Racer* reappeared, with compact close head, hollow front and back forks made of patent weldless steel tubing, rat-trap or ball pedals and ball-bearings to both wheels, and $3/4$" and $1/2$" U-section rims. The prices were "from £17".

# 1884

On 22 February 1884 *The Tricyclist* said, "Starley and Sutton are to the fore with a score of finely-built tricycles of several patterns. Here are a couple of the well-known *Meteor Sociables,* one being most handsome in a glittering coat of nickel plate. Here also are a large number of the newly introduced *Rovers,* as well as children's machines. We also note Starley and Sutton are the first to follow the lead of the Zephyr Tricycle Co. in using an extended wheel-base, the two samples of the *Meteor No. 2* (40" ladies' machines, weighing 70 to 75 pounds) being thus constructed, and we are pleased to note that this is to be the principle on which the *No. 2* is to be constructed for 1884."

Fig. 9

The name *Rover* was first used by the firm in 1884. J.W. Whitehouse of Birmingham had listed a *Rover* bicycle in 1880-1 but not subsequently. Starley produced the *Rover Tricycle* (Fig. 9) "specially constructed for gentlemen requiring a light machine with vertical or bicycle position." On pages 28 to 34 are shown other tricycles and bicycles offered in 1884.

*Ron Miller's 1884 Rover Tricycle. Restoration almost complete.*

# THE "ROYAL METEOR" TRICYCLE, No. 1

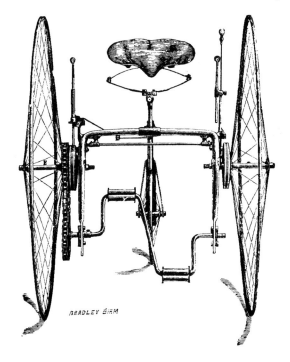

Fitted with a new adjustable band brake, adjustable handles, horn handles and plated hubs, handle brackets, seat and steering rod, new seat-rod adjustment (exceedingly simple), new triangular roller bearing pedals, &c.; ordinary width, 3 feet 3 inches, can be made narrower to order; by unscrewing the foot-rest or cap-nut the side wheel can be taken off, when the machine will pass through a doorway 2 feet 6 inches wide—a very great desideratum.

### PRICES :

|  | | | £ | s. | d. |
|---|---|---|---|---|---|
| **40 inch Wheels** | ... | ... | 17 | 0 | 0 |
| **44 inch Wheels** | ... | ... | 17 | 10 | 0 |
| **48 inch Wheels** | ... | ... | 18 | 0 | 0 |

*BALL BEARINGS TO ALL WHEELS AND CRANK SHAFT, £3 EXTRA.* B. B, pedals, 35s. extra. Enamelled black ground with coloured lines. 12s. 6d. extra. Enamelled black-ground, gold lines, 25s. extra. Plated all over, £8 extra.

*Crates for the above Machines, 4s., not returnable*

*Fig. 10*

# THE "ROYAL METEOR," No. 2,

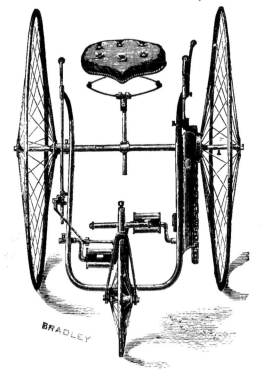

## FRONT STEERER AND DOUBLE DRIVER.

Fitted with Starley's patent automatic balance gear, patent Weldless Steel Tube framework, adjustable double band brake, adjustable handles, plated hubs, handle brackets, seat and steering rod, red moulded tyres, horn handles, new triangular roller bearing pedals, &c. Particularly recommended for rough or hilly work, and its great safety in descending hills.

### PRICES:

*With Ball Bearings to all Wheels.*

| | | | | | | |
|---|---|---|---|---|---|---|
| **40 inch** | ... | ... | ... | ... | **£21** | **0** | **0** |
| **46 inch** | ... | ... | ... | ... | **£21** | **10** | **0** |
| **50 inch** | ... | ... | ... | ... | **£22** | **0** | **0** |

B.B. cranks, 15s. ; Ditto pedals, 35s. Plated all over, £10 extra. Enamelled Black ground, coloured lines. 12s. 6d. extra. Enamelled Black ground, gold lines, 25s. extra.

*Crates for the above Machine, 4s., not returnable.*

Extreme width of Machine, 3 feet 3 inches.

Can be fitted with Seat or Saddle, as preferred. Specify when ordering.

*Fig. 11*

29

# METEOR SOCIABLE

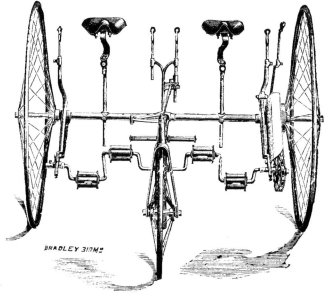

BRADLEY 3/?M?

### PRICE:

*With Ball Bearings to all Wheels.*

| | | | | | |
|---|---|---|---|---|---|
| **40 inch** | ... | ... | ... | ... | **£27 10 0** |
| **46 inch** | ... | ... | ... | ... | **£28 0 0** |

Ball Bearings to Cranks, extra, £1 10s. ; Ditto to Pedals, extra, £3 10s. Enamelled Black-ground, coloured lines, 15s. extra. Enamelled Black-ground, gold lines, 30s. extra.

Fitted with Starley's patent automatic double driving gear, handles adjustable independently of seat, powerful band brake, 1 inch red moulded rubber tyres, new triangular roller bearing pedals.

The 40-inch Meteor Sociable can, with ease, be got into an ordinary guard's van, of any train ; the only Sociable made that can do so. A great advantage to Tourists.

Extreme width of Machine, 5 feet 3 inches.

Can be fitted with seat or saddle, as preferred. Specify when ordering.

*Crates charged 20s., and are returnable.*

*Fig. 12*

# THE YOUTH'S "METEOR"

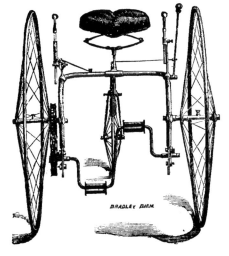

## A THOROUGH RELIABLE MACHINE.

Made on the same lines, and of the same materials as the ordinary "Meteor," with new pan seat, rubber pedals, adjustable handles and seat-rod, efficient double brake, light, yet very strong, and will be found suitable for youths from 10 to 20 years of age ; or for ladies or gentlemen of small size and light weight.

### PRICE:

**36 inch Wheels** ... ... **£10 0 0**

Enamelled Black-ground, coloured lines, 7s. 6d. extra.    Enamelled Black-ground gold lines, 15s. extra.    Half-plated, £3 extra.    Plated all over, £8 extra.

*Crates for the above Machine, 3s. 6d., not returnable.*

SADDLE OR SEAT AS REQUIRED.

*Fig. 13*

31

# The Child's "Meteor."

Made on the same lines, and with the same care, as the ordinary "Meteor"; fitted with an efficient hind-wheel brake, adjustable handles, rubber pedals, pan seat (light and strong), and suitable for children from 4 to 10 years of age.

## PRICE:

**30inch Wheel** ... ... ... ... **£6 6s.**

Half-plated, £2 extra ; plated all over, £6 extra ; enamelled black ground, coloured lined, 5s. extra ; enamelled black ground, gold lines, 10s. extra.

SADDLE OR SEAT AS REQUIRED.

*Crates for the above Machines, 2/6, not returnable.*

*Fig. 14*

32

# THE
# "METEOR" BICYCLE

Each Machine is fitted with Patent Adjustable Ball Bearings to both Wheels.

---

## PRICES :

*Elegantly painted and fitted with front wheel brake.*

|  | | | | £ | s. | d. |
|---|---|---|---|---|---|---|
| **48 inch** | ... | ... | ... | ... | **16** | **0** | **0** |
| **50 inch** | ... | ... | .. | ... | **16** | **10** | **0** |
| **52 inch** | ... | ... | ... | ... | **17** | **0** | **0** |
| **54 inch** | ... | ... | ... | ... | **17** | **10** | **0** |
| **56 inch** | ... | ... | .. | .. | **18** | **0** | **0** |
| **58 inch** | ... | ... | ... | ... | **18** | **10** | **0** |
| **60 inch** | ... | ... | ... | ... | **19** | **0** | **0** |

Enamelled Black-ground, lined colours, 7s. 6d. extra. Enamelled Black-ground, lined gold, 15s. extra.

*Crates charged 2s. 6d., not returnable.*

*Fig. 15*

# "METEOR" BICYCLE NO. 2.

This Bicycle (the best value in the market) is now so thoroughly well-known and appreciated, that it needs little comment. Stock patterns are now constructed upon the interchangeable system.

STANDARD PATTERNS :—Direct spokes in gun metal hubs. adjustable double ball bearings to front wheel, adjustable cones to back, ⅞ red moulded tyres, front ; ¾ in. ditto back. Elegantly japanned, black and yellow, or black and red ; best hogskin saddle.

**Price : £12 0s. 0d.**   Sizes 48, 50, 52, 54, 56.   No other sizes made.

### EXTRAS.

|  |  |  | £ | s. | d. |
|---|---|---|---|---|---|
| All bright except felloes ... ... ... ... | | | 1 | 0 | 0 |
| Nickel Plating, ordinary, bright parts ... ... | | | 1 | 5 | 0 |
| ,, ,, all over, except felloes ... ... | | | 2 | 10 | 0 |
| Ball Bearings to hind wheel ... ... ... | | | 1 | 0 | 0 |
| Harrington's Enamel, coloured lines, 5s ; in gold, 10s. | | | | | |

# THE "METEOR" RACER.

This Machine is fitted with very neat compact close head, hollow front and back forks, made of patent weldless steel tube ; rat-trap, or, if required, ball pedals, ball bearings to both wheels, ¾ and ½ inch U felloes.

**Price, from £17.**

# BOYS' BICYCLES.

Boys' Bicycles are identical with the No. 2, with the exception of bearings, which are parallel. Tyres, ¾ in. front, ⅝ back. They are of great strength, and we have no hesitation in warranting them for any length of time for fair wear and tear.

| Length of Leg. | Size. | Price. | | |
|---|---|---|---|---|
| Inches. | In. | £ | s. | d. |
| 25 | 36 | 8 | 0 | 0 |
| 26 | 38 | 8 | 10 | 0 |
| 27 | 40 | 9 | 0 | 0 |
| 28 | 42 | 9 | 10 | 0 |
| 29 | 44 | 10 | 0 | 0 |

Enamelled Black, coloured lines, 5s. extra.   Enamelled Black, gold lines, 10s. extra.

*Crates charged 2s. 6d., not returnable.*

*Fig. 16*

Another novelty was a bathchair on a tricycle chassis. A few years earlier (the exact date is unknown) James Starley senior had invented a tricycle cab but had not been able to find anyone willing to back it financially. His nephew improved on the idea and the *Coventry Chair* was the result. Beatrix Potter, the creator of Peter Rabbit, kept a diary from 1881 to 1897. It was written in code, and was not deciphered until nearly twenty years after her death. Among the entries is one for 21 February 1885:

"I saw a most extraordinary tricycle pass today. A bath chair made of wickerwork in which reclined a smart lady, and behind, where one should push, a gentleman treadling, puffing and blowing and looking very sheepish. I wonder how anyone will make such an exhibition of themselves. How the bicycles swarm now, and yet a few years since, everyone turned round to stare at a *velocipede!*"

*Fig. 17*

# PART 3 - SAFETY BICYCLES 1885-1899

## 1885

So far this work has taken together all the models catalogued each year but from now it we shall deal first with the safety bicycles and later with their other cycles.

The year 1885 has become a landmark in cycling history, and there are frequent references to it as the year when the safety bicycle was invented. The *Rover*, the bicycle in question, is often said to be the first safety bicycle, the first diamond-framed bicycle, the first bicycle driven by chain to the rear wheel, and the first bicycle with equal-sized wheels. Unfortunately none of these statements is true. Safety bicycles of one kind or another had been around since 1878; if the *Rover* be considered diamond-framed, then the *Humber* and the *McCammon* bicycles (which preceded it) are in the same category; chain-drive to the rear wheel had been advocated in 1869 and had been used (in England) by Shearing, Shergold, Bate, McCammon, Humber, Wallis, Tabor and Pausey - and possibly by others; the wheels of the first *Rovers* were not equal-sized. J.K. Starley resented the idea that his *Rover* was simply the embodiment of safety in a bicycle, as a letter from him demonstrates:

"One would infer from the article on safeties in your last issue that the Rover and various machines of that type are the outcome of an attempt made a few years ago to construct a safety bicycle. It is astonishing to what extent the Rover is spoken of as a return to the lines of the old boneshaker, so that it is not at all to be wondered at that the Rover should be regarded as a rear-driven safety, and nothing more. We deem it our duty to at once dispel this illusion, it being very misleading. The Rover is absolutely the outcome of a determination to obtain advantage previously unknown in a bicycle. We felt confident that a large percentage of unused power could be utilised if the rider were properly placed, particularly with regard to hill-climbing. In this we were not mistaken, as the enormous success of the Rover undoubtedly proves. Being a very safe bicycle, we were induced to call it the Rover Safety, but we have never liked the name Safety, and have debated the matter on many occasions as to the advisability of dropping the word, which we usually have done in our advertisements. We freely assert that if the Rover were a 'safety' bicycle *only*, and with rear-driving *only* to recommend it, few riders would be found for such a machine."

From time to time there is an attempt to change the accepted date of the first *Rover* safety from 1885 to 1884. According to an account in *Coventry Up To Date* published in 1896 a prototype bicycle was built in 1884. A moment's thought reveals that it would have been astonishing had that not happened. But the *Patent Rover Safety Bicycle* (Fig. 18) was first shown to

the public at the Stanley Show held from 18 January to 3 February 1885, and it is customary
to date new machines with the year of
introduction. Unable to obtain a suitable
building, the Stanley Bicycle Club held
the show in a marquee erected near
Blackfriars Bridge; it was labelled The
Wheeleries. As is evident from figs. 1
and 18, the new bicycle was little like
any of its predecessors although it
unfortunately did have the indirect

Fig. 18

steering used by some of them. Despite the catalogue name, it was not
patented; there was nothing about it that was new. Although H.W. Bartleet
said in his *Bartleet's Bicycle Book* that Starley patented the *Rover's* seat-
pillar, reference to the patent (12934 of 19 July 1884) shows that a different
form of saddle-fastening was used. The indirect steering prevented the *Rover*
from realising its full potential, but its large front wheel gave it an advantage
over contemporary safeties such as the *BSA, Marvel, McCammon, Pioneer*
and *Humber*, which had small steerers. Lawson had similarly used a front
wheel larger than the rear in his second safety bicycle, the *Bicyclette*, but
that was not only a much clumsier machine but was also marketed before
the public were ready for it - fatal to any invention. The report of *The
Tricyclist* for 13 February 1885 on the Stanley show commented on "the
Rover safety, for which we suggest the zoological title 'The Camel'." This was
scarcely original, for that name had been given to the Singer *'Xtraordinary
Challenge* some six or seven years previously, and the reporter's suggestion
was not adopted by press or public.

The *Rover* had a 36" front and a 30" rear wheel, and was geared to 50".
Ball-bearings were fitted to wheels, cranks and pedals, and the handlebar
could be adapted to twist sideways for storage. It weighed 45 pounds. The
price was later dropped from £22 to £20, with the twisting bar £1 extra. The
first *Rover* sold was bought by C.W. Lee, 32 Henrietta Street, Covent Garden.
According to Bartleet it was a few weeks later that Stephen Golder, a clerk
in the Coventry offices of Iliffe and Son (publishers of *The Cyclist*) suggested
that the indirect steering should be scrapped.
This was done and what is generally accepted
as the second version (although as we have
seen it was actually the fourth – see
Fig. 20) appeared.

The direct steering was not the
only change; the drive was moved to
the offside. And here we come up
against the difficulties involved in
discussing the 1885-7 *Rover* safeties:
lack of precise information. This
model (Fig. 20) did not appear in any

Fig. 19

37

# The "Rover" Safety

─── NOW HOLDS THE ───

# 50 MILES *AND* 100 MILES

# Road Records of the World.

## 50 MILES IN 3 HRS. 5 MIN.,
By Mr. S. GOLDER, Leamington and S.W.B.C.; and

## 100 MILES IN 7 HRS. 5 MIN. 16 SEC.,
By Mr. GEO. SMITH, Merry Rovers T.C.

# STARLEY & SUTTON,
"Meteor" Works, West Orchard, Coventry.

*Late 1885 advertisement promoting the Rover*
*after its record breaking achievements.*

Rover catalogue and was not mentioned by Sturmey in any of his reference books: yet it was used in an advertisement in *The CTC Monthly Gazette* in December 1885 and January 1886. Bartleet wrote that it was "the model used in the historic 100 miles race of September 1885"; and the wording of the advertisement seems to support that claim. Yet

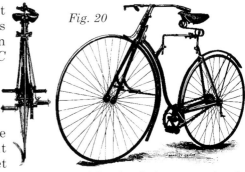

Fig. 20

according to the London Science Museum a machine in their possession is the one ridden by Golder in "the historic race".

This model (Fig. 21) appeared neither in advertisements nor in catalogues. It was illustrated by George Moore in *Wheel World* for November 1885 and it was described in the article by Bartleet. Moore's drawing more or less reproduces the Science Museum model; unfortunately there are differences between that model and the one Bartleet described. Neither Moore nor Bartleet was likely to err

Fig. 21 Rover c Sept. 1885

over detail when it came to giving information about bicycles. To add to the confusion, in his *Bicycle Book* Bartleet said that the second model was fitted with a conventional seat-pillar, yet the illustration he referred to showed plainly that it was not.

The "historic race" was held in September 1885. In 1884 Messrs Hillman, Herbert and Cooper had organised a 100-miles race open to riders of their *Kangaroo* safety bicycle (which had independent chain-drive to each side of the front wheel) and had gained much publicity thereby. Starley and Sutton retaliated with a similar race open to *Rover*-riders. George Smith had won the *Kangaroo* race in 7 hours 11 minutes 10 seconds; he won the Rover race in 7 hours 5 minutes 16 seconds. It was claimed that this result showed that the *Rover* was a faster bicycle than the *Kangaroo*. It probably was, but it seems doubtful whether the race proved anything either way except that George was either faster or luckier than the other riders in each race. In September 1985 the Southern Veteran-Cycle Club organised a ride from Peterborough to Birmingham to celebrate the centenary of the Rover and the famous race (see Appendix 2).

Much interest was being shown in 1885 in the possibility of building an efficient tandem bicycle, and Wilson, Renouf and Howe experimented with designs based largely on the *Rover*. Fig. 23 is a sketch of Wilson's unsuccessful machine, which was known at the time as the Kangarover.

In his *Indispensable Handbook to the Safety Bicycle* published in 1885 Henry Sturmey listed the *Rover* safety which had been at the Stanley Show and mistakenly transposed the sizes of the front and rear wheels; he also got the gear-size wrong, giving it as 55" instead of 50".

On 10th August 1887 the cycling paper *Wheeling* road-tested the *Swift Safety No. 1*. The report said, "It is, with the solitary exception of the original *Rover*, which it equals, the best-steering equal-wheeled safety we have mounted . . ." The Coventry

*Fig. 23 Kangarover*

Machinists' Company were sufficiently proud of this impartial tribute to reprint it in their 1888 catalogue.

# 1886

The 1886 catalogue showed a new design, which was used in an advertisement in *The CTC Monthly Gazette* for March 1886. It was offered with 36" front and 30" rear wheels or two 32" wheels; stock machines were geared to 54" but customers could have that changed. Extras were twisting handlebar £1, hollow rims £1, $7/8$" tyres 10s, tangent spokes 10s and ball-bearing head £1. The photograph is of C.L. Newland of the Bromley Bicycle Club. According to Bartleet it was taken in 1885 (which seems doubtful as the wheels are 34" and 28" - sizes not offered in the 1886 catalogue). Note that the now-conventional saddle-pillar used on the special 1885 racer was not used on this model. Great play was made by Starley and Sutton of the fact that a *Rover* held the record for the greatest distance travelled in an hour (18 $1/2$ miles by Stephen Golder) and for a 50-mile ride (ridden in 3 hours 5 minutes by either Golder or E. Oxborrow, depending on which Rover advertisement you happened to be looking at). That the bicycle used for those records was not the one advertised was clearly not important. Later in the year a racing version of this model was brought out; an advertisement for it appeared in the *Gazette* for May 1886 showing it on a race-track with riders on other makes of safety and a high bicycle lagging despondently far behind.

*Fig. 24*

# 1887

In 1887 there were five *Rover* bicycles in the catalogue: the *Rover Safety*, the *Rover No. 2*, the *Rover Racer*, the *Special Rover* and the *Irish and American Rover*. The *Rover Safety* was unchanged; the *No. 2* had "a cheaper framework" and was £2 cheaper in price but was "still kept up in excellence of workmanship and material to the highest standard". Presumably the *Rover Safety's* workmanship and material were higher than the highest. The *Rover Racer* was illustrated by the advertisement that had appeared in the CTC magazine the previous year, but no particulars of it were given. The *Special* (Fig. 25) was a spring-frame bicycle based on J.K. Starley's patent 12,586 of 4 October 1886. The *Irish and American* model was not described but an entry in the 1888 catalogue gives a clue to what it must have been.

*Fig. 25*

43

# The Rover

## THE MOST POPULAR MACHINE OF THE DAY.
### FITTED WITH A RIGID FRAMEWORK AND ALL THE LATEST IMPROVEMENTS.

**For Testimonials and Press Notices apply to**

# STARLEY <small>AND</small> SUTTON

## METEOR WORKS, WEST ORCHARD, COVENTRY.

Abridged Lists free.   Full Illustrated Catalogue, Two Stamps.

The badge on this machine reads "The Rover, Starley & Sutton, Coventry"; the authors have been unable to find any catalogue illustration of it. The company name, and presumably head badge, was changed in September 1888 with the formation of JI. K. Starley & Co Ltd.
Museum of Irish Transport, Killarney, Ireland.

# 1888

The 1888 catalogue began with an explanation of why the tried and tested Rover frame with its straight forks and hinged steering was the best possible pattern. It then went on to explain that in response to growing demand there would be new models. The *Special* was renamed *Spring Frame* but there were no other changes. The *No. 1* was similar to the 1887 *Rover Safety* but the exaggerated curve in the top tube had been lost. Although the machine is listed and illustrated in the 1888 catalogue no specification is given. It is illustrated in the 1889 catalogue and renamed the *Rover Safety*. Strangely, it was used in the *Gazette* from February to July 1888; in January, November and December that year the 1887 *Rover Safety* was used to advertise the bicycle which had "set the fashion to the world". As the 1888 catalogue had been prepared either in 1887 or very early in 1888 this does not suggest that the firm thought their new models were all that appealing.

The 1888 *Rover Safety* (Fig. 26) had a new frame; still a curvilinear curiosity, but different from previous ones. It had a socket head and detachable cranks, and cost £20; a ball-bearing head cost £1 extra. The specification was unchanged from that of the 1886-7 *Safeties*. If fitted with larger tyres for Irish and American roads it cost £21, with 30s extra for a band-brake. This Irish-American version was "geared and finished in the same style as the *No. 1* ", but here *No. 1* seems more likely to refer to the *Rover Safety* than to the *No. 1*.

*Fig. 26*

46

The *Universal Rover* was a complete departure from Rover practice. Early in 1886 Messrs Hillman, Herbert and Cooper had brought out a *Premier* cross-frame, which was closely followed by Dan Albone's *Ivel* and then a host of others. Unfortunately we are unlikely to know exactly what the *Universal* cross-frame looked like. As the catalogue said, the illustration (Fig. 27) did not fairly represent the machine, and it was neither advertised nor listed again.

*Fig. 27*

The *Popular Rover* (usually known nowadays as a semi-diamond) apparently contradicted what had been said in the catalogue introduction. Although straight forks were better than curved forks with hinge steering, and curved forks were needed with socket steering, the *Popular* was hinged and curved. The note beneath the *Popular* refers to the *Rover No. 2,* presumably another name for the machine. As with the *Universal,* we remain ignorant of the improvements due to be revealed in the new block being prepared. The *Popular* does not seem to have been advertised except in the catalogue.

*Fig. 28*

There were no particulars of the *Racer,* only the 1886 CTC advertisement. One other item that may be mentioned here is the Cyclist Spring, which as the text explains was designed to overcome the bumping and jarring occasioned by solid tyres on rough roads. As this was introduced in 1888 one would have thought it likely to be a standard fitting on the 1889 models. Alas! it never made the catalogues.

*Fig. 29*

As stated earlier, there are problems over identifying early Rovers; this photograph (Fig. 30) illustrates the point perfectly. The rear part is reminiscent of that of the 1886 *Safety;* but the front part (with hinge steering and straight forks) is that of the 1886-8 *No. 1.* The machine is not listed anywhere or advertised, and this photograph is the only available evidence that it ever existed. Note the lamp-holder screwed on the front spindle. That was used to carry the type of lamp designed to fit on the hub of an ordinary.

*Fig. 30*

*Electric Car of 1888*

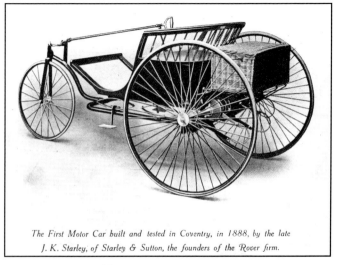

The First Motor Car built and tested in Coventry, in 1888, by the late J. K. Starley, of Starley & Sutton, the founders of the Rover firm.

48

# 1889

In 1889 full specifications were given for all machines except the *Racer,* which had disappeared from the catalogue. As mentioned earlier, the company's name had changed, in September 1888, to J.K. Starley and Co.

The *No. 1* reverted to its old name of *Rover Safety.* It had 30″ wheels geared to 54″ (unless otherwise ordered) but could also be obtained with 33″ or 36″ front wheels, direct spokes, adjustable ball-bearings to wheels, bracket and pedals, $3/4$″ front and $7/8$″ rear tyres, adjustable handlebar, spoon-brake to front wheel, mudguards, footrests, lamp-bracket etc., valise and oilcan. It was black-enamelled, or painted and lined in two colours with all bright parts plated, and cost £20. Extras were a twisting handlebar £1, hollow rims £1, $7/8$″ tyres 10s, tangent spokes 10s, ball-bearing head £1, band-brake 30s,

## The "Socket-steerer Rover"

### WITH BALL-BEARING HEAD.

SPECIFICATION.—30in. wheels, geared to 54in. (unless otherwise ordered) ; improved ball-bearing head ; ball bearings to both wheels, crank-axle, and pedals ; tyres, ¾in. to front and ⅞in. to back wheel ; adjustable handle-bars ; vertical seat adjustment ; spoon brake ; chain and wheel-guards ; best saddle and spring ; lamp-bracket ; foot-rests ; valise, spanner, and oilcan ; finished in best black enamel, or painted and lined in two colours ; all bright parts plated.

## Price £21.

EXTRAS.—Twisting handle-bars for storing, £1. Hollow rims, £1. ⅞in. tyres, 10/- Tangent spokes, 10/- Band brake, 30/- Gold lining, 15/- Crates, 2/6 each, not returnable.

"THE 'ROVER' IS A PERFECT DEMON."—*Wheeling.*

*Fig. 31*

49

gold lining 15s, and larger tyres for Irish and American roads £1. It was advertised in the *Gazette* until July.

The 1888 *Rover Safety* became the *Socket-steerer Rover* in 1889. As will be seen in Fig. 31, there were one or two changes. The seat-stays were more upright and the rider was further back over the back wheel. The wheels were 30" geared to 54" (unless otherwise ordered) and an improved ball-bearing head was no longer an extra. The rest of the specification was as for the 1888 *Safety* except that the brake was slightly different and there was no mention of the Irish and American connection. The price increased to £21 - probably to pay for the ball-bearing head.

The *New Light Rover Safety* was 12 pounds lighter than the *Safety* but as the weight of the *Safety* was not given we are little wiser. It was claimed

# The "New Light Rover" Safety.

THIS Machine is about 12lbs. lighter than our " Rover " Safety, and will not stand so much rough usage, but with reasonable care it will be found amply strong enough, and is quite capable of carrying any rider up to twelve stone weight. Should intending purchasers consider our " Rover" Safety too heavy, we would strongly recommend them to give this Machine a trial. Wherever we have supplied them they have given universal satisfaction.

SPECIFICATION.—30in. front and 28in. rear wheel (driver), geared to 56in. (unless otherwise ordered). Adjustable ball bearings to both wheels, crank-axle and pedals. Tyres, ⅞in. and ¾in. to front and back wheels respectively. Direct spokes (or tangent if preferred). Lighter framework, saddle and pedals. Adjustable handles. Vertical adjustment to seat pillar. Spoon brake. Wheel and chain-guard. Spanner oilcan, and valise. Finished best black enamel, or painted and lined in two colours

## Price £20.

EXTRAS.—Twisting handle-bar for storing, £1. Gold lining, 15/- Hollow rims, £1. ⅞in. tyres, 10/- Ball-bearing head, £1. Band brake, 30/- Crates, 2s. 6d. each nett, not returnable.

" THE ' ROVER' HAS SET THE FASHION TO THE WORLD."—*Cyclist.*

*Fig. 32*

that this machine was ridden by S.G. Whittaker when he broke two world's records in one day - five miles in 13 minutes 33 $2/_3$ seconds and 21 miles 126 yards in one hour. Although there are affinities with the 1888 *Rover Safety* the steering is hinged and the head shorter. It appears that Starley had had second thoughts about the undesirability of combining hinge steering and curved forks. This model was used for advertising in the *Gazette* from August 1889 onwards.

The *Popular Rover Safety* had a slightly different frame and straight forks; equal-sized wheels were offered but a 33" front wheel could be provided. It does seem strange that there were so many variations in wheel sizes. The steering must have been affected by fitting a larger wheel and it is surely unlikely that the firm kept a stock of special frames just in case a customer happened to ask for a larger steerer.

# The "Popular Rover" Safety.

SPECIFICATION.—30in. wheels, geared to 54 inches (unless otherwise ordered); adjustable ball bearings to both wheels and crank-axle; tyres, ¾in. and ⅞in. to front and back wheels respectively; adjustable handles, vertical seat pillar adjustment; spoon brake on front wheel; mud-guards; Starley's patent detachable cranks; best saddle and spring; lamp-bracket, foot-rests, valise, spanner and oilcan; finished in plain black enamel, or painted and lined in two colours; all bright parts plated.

## Price £18.

Also made with 33in. front wheel.

EXTRAS.—Twisted handles for storing, £1. Ball pedals, 15/- Lamp, to fit lamp-iron, specially made, 12/6. Hollow rims, £1 ⅞in. tyres, 10/- Gold lining, 15/- Crates, 2/6 each, not returnable.

●●●●●●●●●●●●●●●●●●●●●

SPECIAL NOTICE.—We have the greatest confidence in recommending the "Popular Rover" as a thoroughly sound, reliable machine, in the framework of which we are enabled to retain the direct connection between the two chain wheels, and from the rear chain wheel to seat of rider, points we considered indispensable when first introducing the "Rover."

"THE 'ROVER' IS A PERFECT DEMON."—*Wheeling.*

*Fig. 33*

The *Universal Rover Safety* replaced the 1888 *Universal,* the firm's solitary venture into the cross-frame field. As the extract explains, it was a cheap model by the firm's standards; but not all that cheap when compared with some of the other cross-frames on the market: *Brookes No. 2* £13 10s, *Ormonde* £12 12s, *Phoenix* £12, *Express* £8, *Cycledom R.D. Safety* £7 10s and *Jubilee* £6 5s.

# The "Universal Rover" Safety.

A S there is a large demand for a cheaper safety than those we have hitherto sold, we have added the above to our list, and can thoroughly recommend it as being a sound and serviceable machine. We have carefully considered where we could take out the expense of construction without reducing the strength and stability of the machine, and, where a cheap but reliable mount is required at a little above the cost of the ordinary common machines, we can confidently offer the above.

SPECIFICATION.—30in. front and 28in. back wheels, geared to 54in.; curved front forks; ball bearings to both wheels and crank-axle; tyres, ⅞in.; adjustable handles; vertical seat adjustment; mud-guards to both wheels; lamp bracket and foot-rests, saddle, spanner, and oilcan. Finished plain black enamel; bright parts plated. Foot-rests are attached to this machine, although not shown in the above illustration.

## Price £14.

### No deviation can be made from the standard pattern.

Crates, 2/6 each nett, not returnable.

"THE 'ROVER' HAS SET THE FASHION TO THE WORLD."—*Cyclist.*

*Fig. 34*

The *Spring-frame Rover Safety* was unchanged except for the addition of the specification, as follows: 30" wheels geared to 54" (unless otherwise ordered), ball-bearings to wheels, bracket and pedals, $^3/_4$" front and $^7/_8$" rear tyres, adjustable handlebar, rear brake, mudguards, lamp-bracket, footrests, valise, spanner and oilcan; black-enamelled or painted and lined in two colours, with all bright parts plated. It cost £21 10s; extras were ball-bearing link connection £1, hollow rims £1, $^7/_8$" tyres 10s and gold lining 15s.

The *Rational Rover* was an emphatic return to the principle of the large front wheel that gave the 1885 safety such an advantage over the other safeties on the market when it was introduced. The explanation given could perhaps be better expressed but it does make sense when studied.

# The "Rational Rover."

WE consider the "Rover" as introduced by us with 36in. front wheel did not meet with the appreciation we feel it deserved, and take this opportunity of re-introducing it to the notice of our readers as the "Rational Rover," and append a few remarks, taken from the introduction of our list, which will explain our reasons for again calling your attention to this Machine.

We may mention that the steering of a safety bicycle is difficult in consequence of its great ease, and, strange as it may appear, it would be easier if it were harder. There is a point at which exertion is easy, below which it becomes as difficult as it would be hard above that point, and with a straight fork the line of the pivot is carried in advance of the point of contact of the wheel with the ground, producing a steadying effect upon the hands, and together with a 36in. front wheel forms one of the easiest machines to steer that can possibly be made. *For remarks by E. R. Shipton, Esq., C.T.C., re the "Rational Rover," see page 31.*

SPECIFICATION.—36in. front and 30in. rear (driver) wheels, geared to 54in. (unless otherwise ordered) ; adjustable ball bearings to both wheels, crank-axle, and pedals ; tyres, ¾in. and ⅞in. to front and back wheels respectively ; patent detachable cranks ; adjustable handles ; vertical seat adjustment ; spoon-brake to front wheel ; chain and wheel guards ; oilcan, spanner, valise, etc. ; finished best black enamel, or painted and lined in two colours ; all bright parts plated.

## Price £20.

EXTRAS.—Twisting handle-bar for storing, £1.   Hollow rims, £1.   ⅞in. tyres, 10/-.
Ball-bearing Head, £1.   Band brake, £1 10s.   Gold lining, 15/-

Crates, 2/6 each net, not returnable.

*Fig. 35*

*Rational Rover c 1889/90.*

The entry for the *Lady's Rover Safety* is a little puzzling. It says "the rear wheel is now fitted with a dress-guard"; but this is the first time the model has appeared in a catalogue.

Although the short-lived addiction of the "upper classes" to the pastime of cycling in the 1890s had made it fairly respectable for women to indulge in it, public opinion in general looked upon any form of dress that betrayed the fact that women had two legs, or showed more than about an inch or so of ankle, as indicative of the moral depravity of the wearer. Hence the insistence on frames that could safely accommodate the voluminous skirts that were then the fashion.

# The " Lady's Rover " Safety.

SPECIFICATION.—28in. and 26in. wheels geared to 51in. unless otherwise ordered. Adjustable ball bearings to both wheels, crank axle and pedals. Tyres, ⅞in. and ¾in. Adjustable handles and seat. Spoon brake to front wheel. Chain and wheel guards. Best saddle and spring. Lamp bracket, foot-rests, valise, spanner and oilcan, etc.

The rear wheel is now fitted with a dress-guard, so that by no possibility can a lady's dress become entangled in the chain or spokes.

We have thoroughly tested the above machine, and can confidently recommend it either for ladies' or gentlemen's use.

*Finished in best black enamel, or painted and lined in two colours. All bright parts plated.*

# Price £20.

EXTRAS.—Twisting handle-bar for storing, £1 ; hollow rims, £1 ; ⅞in. tyres, 10/- ; tangent spokes, 10/-
Gold lining, 15/-

CRATES 2s. 6d. each NET—not returnable.

*Fig. 36*

At the Stanley Show in January 1889 the firm showed what they called a *Rover Rational Tandem* with a 48" front and a 36" back wheel, the former pedalled as on an ordinary and the latter geared to 54" as a safety. *Bicycling News* reported that the tandem was fast and comfortable, although the rear rider might grumble about the view. The machine is similar to a prototype built by William Gwinnett in 1884 when he filed a provisional specification for a patent; the main difference is that his rear portion had no chainstays. Not that Gwinnett or Starley achieved much with their tandems; neither succeeded. The main reason for failure is obvious to any tandem-rider - the two riders must be in physical accord (better known as "nicking together") for successful tandeming. If their pedalling rates are different there is no possibility of the co-operation essential for smooth running - there is at best a weaving progression and at worst a fearsome wobbling.

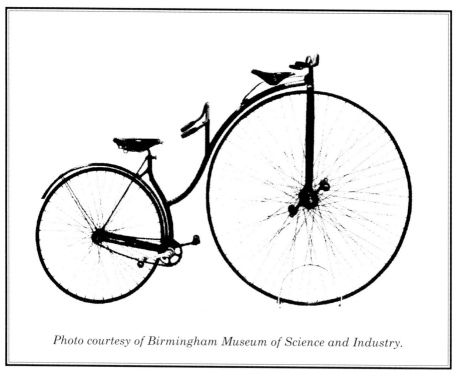

*Photo courtesy of Birmingham Museum of Science and Industry.*

*Fig. 37*

Useful instructions on cleaning and replacing bearings and adjusting the bearings and chain were given for the first time in this catalogue.

*c1889*
*Not illustrated in any known catalogue. The badge reads J. K. Starley & Co,*
*Late Starley & Sutton,West Orchard Coventry.*

*c.1890 New Light Rover.
Photographed at an International Veteran-
Cycle Rally in Switzerland 1986.*

# 1890

The first straight-tubed *Rovers* with true diamond frames appeared in 1890, although the persistence of curved tubing betrayed the apparent obsession with it that was shared by other Starleys. The offer of the twisting handlebar to ease problems of storage disappeared from the catalogue. The *Rover Safety* changed its name again; it became simply the *Rover*. According to the catalogue it was improved for 1890 but the specification was unchanged. The *New Light Rover* was now "much lighter" instead of "about 12 lb lighter" than the *Rover*. The *Rational Rover* was unchanged. The *Socket-steerer Rover* became the *Socket-steering Rover*. The *Lady's Rover Safety* became the *Lady's Rover* and the previous year's incorrect gear of 51" was altered to 52". The *Popular* had 30" wheels or 30" front and 28" rear, geared to 54" (unless otherwise ordered). A 33" front wheel could also be fitted. The *Universal Rover Safety* became the *Universal Rover* and was fitted with a hollow handlebar; the price dropped to £12 12s. The *Spring-frame Rover* had new springing. Although the catalogue says it is a new patent this seems doubtful. The only patent granted to J.K. Starley for a spring-frame before 1890 was the 1886 one he was already using. He was to have a later patent, in 1891, but that was for springing the rear wheel. Perhaps he was using someone else's patent under licence. The additions to the range are shown here: The *Diamond Rover* (Fig. 38), the *Rover Racer* (Fig. 39), the *Rover Semi-racer* (Fig. 40) and the *Universal Diamond Rover* (Fig. 41). In the introduction to the catalogue the firm said that there were only three additions to their range: the *Diamond Rover*, the *Stayed Diamond Rover* (both weighing about 33 pounds and costing £20) and the *Universal Diamond Rover*. As we have

*Fig. 38*

seen, this conflicts with what is listed. Unfortunately, two pages are missing from the catalogue and we have not found any information on the stayed model. The machines chosen to advertise *Rovers* in the *Gazette* were the *Rover*, the *Lady's Rover* and the *Rover Sociable* (which will appear later).

Fig. 39

Fig. 40

*Fig. 41*

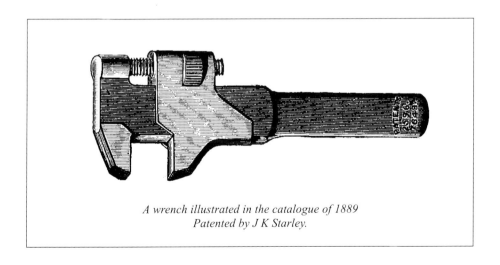

*A wrench illustrated in the catalogue of 1889*
*Patented by J K Starley.*

# 1891

During 1890 there had been much argument over the value of the pneumatic tyre, and some firms had started to fit them. Others had resurrected the cushion tyre of the 1880s in an attempt to provide the admitted comfort of the pneumatic without the fear of puncture or - so they claimed - of sideslip. On 26 November 1890 *The Cyclist* published the following letter from J.K. Starley:

"Before the matter goes too far, we think it is quite advisable that some distinct expressions of opinion should be given on the question of the cushion tyre. For our own part we consider it absolutely necessary to bear in mind that to be effective, it must be very elastic, and if it is very elastic it will not bear the weight of the rider, and, as a consequence, becomes a flattened-out mass of rubber. A cavity in a tyre, with air as a neutral pressure, offers absolutely no resistance, and therefore the whole weight of the rider comes upon the rubber. If the rubber is as flexible as it should be it is not able to stand the weight of the rider or anything like it, so that the object aimed at, i.e. greater elasticity, is not obtained. Some are trying a stiffer kind of rubber that will withstand the weight of the rider, but in this they reduce the elasticity, thus neutralising the advantage they seek to obtain. It might also be worth while to consider whether a larger diameter does not offer a greater mark for obstacles met with which would set up a tendency to press down on one or the other side of the tyre, and bring a great deal of lateral pressure on the spokes that would gradually tend to make the wheel become loose. Our own impression is that the outcome of this matter will be a greater demand for larger solid tyres, and we think, if made of best quality flexible rubber, they will prove the best in the end."

This letter has been quoted as proof that J.K. Starley was against the use of the pneumatic tyre. It is more likely that he was simply arguing that a solid tyre was better than a cushion. On 3 July 1897 John Boyd Dunlop wrote to Starley:

"Every body knows that you set the fashion to the introduction of the rear driven safety, but, few know that you were the first gentleman in England to appreciate the Pneumatic Tyre. Long before the Pneumatic Tyre Co. was floated you sent hubs and spokes to Edlin & Co., Belfast, to have wheels built and fitted with pneumatic tyres. It was my intention to take the wheels, when built, over to you with a view to a floatation (sic). Edlin was in a small way and was very busy, and therefore unable to complete the wheels in a reasonable time, hence the project fell through. I have pleasure in sending at your request two photos and hope to have yours in return."

The specification of the *Rover* ("improved for 1891") was unchanged but the extras were different. Thoroughly recommended were $7/8$" and 1" Best Black tyres for 25s; $1^1/4$" cushions cost £2 15s, pneumatics £5, hollow rims 10s, $7/8$" tyres 10s and gold lining 15s. Fitting with larger tyres for Irish and

# 1891.

## YORK TO LONDON IN 14 hrs. 33 min.

*Wheeling* says, October 27th, 1890 :—

"LONDON TO YORK RECORD BEATEN BY 2H. 19M.—THE ROVER STILL LEADS THE WAY.

" We question whether any ride has received so much attention as ' Dick Turpin's jaunt to York.' It will leave its traces in the good old stories told by our nurses to the children of England for many generations to come. No road has received so much attention from journalists as the road between the 'Little Village ' and York—none so often described. Poor Dick Turpin! Poor Black Bess! The cycle has put into the shade—that is, when ridden by one of our present fast road-riders—the wonderful performance, if it were ever accomplished, of that grand old mare, Black Bess: and though Dick Turpin's ride may never be forgotten, it will, doubtless, be many times eclipsed by the future fast-riding cyclist, as it has been by the present-day scorcher. The latest Dick Turpin is one T. A. Edge, of *Wheeling*, and editor of *British Sport*, who, mounted on the famous ' Rover ' Safety Bicycle, the first rear-driver safety made and fore-runner of our modern fashionable mount, started from York at 6.45 a.m. on Thursday morning, and rode through to London in 14h. 33m., beating the previous record by 2h. 19m."

# J.K.STARLEY & Co., Ld.,

### Manufacturers,

## METEOR WORKS, WEST ORCHARD, COVENTRY.

Telegraphic Address –" METEOR," COVENTRY.                    Telephone 56.

London Depôt : 5, HOLBORN VIADUCT, E.C.

FRENCH AND GERMAN EDITIONS OF CATALOGUE CAN BE OBTAINED ON APPLICATION.

*Back cover of 1891 abridged illustrated list.*

American roads cost £1, and only a 33" front wheel was offered as an option. The offer of $^7/_8$" tyres for 10s is puzzling. It was the standard size for the rear wheel - why not say $^7/_8$" front tyre? And what size tyres were fitted for those Irish and American roads that must have been so terrible? Best Black Tyres (throroughly recommended) cost 25s, yet the special tyres for Ireland and America were obtainable for a mere £1. It seems likely that the black tyres were either more resilient or tougher - or both. Most tyres were red; very few firms offered black or grey. Long after solid tyres were obsolete - except on trade cycles - H.W. Bartleet, who was much involved with racing on high bicycles in this century, referred wistfully to the soft grey tyres that were obtainable in his younger days.

The *New Light Rover* with socket ball steering had the specification of the 1889 model with hinged steering but with different extras: $^7/_8$" and 1" solids were 25s, $1^1/_4$" cushions £2 15s, pneumatics £5 and gold lining 15s. (Fig. 42). Some light was thrown on "lined in two colours" that appeared in some specifications. In the 1891 catalogue was a letter from a customer who had returned his *Light Rover* (which he said he bought at the Stanley Show held in February 1888) for overhaul; in the letter he asked for it to be re-enamelled and thought that "the regulation blue and yellow lines would improve it". The machine was doubtless the *New Light Roadster,* so if the customer was right that model was available in 1888 although it was neither catalogued nor used for advertising until 1889.

The *Universal Diamond Rover* again carried a warning that no deviation could be made from the standard specification yet offered extras: $^7/_8$" back tyre 5s, ball pedals 10s and cushions £2 15s. The *Universal Diamond Rover* with pneumatic tyres was listed separately in the catalogues and offered as extras only ball pedals for 10s. The *Rover Racer* was still offered at £19 10s, with extras $1^1/_4$" cushions 35s and pneumatics £5; the model with brake and mudguards had been withdrawn. The *Spring-frame Rover* was unchanged, as was the *Universal Rover*; but the latter could be fitted with cushions for 35s and pneumatics for £5. Two models disappeared from the catalogue: the *Popular Rover* and the *Rational Rover*. There was probably little demand for a relatively expensive semi-diamond machine and one cannot imagine Starley lamenting its demise, but we suspect that he may have been sad to see the end of a model that was near to his 1885 Rovers. One oddity of the Starley catalogues was the cavalier attitude towards the word "tyre". In some years it was tyre, in others it was tire. In 1891 they used both spellings.

In March a new model was used to advertise in the *Gazette* - the *Rover Light Roadster*. No such model was listed in the catalogue and the illustration was clearly that of the *Universal Diamond Rover*; the text claimed that it weighed 35 pounds with solid tyres - information not given in the catalogue. In August the *Socket-steering Rover* was portrayed but not named. In September and October the *Universal Diamond Rover* appeared labelled *Rover Light Roadster* and was said to weigh 28 pounds without guards or brake. In December it appeared without reference to weight but named

*Rover Safety* (the name that J.K. Starley had said he objected to).

The *Socket-steering Rover* was "also made with 33" and 30" wheels"; extras were as for the *New Light Rover*. The *Lady's Rover* had an unchanged specification but could be provided with 28" and 30" wheels and fitted with a removable stay which made it "suitable for gentlemen's use"; extras were $^7/_8$" tyres 10s, cushions (1" and $1^1/_4$") £2 15s, pneumatics £5, hollow rims £1, tangent spokes 10s, ball socket £1 and gold lining 15s.

# THE NEW LIGHT "ROVER,"

## Fitted with Short Socket Ball Steering.

@HIS machine is the same as our New Light "Rover," but is fitted with the popular socket ball steering in place of the ordinary pivot.

SPECIFICATION.—30in. front and 28in. rear wheel, geared to 56in. (unless otherwise ordered); adjustable ball bearings to both wheels, crank-axle and pedals; ⅝in. and ¾in. tires; direct spokes; adjustable handles and seat-pillar; plunger spoon brake; wheel and chain-guards; plated lamp bracket, foot-rests; spanner, oilcan, and valise; finished best black enamel, and lined in two colours.

### PRICES.

| | | | | | | | | |
|---|---|---|---|---|---|---|---|---|
| Ordinary Tires | ... | ... | ... | ... | ... | £21 | 0 | 0 |
| Black Tires (1in. and ¾in.) Special | .. | | ... | ... | 22 | 5 | 0 |
| Cushion Tires (1¼in. both wheels) | ... | | ... | ... | 23 | 15 | 0 |
| Pneumatic Tires | | ... | ... | ... | ... | ... | 26 | 0 | 0 |

Extras.—Gold lining, 15/-; hollow rims, £1; ¾in. tires to both wheels, 10/-
Crates, 2/6 each, not returnable.

*Fig. 42*

The *Rover Semi-racer* was still obtainable with the 1890 specification at £21 but with hinge steering it cost only £20; the only extras listed were ⁷/₈" and ¾" solids 15s, cushions £2 15s and pneumatics £5. The *New Diamond Rover* is shown in Fig. 43.

THE

# NEW DIAMOND ROVER.

⊙O meet the demand that has arisen for a medium priced and thoroughly reliable machine we have introduced the New Diamond "Rover" for next season. Having spent a considerable time in experimenting and testing, we can confidently recommend it to gentlemen desiring a mount at a less cost than our "Rover."

SPECIFICATION.—30in. front, 28in. back wheel, gear 54in.; curved front forks; ball bearings to both wheels and crank axle, also pedals; adjustable handles; mud-guards to wheels; chain-guard; foot rests; saddle, spanner, and oilcan. Finished best black enamel, and bright parts plated. With plain socket steering, price £17; with ball socket steering, £18.

⅞in. and 1in. Solid Tyres, £1 extra.

Penge, S.E., 1/6/90.

Dear Sirs,—No doubt you would like to hear what I think of the machine now that I have had sufficient time to test it. All I can say is that if any one had asked me the question, "Is life worth living?" before and after the machine was in my possession, my answers would have been very different. Now I should answer, "Certainly, if you possess a 'Rover' Safety;" then I should have been tempted to answer, "No." For ease in driving, comfort in riding, recommend me to the "Rover" Safety. The saddle suits me A1—never given me a moment's uneasiness. I think upon the whole I have to thank my friend for persuading and you for supplying a tonic that will dispel melancholy and change a misanthrope into an optimist.

I am, faithfully yours,

J. ROE.

*Fig. 43*

# 1892

The *Rover* was unchanged but the options of a 33" front wheel and pneumatics were withdrawn. The *New Light Rover* with hinge steering was unchanged but the price for the solid-tyred version had risen from £20 to £21 and the extras were slightly different: Special Black $^7/_8$" and 1" tyres 25s, cushions £2 15s, 2" pneumatics £5 and Clincher pneumatics £5 10s. The option of pneumatics on the *Socket-steering Rover* had been withdrawn, the *Lady's Rover* (Fig. 44) had a new frame and socket steering, and cost more. Tangent spokes were specified, but they were listed among the extras at 10s!

The solid-tyred *Universal Diamond Rover* was unchanged but Clincher pneumatics were offered at £4 10s extra. The pneumatic-tyred *Universal Diamond Rover* (Fig. 45) had a new frame and socket steering. It will be noticed that there is a reversion to the underslung bracket; possibly it was decided that that type of frame was nearly obsolescent and that stocks should be used up on one of the second-rank models. There was a new version of the *Rover Racer* (Fig. 46) which reverted to the straight forks once advocated so strongly by Starley and had the rising top-tube that became fashionable in the early 1890s; and there were two versions (figs. 47 and 48) of another model, the *Rover Light Roadster* (the name that had been used in the *Gazette* in 1891 for advertising the *Universal Diamond Rover*). The *Rover Semi-racer*, the *New Diamond Rover* and the *Spring-frame Rover* had disappeared from the catalogue. The models used during 1892 to advertise in the *Gazette* were as follows: in January, a solid-tyred *New Light Roadster* labelled *The Rover*; from April to June, a new model (labelled *The Rover*) which proved to be the *New Popular Rover;* in July, no cycle but an announcement that light roadsters were available at 35 pounds complete; in August, a *Lady's Rover;* from September to December, the *New Popular Rover* under its own name. In April the "actual weights" of the *Rovers* were given: a racer from 26 pounds; a racer with roadster tyres from 30 pounds; a racer with roadster tyres, brake and mudguards from 35 pounds; and a light roadster with cushion tyres (1" and $1^1/_4$" with $^1/_4$" hole) at 35 pounds or 41 pounds with pneumatic tyres. (Note: It seems advisable to be suspicious of the weights given for the 1892 Rover Light Roadsters, even though they appeared in the firm's advertisement in "The CTC Gazette". No evidence has been found that cushion or pneumatic tyres were noticeably heavier than solids.)

# THE "LADY'S ROVER,"

### WITH

## BALL SOCKET STEERING.

**SPECIFICATION.**—28in. front, and 26in. rear wheels, geared to 52in. (unless otherwise ordered); improved adjustable ball bearings to head, both wheels, crank-axle, and pedals; ⅝in. and ¾in. tires; tangent spokes; adjustable handles and seat-rod; plunger spoon brake; chain and mud guards laced for the protection of the dress; finished best black enamel and lined in two colours; all bright parts plated. Best saddle and spring, plated lamp bracket, foot-rests, valise, spanner, and oil-can.

## PRICES.

| | | | | | |
|---|---|---|---|---|---|
| Ordinary Tires (⅝in. and ¾in.) | ... | ... | ... | ... | £21 0 0 |
| Black Tires (⅞in. and 1in.) Special | ... | .. | ... | | 22 5 0 |
| Cushion Tires, (1¼in. and 1in.) | ... | ... | ... | ... | 23 15 0 |
| Pneumatic Tires (1¾in. and 2in.) | ... | ... | ... | ... | 26 0 0 |
| Clincher Pneumatics... | ... | ... | ... | .. | ... | 25 10 0 |

**Extras.**—Hollow rims, £1. ⅞in. tires, 10/- Tangent spokes, 10/- Gold lining, 15/-

Crates, **2/6** each, not returnable.

### Extended Purchase where desired.

*Fig. 44*

69

# THE
# UNIVERSAL DIAMOND "ROVER."

**SPECIFICATION.**—Long Ball Socket Steering and extended wheel base ; 30in. front and 28in. rear wheels, geared to 56in. ; improved adjustable ball bearings to head, both wheels and crank-axle ; ⅞in. and ⅝in. tires ; direct spokes ; adjustable handles and seat-rod ; plunger spoon brake ; chain and mud guards ; finished black enamel ; all bright parts plated. Saddle and spring, plated lamp bracket, foot-rests, valise, spanner, and oil-can. Plain pedals.

## PRICES.

| | | | | | | | |
|---|---|---|---|---|---|---|---|
| Ordinary Tires... | ... | ... | ... | ... | ... | £15 | 15 0 |
| Cushion Tires ... | ... | ... | ... | ... | ... | 18 | 10 0 |
| Pneumatic Tires (2in. both wheels) | | | ... | ... | 20 | 15 0 | |
| Clincher Pneumatics ... | ... | ... | ... | ... | 20 | 5 0 | |

Ball pedals, 10/- extra.

No deviation can be made from Standard Pattern.

Crates, **2/6** each, not returnable.

**Extended Purchase where desired.**

*Fig. 45*

70

# THE "ROVER"
## SAFETY.

"Has set the fashion to the World."—*Cyclist*.     "The King of Safeties."—*Irish Cyclist*.

# 70,000 Miles on a "ROVER" without a Breakdown.

### THE FOLLOWING PROVES CONCLUSIVELY THE STABILITY OF OUR MACHINES:—

Messrs. J. K. Starley & Co., Coventry.                                              Drybriggs, Cupar Fife.
    Dear Sirs,—Nearly six years ago I purchased one of your "Rovers," and have very much pleasure to testify to its excellence.   I have ridden it over 70,000 miles, and it is still likely to run as many more.   The only thing at all wrong with it is the crank axle adjustment, it is getting quite low, and no wonder after such a performance ; besides riding it for that distance, one of my sons has ridden a few hundred miles on it.   I could not say how many. As for repairs during that time I have found rubbers for the wheels has been my heaviest expense, as I have had two new rubbers put on front wheel, and four on the back wheel.   I have also worn out two chains during the last two and a half years.   For actual repairs, it has not cost me 5s., with the exception of two new chain wheels, and new chain, which is not, of course, included under repairs.   I may also state the extra load the machine has had to carry.   I have a country postal delivery to make each day, distance between 19 and 20 miles, so that, in addition to carrying myself, 11½ stones, I had also from 20 to 35lb. on my back, and on very exceptional days, I have had as far as 60lb., which says a great deal for the excellent material the machine must have been made of.   I can recommend the "Rover" with every confidence to any one wishing a machine—and especially for postmen, or any one who has heavy work to do.   I do not think they can buy anything to beat a No. 1 "Rover."—Yours truly,      E. WALTON,
                                                              Pensioner, Late Colour-Sergeant the Black Watch, Royal Highlanders.

FOR PRICE LIST AND FULL PARTICULARS, APPLY

# J. K. STARLEY & Co. Ltd.
## METEOR CYCLE WORKS, COVENTRY.

LONDON—5, HOLBORN VIADUCT, E.C.              13, PARIS—RUE TAYLOR

71

# THE "ROVER" RACER.

SPECIFICATION.—Long Ball Socket Steering and extended wheel base; 30in. front and 28in. rear wheels; geared to 63in. (unless otherwise ordered); improved adjustable ball bearings to head, both wheels, crank-axle, and pedals; 1⅜in. racing pneumatic tires; tangent spokes 14 and 15 gauge; adjustable handles and seat-rod; racing chain; rat-trap pedals; finished best black enamel; all bright parts plated. Racing saddle, valise, spanner, and oil-can.

Weight, to above Specification, 28lbs. all on.

Or with 26in. front and rear wheels, 25lbs., all on.

## PRICE, £25 10 0

Also made with Roadster Tires, Brake, and Guards; easily detachable. Weight, 35lbs. Price, £26 10 0

Crates, 2/6 each, not returnable.

## Extended purchase where desired.

*Fig. 46*

72

# THE "ROVER" LIGHT ROADSTER,

## With Short Ball Socket Steering.

**SPECIFICATION.**—30in. front and 28in. rear wheels, geared to 60in. (unless otherwise ordered); improved adjustable ball bearings to head, both wheels, crank-axle, and pedals; ⅝in. and ¾in. tires, tangent spokes, 12 and 14 gauge for solid and cushion tires, 14 and 15 gauge for pneumatic tires; adjustable handles and seat-rod; plunger spoon brake; mud guards; finished best black enamel, and lined in two colours; all bright parts plated. Best saddle and spring, plated lamp bracket, foot-rests, valise, spanner, and oil-can.

### This Machine is specially suited for Short Riders.

## PRICES.

| | £ | s | d |
|---|---|---|---|
| Ordinary Tires (⅝in. and ¾in.) ... ... ... | £21 | 0 | 0 |
| Best Black Tires (1in. and ⅞in.) Special ... ... | 22 | 5 | 0 |
| Cushion Tires ... ... ... ... ... ... | 23 | 15 | 0 |
| Pneumatic Tires (1¾in. and 2in.) ... ... ... | 26 | 0 | 0 |
| Clincher Pneumatics ... ... ... ... ... | 25 | 10 | 0 |

Crates, **2/6** each, not returnable.

### Extended Purchase where desired.

*Fig. 47*

# THE "ROVER" LIGHT ROADSTER.

SPECIFICATION.—Long Ball Socket Steering and extended wheel base; 30in. front, and 28in. rear wheels, geared to 60in. (unless otherwise ordered); improved adjustable ball bearings to head, both wheels, crank-axle, and pedals; ⅞in. and ¾in. tires; tangent spokes; 12 and 14 gauge for solid and cushion tires, and 14 and 15 gauge for pneumatic tires; adjustable handles and seat-rod; plunger spoon brake; mud guards; finished best black enamel, lined in two colours; all bright parts plated. Best saddle and spring, plated lamp bracket, foot-rests, valise, spanner, and oil-can.

### This Machine is specially suited for Tall Riders.

## PRICES.

| | £ | s | d |
|---|---|---|---|
| Ordinary Tires (⅞in. and ¾in.) ... ... ... ... | £21 | 0 | 0 |
| Best Black Tires (1in. and ⅞in.) Special ... ... | 22 | 5 | 0 |
| Cushion Tires ... ... ... ... ... ... | 23 | 15 | 0 |
| Pneumatic Tires (1¾in. and 2in.) ... ... ... ... | 26 | 0 | 0 |
| Clincher Pneumatics... ... ... ... ... | 25 | 10 | 0 |

Crates, 2/6 each, not returnable.

### Extended Purchase where desired.

*Fig. 48*

75

# "ROVER" SEMI-RACER.

## Pivot Steering.

### FITTED WITH PNEUMATIC TIRES.

**SPECIFICATION.**—30in. front, 28in. rear wheel, geared 60in. (unless otherwise ordered); tangent spokes; adjustable handle-bar and seat rod; foot-rests; adjustable ball bearings to all parts; plated lamp bracket, best saddle and spring, valise, oilcan, and spanner; finished best black enamel; bright parts plated.

## PRICES.

| | | | | | |
|---|---|---|---|---|---|
| Ordinary Tires (⅝in. and ¾in.) | ... | ... | ... | £20 | 0 0 |
| Best Black Tires (⅞in. and 1in.) Special | ... | ... | 21 | 5 0 |
| Cushion Tires (1¼in. to both wheels) | ... | ... | 22 | 15 0 |
| Pneumatic Tires | ... | ... | ... | ... | ... | 25 | 0 0 |

Crates, **2/6** each, not returnable.

*Fig. 49*

# 1893

This year saw a break with the past. The *Rover*, the *New Light Rover*, the *Socket-steering Rover*, *Rover Semi-Racer* and the *Universal Diamond Rover* disappeared, and with them went solid tyres and curved tubing in men's cycles. A curved frame was still used for the *Lady's Rover* but that was partly to give skirt-room and partly to appeal to ladies, who were believed to think the curves pretty. A Carter gearcase was obtainable at 30s. Spoking was tangent or direct as required. Only Dunlop and cushion tyres were offered, the prices of the models so fitted being £26 and £24 5s respectively. The new models, (figs. 51, 52, 53 and 54) are the *New Popular Rover*, the *Rover Roadster*, the *Rover Light Roadster* and the *Rover Racer*. The *New Popular Rover*, which as we have seen was being advertised in April 1892, was clearly a replacement for the socket-steering *Universal Diamond Rover* but it was much cheaper; even when fitted with a Carter gearcase it cost only £17, at least an 18% reduction on the price of a machine with an inferior frame and without a gearcase. The name *Rover Racer* was kept, but the new model was little like the ungainly racer of 1892. Two versions were available, the one shown in Fig. 54 and one with two 28" wheels "for short riders".

Much ingenuity was shown last century in getting the drive in line with the bracket bearing and in separating the ball-races as widely as possible; the Rover solution with its positive adjustment was one of the neatest (see Fig. 50).

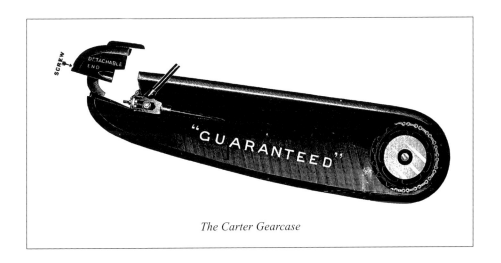

*The Carter Gearcase*

# CRANK BEARINGS.

The following illustration shows our crank bracket for 1893. As will be seen our ball races are placed wide apart by a special arrangement of attaching the crank chain wheel, while the hardened cones are placed upon the spindle in such a manner that they may be easily replaced. The bracket is quite dust-proof, easily adjusted, and cannot well be broken or get out of order. Most of the leading makers are now using this form of bracket and chain adjustment.

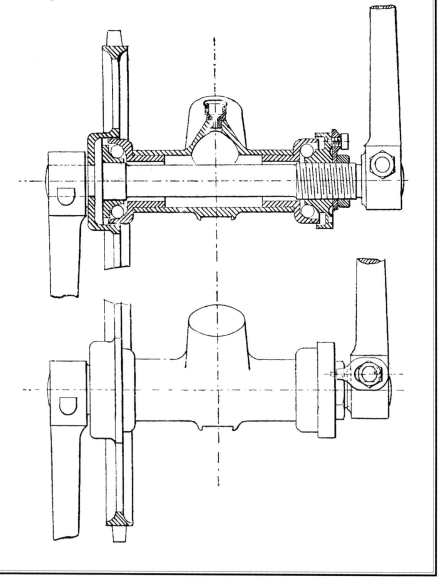

*Fig. 50*

# THE NEW POPULAR "ROVER."

**SPECIFICATION.**—Long Ball Socket Steering and extended wheel base; wheels 30in. and 28in., or two 28in., geared to 60in.; improved adjustable ball bearings to head, both wheels, crank-axle and pedals; tires to order; direct spokes; adjustable handles and seat-rod; roller chain; rubber ball pedals; finished black enamel; all bright parts plated. Good saddle, inflator, valise, spanner, and oilcan

Weight under 40lbs.

## PRICES.

The following prices are net, and not subject to discount:—

|  | | | On Easy Terms. |
|---|---|---|---|
| Dunlop Pneumatic Tires (1¾in. and 2in.) ... ... | £15 0 0 | ... | £18 0 0 |
| Cushion Tires ... ... ... ... ... ... ... | 13 0 0 | ... | 15 15 0 |

Chain Cover, 20/- extra; weight 1lb extra.

Crates, 2/6 each, not returnable.

Carter's Gear Cover, 40/- extra; weight 2lbs. extra.

*Fig. 51*

79

# THE "ROVER" ROADSTER.

## SPECIALLY RECOMMENDED FOR TOURING.

SPECIFICATION.—Long Ball Socket Steering and extended wheel base; 30in. front and 28in. rear wheels, geared to 60ln. (unless otherwise ordered); improved adjustable ball bearings to head, both wheels, crank-axle, and pedals; tires to order; tangent or direct spokes; adjustable handles and seat-rod; plunger spoon brake; mud-guards, easily detachable; finished best black enamel, lined in two colours; all bright parts plated. Best saddle and spring, plated lamp-bracket, foot-rests, inflator, valise, spanner and oilcan.

Weight 38lbs.; direct spokes, if required, 1lb. extra

## **PRICES** (Including Chain Cover).

Dunlop Pneumatic Tires (1¾in. and 2in.) ... ... ... ... £26 10 0

Cushion Tires ... ... ... ... ... ... ... ... 24 5 0

Crates 2/6 each, not returnable.

## EXTENDED PURCHASE WHERE DESIRED.

Carter's Gear Cover, 30/- extra; weight 1lb. extra.

*Fig. 52*

# "ROVER" LIGHT ROADSTER.

SPECIFICATION.—Long Ball Socket Steering and extended wheel base; wheels 30in. and 28in., or two 28in.; geared to 60in. (unless otherwise ordered); improved adjustable ball bearings to head, both wheels, crank-axle, and pedals; roadster Dunlop pneumatic tires and spokes; adjustable handles and seat-rod; plunger spoon brake; light mud-guards, easily detachable; racing block chain rat-trap pedals; cork handles; finished best black enamel and lined in two colours all bright parts plated. Racing saddle, inflator, valise, spanner, and oilcan

Weight (including chain cover) to above Specification 34lbs. all on.

**Price** (including chain cover)   -   -   **£27.**

Crates, 2/6 each, not returnable.

**EXTENDED PURCHASE WHERE DESIRED.**

Carter's Gear Cover, 30/. extra   weight 1lb. extra.

*Fig. 53*

# THE "ROVER" RACER.

### 30in. Front and 28in. Rear Wheels.

SPECIFICATION.—Long Ball Socket Steering and extended wheel base; geared to 63in. (unless otherwise ordered); improved adjustable ball bearings to head, both wheels, crank-axle, and pedals; 1⅝in. racing Dunlop pneumatic tires; light tangent spokes; adjustable handles and seat-rod; racing block chain; rat-trap pedals; cork handles; finished best black enamel; all bright parts plated. Racing saddle, inflator, valise, spanner, and oilcan.

Weight, to above Specification, 22lbs. to 23lbs. all on.

## Price   -   -   -   £25 10s.

Crates, 2/6 each, not returnable.

### EXTENDED PURCHASE WHERE DESIRED.

Toe Clips, 2/6 per pair extra.   Chain Cover, 10/- extra; weight 1lb.

Carter's Gear Cover, 40/- extra; weight 2lbs.

*Fig. 54*

# 1894

Unfortunately the only 1894 Rover catalogue the authors have found was issued from the Starley depot at 52 rue de Dunkerque in Paris, and we have had to rely on a list of models and prices printed in the January *Gazette*. There were:

| | |
|---|---|
| *Rover Roadster*, 38 pounds with pneumatic tyres and chain cover | £26 10s |
| *Light Roadster*, 34 pounds with pneumatic tyres and chain cover | £26 10s |
| *Rover Racer*, 23 pounds with racing pneumatic tyres | £25 10s |
| *High Rover*, 38 pounds with pneumatic tyres and chain cover | £25 10s |
| *Ladies' Rover*, 32 pounds with pneumatic tyres, chain cover and wheel guards | £26 10s |
| *Ladies' Popular Rover*, 36 pounds with roadster pneumatic tyres | £16 |
| *No. 2 Rover Racer*, 28 pounds with roadster pneumatic tyres | £18 |
| *New Popular Rover*, 40 pounds with roadster pneumatic tyres | £15 |

The May advertisement carried a testimonial from Seddon's Pneumatic Co. Ltd complimenting the firm on a *Rover Road Racer* built for the Anfield Bicycle Club captain; it weighed $26^1/_2$ pounds equipped for the road, with gearcase. The June advertisement was for a *Rover Light Roadster*. Fitted with guards, brake, gearcase and Brooks B28 saddle it weighed 34 pounds and cost £26 10s (the January figure); without guards, brake or gearcase it weighed 26 pounds and cost £25 10s. In July the *New Popular Rover* was offered at £13 with $1^1/_4$" cushion tyres.

In the French catalogue the *Rover de Route* (the *Rover Roadster*) was designed for tourists using bad roads (possible Irish or American?) and riders weighing up to 19 stones. With pneumatic tyres it cost 850 francs and the only extra offered was a Grose chain-lubricator (unfortunately not described) at 30 francs. The *Rover légère de Route* (The Light Roadster) had a similar option; it was suggested that a rider might remove brake and guards, so saving about a pound in weight, and use the bicycle for road-racing. The *High Rover* (Fig. 55) was based on patent 10,153 granted to S. McCormack of Dublin in 1893. Quite a few makers, including Humber and Raleigh, turned out a similar machine (which is generally known as the *Giraffe*, the name of the Humber version). Its main appeal would

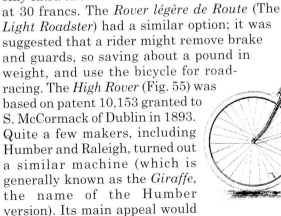

*Fig. 55*

have been to the rider who missed the view from the seat of a high bicycle and the absence of side-slip with the high bicycle. Another advantage was that water and mud were unlikely to reach the feet. The machine in the illustration faithfully follows McCormack's patent, which makes one wonder whether the English version was slightly different. In his review of the 1893 National Cycle Show C.W. Brown complained that the *High Rover* and one of the Raleigh patterns were a cross between a *Giraffe* (he was using the Humber name even then) and the "rear-driver proper", as the lower or main backbone was bent at the bracket so that the pedals were some three inches lower than those on machines of the *Giraffe* pattern. There is no sign of such a bend in the Paris catalogue. Furthermore, a *High Rover* (complete with Rover badge) in the Museum of British Road Transport has its chainstays in an almost direct line with the frame-tube; the pedals would be less than three inches lower than those on the *Giraffe*. Either the Rover at the cycle show, or this sole (?) remaining example of the model, was not typical of what Rover had on offer. There is also the possibility that Brown had seen this version and thought that the "bend" at the bracket was greater than it really was. This episode is another example of the need for caution when compiling history on the evidence provided in manufacturers' catalogues.

The *Rational Rover* was built for the tall rider. It was on the lines of the roadster but had a bigger frame and two 30" wheels. These first four machines and the *Bicyclette Rover pour Dames* were fitted with Southard cranks. Patent 17,408 was granted to F. Southard on 29 November 1888 for cranks made of solid steel rods that were twisted cold to increase their strength. This last bicycle had a new frame with 28" front and 26" rear wheels. Judging from the catalogue drawings, the *Ladies' Rover* and the *Ladies' Popular Rover* must have looked almost identical. The cheaper model had plain cranks, a slightly larger chain and - obviously - lower quality tubing, and it was unlined.

The curved frame was not illustrated.

The *Rover de Course No. 2* (the *No. 2 Rover Racer*) was produced in response to the demand for a light bicycle at a relatively low price. The illustration was similar to that of the 1893 *Rover Racer*. The *Rover Populaire* (the *New Popular Rover*) had a 30" front and 28" rear wheel; there was no mention of the two 28" wheels available in the 1893 English version. It cost 700 francs. A French model that was not advertised in England was the *Rover de Route No. 2*. It looked very like the *Rover Populaire* but weighed just over a couple of pounds less and cost 50 francs more; and the frame was lined instead of being simply enamelled.

c1894
Three young men ready for a day's cycling; two were riding Rovers. Rod Safe Photographic Collection.

# 1895

This was another year of major change, and the catalogue was well behind with its announcements. The January advertisement in the *Gazette* claimed that "The *Imperial Rover* met with a grand reception", and "*Imperial Rover*" was used instead of the plain "*Rover*" for the rest of the year. In May the *Imperial Rover Light Roadster* was advertised; it weighed 27 pounds with leather gearcase and detachable brake. It was not listed in the catalogue, and there are no details of the specification. In appearance it was similar to the *Rover Light Roadster*. The third edition of the 1895 catalogue contained the *Imperial Rover Racer* (Fig. 57) for road or path.

Three names had disappeared: *High Rover, Rover Racer* and *No. 2 Rover Racer*. The first was obsolescent - there had been none exhibited at either the National or the Stanley Shows at the end of 1894 - and the two racing models were replaced by the *No. 2 Rover Light Roadster,* (Fig. 56). Another problem now arises. The catalogue says that the machine was introduced a year previously, yet it bears little resemblance to the 1893 or 1894 *Rover Light Roadsters.* The former weighed 34 pounds with gearcase, brake and mudguards; the latter weighed 30 pounds without those appendages. This *No. 2* weighed 28 pounds, was intended for speed work on road or path and, like all the other diamond-framed models, had a new frame. The steep top-tube slope up to the head had gone although there was still a slight inclination.

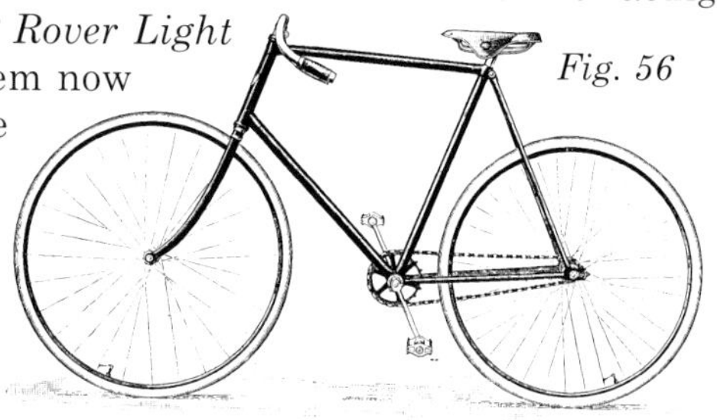

Fig. 56

*The No. 2 Rover Light Roadster,* (Fig. 56) the *New Popular Rover,* (Fig. 58) the *New Light Popular Rover* (Fig. 59) and the *Lady's Rational Rover* (for use also by small men and boys – Fig. 60) were all new, as can be seen. The *Rover Roadster* had the new diamond but was otherwise unchanged. This curved-tube *Lady's Rover* (Fig. 61) was reintroduced "in response to many applications from all parts of the world". Many alterations in detail had been made to bring the weight down to 30 or 32 pounds. On one page the catalogue said that the machine could be made with a single straight tube; on the next page that it could be made with double straight tubes to order. Although this option appeared under the *Lady's Rover* it seems likely that it was misplaced. In the first edition of the 1895 catalogue was the *Ladies' Popular Rover* (Fig. 62) with the single down-tube. In the third edition that version was replaced by the one with two down-tubes (Fig. 63), specification and price being unchanged. Comparison of the two shows that in addition to the extra tube there was a slight change in construction when the junction of the upper down-tube and the cross-stay with the lower down-tube was strengthened. Although the specification lists direct spokes, tangent spokes are depicted in the drawing. This illustration of the curved-tube version appeared on the back cover of the first 1895 catalogue; on the third edition it was replaced by an *Imperial Rover Path Racer (see fig. 69).*

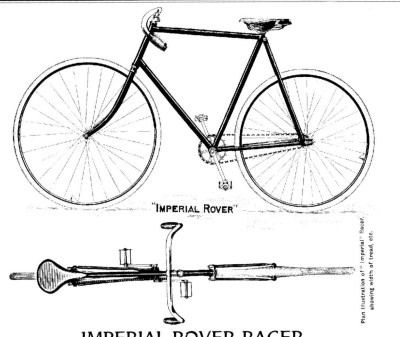

# IMPERIAL ROVER RACER.

## FOR PATH OR ROAD.

This machine has been specially designed for speed, and it is remarkable that within two weeks from the time the first was finished it scored the four following records:

Edinburgh to Liverpool, 22$^1$/$_2$ miles over very rough roads in 15 h., 3m, by Mr. H. B. Saunders, Anfield B.C., beating record by thirty-one minutes.

Northern twenty-four hours' record, 357$^1$/2 miles, by Mr. W. J. Neason, Anfield B.C., beating record by ten miles. (Only three men have previously beaten this distance on the road, Messrs.Holbein, Shortland, and Fontaine, and they on the great North Road.)

Birmingham to London and back, 208 miles, in 12h. 35m., by Mr. W. J. Goodwin, of Coventry, beating record by 24 minutes, and establishing a new Midland record of 197 miles in twelve hours *en route.*

And it is remarkable that this machine should have gone through the whole of these rides without showing the slightest signs of a defect of any kind, not withstanding the fact that Neason in his twenty-four hours' Northern record ran into the side of the road twice and once into a gate, owing to the night being dark and foggy. Racing men have not been slow to realise that there are many very valuable points in the construction of this machine, and we have already received orders from some of the fastest and best riders of the day.

WEIGHT, for path, 20$^1$/$_4$ lbs.; for road, with special road racing tyres, 24lbs. Any deviation from standard pattern will of necessity alter the weight.

**Price**  (including interchangeable gear)  ..  ..  ..  ..  **£27 10 0**

### SPECIFICATION.

SADDLE.- Brooks's B11 for path, or B10 for road..

FRAME. - Best weldless tubes;1in. connecting (parallel with ground) and seat tubes;1$^1$/$_8$in. backbone; $^3$/$_4$in. back tubes; $^{11}$/$_{16}$in. back stays.

CRANK BRACKET. -New and improved barrel shape.

WIDTH OF TREAD. - Path racer, 4$^1$/$_2$in.; road racer (to take chain cover), 5in.

GEAR. -"Rover" interchangeable; 66in. and 72in.for path, 63in. and 69in. for road, or other speeds to order.

CRANKS. - 6$^1$/$_4$in. or 6$^1$/$_2$in., square.

CHAIN. - $^1$/$_4$in.Perry's or Appleby's "Rover" block.

HANDLE-BAR. - $^{15}$/$_{16}$in. best weldless tube; special drop for path; Rational or modified drop for road; cork handles, celluloid rips.

WHEELS. - 28in. back and 30in. front, hollow rims.

SPOKES - SPECIAL DOUBLE BUTTED TANGENT, FOR GREATER STRENGTH AT RIM AND HUB.

TYRES. - 1$^3$/$_4$in. for path, 1 $^5$/$_8$in. for road.

FORKS. - best weldless steel tube; double fork crown, with broad plate edges, new curve and rake.

STEERING. - Improved ball; new dust-proof bearings top and bottom.

PEDALS. - Special "Rover" racing rat-trap; new method of fstening, dispensing with nuts and washers.

CONES AND BEARINGS. - All our cones and bearings are made of special diamond cast steel, separately hardened in water.

FINISH. - Best black enamel; bright parts plated on copper.

*Fig. 57*

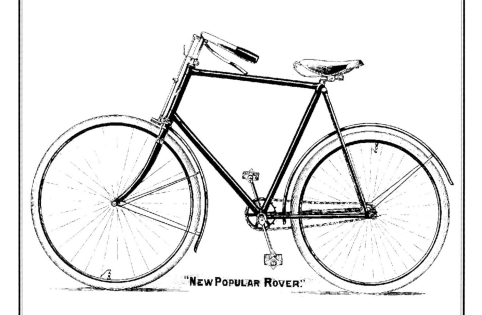

# THE NEW POPULAR ROVER.

We again have great pleasure in recording a most successful year with this now very popular machine. It has stood the test of the past three seasons in a very satisfactory manner, and we have very many testimonials from riders of all grades of society, expressing the great feeling of safety and comfort they have when riding this machine. It is not, of course, such a high-class machine as our Light Roadster or Roadster, but we can conscientiously say it is equal to nine-tenths of the so-called "best makes" on the market. We build it in two sizes to suit short and tall riders; it will be found up-to-date in every detail, and we think quite as popular with cyclists during '95 as it has been up to the present time.

The weight of this machine has been reduced somewhat, and we trust that this fact, together with the others mentioned above, will insure a continuance of the valued support of our numerous friends.

WEIGHT. - Complete 37lbs.

| | NETT CASH. | DEFERRED PAYMENTS. |
|---|---|---|
| **Price,** Pneumatic tyres   ..      ..      ..      .. | £15 0 0   .. | £18 0 0 |
| ··     Cushion tyres   ..      ..      ..      .. | 13 0 0   .. | 15 15 0 |

These prices are strictly nett, and not subject to discount.

## SPECIFICATION.

SADDLE.- Lamplugh's 410A.
FRAME. - Open diamond, large tubes.
CRANKS. - $6^1/_2$in. throw.
GEAR. - 60in.
CHAIN. - $5/_{16}$in. hardened block
HANDLE-BAR. - $15/_{16}$in. "Rover" Rational; horn handles.
WHEELS. - 28in. back and 30in. front, direct spokes.
TYRES. - $1^3/_4$in. pneumatic to both wheels, or $1^3/_4$in. and 2in. to order.
BRAKE. - "Rover" plunger, with rubber pad to spoon.
FORK. - Specially toughened steel sides, double plate crown, detachable footrests and lamp bracket.
GUARDS. - Steel, easily detachable without removing wheels.
STEERING. - Improved ball, top and bottom.
PEDALS. - Rubber, covered centres.
FINISH. - Best black enamel; bright parts plated on copper.

*For list of Extras see page 28. Testimonials, page 33.*

*Fig. 58*

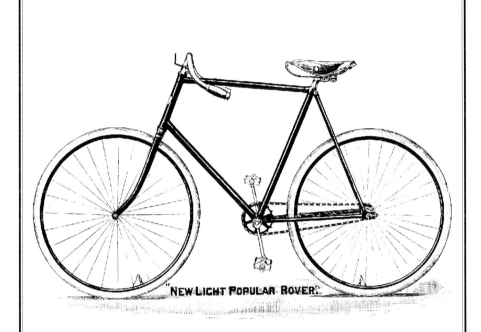

# NEW LIGHT POPULAR ROVER.

Since introducing our list for '94, we have placed upon the market a machine built upon similar lines to the "New Popular Rover", but without brake and guards, for strong and fast road riders who do not require the usual extras that are fitted to an ordinary roadster machine, and the success that this machine has met with is extraordinary, considering that we did not introduce it until very late in the season. It will be seen from teh following specification that it is thoroughly up to date in every respect, and a machine in which riders can place every confidence.

WEIGHT, with pneumatic tyres, 30lbs.

| | NETT CASH. | | DEFERRED PAYMENTS. |
|---|---|---|---|
| **Price,** Pneumatic tyres    ..    ..    ..    .. | £15 0 0 | .. | £18 0 0 |
| Cushion tyres    ..    ..    ..    .. | 13 0 0 | .. | 15 15 0 |

These prices are strictly nett, and not subject to discount.

## SPECIFICATION.

SADDLE.- Lamplugh's 410A.
FRAME. - Open diamond, large tubes.
CRANKS. - Round, $6^{1}/_{2}$in. throw
GEAR. - 63in.
CHAIN. - $^{5}/_{16}$in. block.
HANDLE-BAR. - $^{15}/_{16}$in., modified drop or rational to order.
WHEELS. - 28in. back and 30in. front, direct high tension spokes.
TYRES. - $1^{3}/_{4}$in. pneumatic to both wheels.
FORK. - Best toughened steel.
STEERING. - New ball, top and bottom.
PEDALS. - "Rover" rat trap.
FINISH. - Best black enamel; bright parts plated on copper.

*For list of Extras see page 28. Testimonials, page 33.*

*Fig. 59*

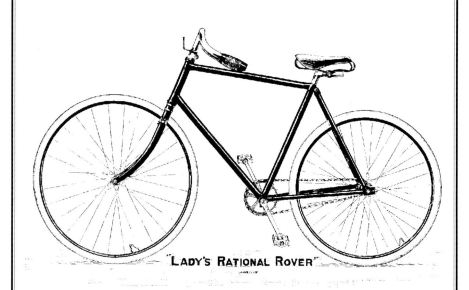

"LADY'S RATIONAL ROVER"

# LADY'S RATIONAL ROVER.

In response to the increased demand for the ordinary "Rover" frame for the use of ladies who have adopted the rational dress, we are building a machine with 25in. and 28in. wheels to the following specification, and we can, at the same time, thoroughly recommend it for youths, or very short riders who cannot reach teh ordinary size frame. It is practically the "Rover" Light Roadster with small wheels and without guards or brake.

WEIGHT. - Complete 25lbs.

              **Price,** Pneumatic tyres           ..       ..       ..       ..       **£25 10 0**

## SPECIFICATION.

SADDLE.- Brook's B10.

FRAME. - 1in. connecting and seat tubes; $1^{1}/_8$in. backbone; $^{3}/_4$in. back tubes; $^{11}/_{16}$in. back stay tubes; very narrow tread; "Rover" barrel crank bracket.

CRANKS. - Square, 6in. throw.

GEAR. - 60in.

CHAIN. - Perry's or Appleby's $^{1}/_4$in. "Rover" block

HANDLE-BAR. - $^{15}/_{16}$in. tube, "Rover" Rational pattern.

WHEELS. - 26in. back, 28in. front, double-butted tangent spokes.

TYRE. - 1 in. back, $1^{5}/_8$in. front, pneumatics.

FORKS. - Best weldless steel tube, new curve and rake.

STEERING. - Improved ball with large socket tube, and new dust-proof bearings top and bottom.

PEDALS. - "Rover" rat-trap, with new method of fastening dispensing with nuts and washers.

CONES AND BEARINGS. - Best diamond cast steel, separately hardened in water.

FINISH. - Best black enamel; bright parts plated on copper.

*Fig. 60*

# THE LADY'S ROVER.

In response to many applications from all parts of the world for Lady's "Rovers" of the old curved tube pattern, we have decided to continue manufacturing this style of frame, and, as will be seen by teh illustration opposite, a curved tube gives more room for the dress, and for mounting or dismounting, than the straight tube, in addition to which it is quite as fast and as easy to steer as the latter. For those who porefer it, however, we are also making the Lady's "Rover" with the single straight tube as last year. We have also made many alterations in detail which will bring the machine down in weight to 30lbs. or 32lbs. only.

**Price,** including chain and wheel guards    ..        ..    ..        **£26 10 0**

### SPECIFICATION.

SADDLE.- Brook's special.
FRAME. - Best weldless steel tubes, narrow tread, and improved bottom bracket.
CRANKS. - Square, 6in. throw.
GEAR. - 56in.
CHAIN. - Perry's or Appleby's "Rover" $1/_4$in. block
HANDLE-BAR. - $15/_{16}$in. tube, "Rover" Rational pattern.
WHEELS. - 26in. back and 28in. front, double-butted tangent spokes.
TYRES. - $1^3/_4$in. pneumatic to both wheels.
BRAKE. - "Rover" plunger, with rubber pad to spoon.
FORKS. - Best weldless steel tube, with detachable foot-rests and lamp bracket.
GUARDS. - Best corrugated steel, with patent leather chain cover, and laced back-guard to protect dress.
STEERING. - Improved ball, with large socket tube, and new dust-proof bearings top and bottom.
PEDALS. - Best "Rover" rubber, dust-proof covered centres, ends specially finished to prevent catching the dress.
CONES AND BEARINGS. - All best diamond cast steel, separately hardened in water.
FINISH. - Best black enamel, lined in two colours; bright parts plated on copper.

*Fig. 61*

# THE LADIES' POPULAR ROVER.

We are very pleased to be able to say that this really high-grade machine has been most favourably received during season '94 at home and abroad, and has given every satisfaction with regard to weight, price and stability. We have improved this machine up to date, and it will be found rather lighter than formerly, while the essential features of strength and finish have not been lost sight of. WEIGHT. - Complete 34lbs. to 35lbs.

| | Nett Cash. | Deferred Payment. |
|---|---|---|
| **Price,** including chain and wheel guards | £16 0 0 | £18 0 0 |

These prices are strictly nett, and are not subject to discount.

## SPECIFICATION.

SADDLE.- Brook's or Middlemore's, to order.
FRAME. - Weldless steel tube.
CRANKS. - 6in. round.
GEAR. - 56in.
CHAIN. - $5/16$in. hardened block
HANDLE-BAR. - Rational pattern; horn handles.
WHEELS. - 26in. back, 28in. front; direct spokes.
TYRES. - $1^3/4$in. pneumatic to both wheels.
BRAKE. - "Rover" plunger, with rubber pad to spoon.
FORK. - Specially toughened steel sides; double plate crown; detachable foot-rests and lamp bracket.
GUARDS. - Steel, easily detachable, with patent leather chain gurad, back guard laced to protect dress.
STEERING. - Improved ball, with large socket tube, and new dust-proof bearings top and bottom.
PEDALS. - "Rover" rubber, dust-proof centres, ends specially finished to prevent catching the dress.
FINISH. - Best black enamel; bright parts plated on copper.

*Fig. 62*

# THE LADIES' POPULAR ROVER.

We are very pleased to be able to say that this really high-grade machine has been most favourably received during season '94 at home and abroad, and has given every satisfaction with regard to weight, price and stability. We have improved this machine up to date, and it will be found rather lighter than formerly, while the essential features of strength and finish have not been lost sight of.

WEIGHT. - Complete 34lbs. to 35lbs.

Nett Cash. Deferred Payment.

**Price,** including chain and wheel guards     ..     ..    ..     **£16**     **£18**

These prices are strictly nett, and are not subject to discount.

## SPECIFICATION.

SADDLE.- Brook's or Middlemore's, to order.
FRAME. - Weldless steel tube.
CRANKS. - 6in. round.
GEAR. - 56in.
CHAIN. - $^5/_{16}$in. hardened block
HANDLE-BAR. - Rational pattern; horn handles.
WHEELS. - 26in. back, 28in. front; direct spokes.
TYRES. - $1^3/_4$in. pneumatic to both wheels.
BRAKE. - "Rover" plunger, with rubber pad to spoon.
FORK. - Specially toughened steel sides; double plate crown; detachable foot-rests and lamp bracket.
GUARDS. - Steel, easily detachable, with patent leather chain gurad, back guard laced to protect dress.
STEERING. - Improved ball, with large socket tube, and new dust-proof bearings top and bottom.
PEDALS. - "Rover" rubber, dust-proof centres, ends specially finished to prevent catching the dress.
FINISH. - Best black enamel; bright parts plated on copper.

*Fig. 63*

# 1896

The 1896 catalogue was an elaborate production. J.K. Starley wrote an introduction reviewing the ten years that had elapsed since the introduction of the *Rover*, and there was an article on the Rover specialities. Ten bicycles were listed. The *Rover Light Roadster* (Fig. 64) had been "improved wherever possible". The *Rover Roadster* was similar to the 1895 model except that it had hollow rims and a $5^3/_4$" tread (the distance between the outer faces of the cranks). The *Royal Rover* (Fig. 65) replaced the *No. 2 Rover Light Roadster*; it had a 5" tread. The *New Light Popular Rover* (Fig. 66) had some alterations from the 1895 model; note that with extra fittings it was known as the *New Popular Rover*. The *Ladies' Royal Rover* was a dearer version of the 1895 *Ladies' Popular Rover* with two down-tubes. The *Ladies' Popular Rover* was "a reproduction of the *Ladies' Royal Rover* at a lower price" (£16). It had a 5" tread, and was heavier; the weight was not revealed. The *Gentleman's Rover* (Fig. 67) and the *Ladies' Imperial Rover* (Fig. 68) were new models. In the notes on the latter it is said that it was made with a double straight tube frame; that was the machine listed as the *Ladies' Royal Rover*. The *Imperial Rover Path Racer* (Fig. 69) was listed for the first time, although it had clearly been on sale during 1895 and had appeared (minus specification) on the back cover of the third edition of the 1895 catalogue. The *Imperial Rover Road Racer* (Fig. 70) is also listed for the first time but was clearly produced in quantity during 1895.

# The Rover Light Roadster.

**price,**

**including leather chain cover,**

**£26 10s.**

THIS bicycle has been improved wherever possible for the coming season; we have fitted steering lock, and brought it well up to date in every detail, so that it makes a really reliable touring machine for riders up to twelve stone in weight. This machine has met with unqualified success; the brake and mud-guards are easily detachable, and consequently the machine can be considerably lightened, if required, at any time.

We have, for the coming season, decided to fit this bicycle with hollow rims, as they have proved themselves during the past year to be more reliable than solid rims, a reputation they had not earned in time past.

We make this machine (as all our other best models) in three heights of frame to suit short, medium, and tall riders, as per our illustration on page 10, viz., 22½in., 24in., and 26in. seat tubes.

WEIGHT, complete as per illustration, with chain cover, 32 lbs.

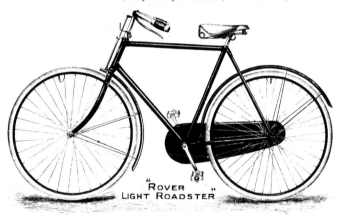

"ROVER" LIGHT ROADSTER

## Specification.

**Saddle.**—Brooks's B28, size 2.

**Frame.**—As described on page 10 (above illustration shows the medium-size frame).

**Width of Tread.**—5in. wide.

**Gear.**—"Rover" interchangeable (see page 11), the standard being 63in.; eight teeth on back, eighteen teeth on crank-axle chain wheel.

**Cranks.**—"Rover" pattern, square; 6½in. long (see page 11).

**Pedals.**—"Rover" rat-trap, special dust-proof capped ends.

**Chain.**—Best "Rover" block.

**Handle-bar.**—"Rover" rational shape; 1½in. best weldless steel tube; felt grips, with white tips.

**Wheels.**—30in. front and 28in. back; hollow rims.

**Spokes.**—Tangent, double butted, of the highest quality.

**Tyres.**—1⅜in. and 1¾in. Dunlop or Clincher detachable.

**Forks.**—Best weldless steel tube; detachable footrests and lamp bracket.

**Brake.**—"Rover" detachable, fitted with rubber block and improved connections.

**Guards.**—Best corrugated steel; detachable without removing wheels.

**Steering.**—Special ball bearings, dust-proof, with "Rover" steering lock (see page 11).

**Bearings.**—All cones, cups, and bearings are made of special diamond cast steel, specially hardened.

**Finish.**—Best black enamel; bright parts plated on copper.

*Fig. 64*

95

# The Royal Rover.

THE wonderful amount of success our No. 2 Rover has met with in the past has prompted us to place on the market a specially high grade, moderate-priced machine, and this we have pleasure in doing in our Royal Rover.

**Price**

**£20.**

This is practically identical with our Imperial Road Racer, but is not so light and well finished, nor are the fittings so good; at the same time all wearing parts are of the very best quality and workmanship, we cover it with the same guarantee as our best machines, and, as will be seen by the specification herewith, it has many of the other " Rover " specialities in addition.

We are making the Royal Rover in two sizes of frames only, viz., the 22½in. and 24in. seat tubes, the weight being 29 lbs.

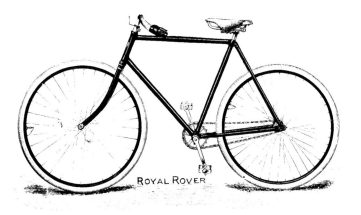

## Specification.

**Saddle.**—Middlemore's 661.

**Frame.**—As described on page 10 (the above illustration shows the medium-sized frame).

**Tread.**—5in. wide.

**Gear.**—63in.; eight teeth on back wheel, eighteen on front.

**Cranks.**—" Rover " pattern, square ; 6¾in. long (see page 11).

**Pedals.**—" Rover " rat-trap; dust-proof capped ends (see page 12).

**Chain.**—" Rover " block.

**Handle-bar.**—" Rover " medium drop ; 15/16in. best weldless steel tube ; cork handles, white tips.

**Wheels.**—30in. front, 28in. back ; solid rims.

**Spokes.**—Tangent, of the best quality.

**Tyres.**—1¾in. Dunlop or Clincher detachable.

**Forks.**—Specially toughened steel ; double plate crown.

**Steering.**—Special ball bearings, dust-proof.

**Bearings.**—All cones, caps, and bearings are made of special diamond cast steel, specially hardened.

**Finish.**—Best black enamel ; bright parts plated on copper.

*We can supply this machine with a 26in. frame at a charge of £1 extra net.*

*Fig. 65*

# The New Light Popular Rover.

Price,
with pneumatic tyres
**£15 10s.**
Deferred payments,
**£18** net.

THIS really low-priced reliable mount has met with a wonderful amount of success in the past. We have brought it up to date, and are now fitting tangent spokes, besides having devoted great care and attention to the details of this bicycle.

It is light and strong, and the price brings it within the reach of all who desire a high-class bicycle without paying a top price for same; it is a machine in which riders can place every confidence. Its low price makes it command a very ready sale all over the world.

As illustrated, the weight of the machine is 30 lbs., with brake and guards it is 37 lbs.

We make this machine in two sizes, i.e., with our 22½in. and 24in. seat tubes.

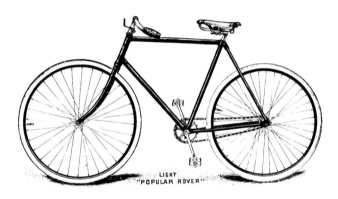

## Specification.

**Saddle.**—Mason's No. 562.
**Frame.**—As described on page 10 (above illustration shows a medium-sized frame).
**Tread.**—5in. wide.
**Gear.**—63in.; eight teeth on back wheel, eighteen on front.
**Cranks.**—"Rover" pattern, square; 6½in. long (see page 11).
**Pedals.**—"Rover" rat-trap, dust-proof.
**Chain.**—"Rover" block.
**Handle-bar.**—"Rover" medium drop; ⅞in. weldless steel tube; cork handles, black tips.

**Wheels.**—30in. front and 28in. back ; solid rims.
**Spokes.**—Tangent, of the best quality.
**Tyres.**—1⅝in. Clincher and Dunlop detachable.
**Forks** —Specially toughened steel ; double plate crown.
**Steering.**—Special ball bearings ; dust-proof.
**Bearings.**—All cones, cups, and bearings are made of special diamond cast steel, specially hardened.
**Finish.**—Best black enamel ; bright parts plated on copper.

*N.B.—This machine, fitted with guards and brake (rational, not dropped, handle-bar), is offered to the public as the* **NEW POPULAR ROVER** *at £16 net cash. Deferred payments £18 net.*

*We can supply these machines with a 26in. frame at a charge of £1 extra net.*

*Fig. 66*

# The Gentleman's Rover.

THIS, a new introduction for 1896, we have placed on the market to meet a want for a bicycle combining everything that is necessary to make a perfectly reliable, easy running machine, one that is made and finished with scrupulous care, and cannot possibly be excelled in detail by any manufacturer. We make this machine in the three different heights of frame, as per our illustration on page 10, viz., 22½in., 24in., and 26in. seat tubes.

We are also building each size in two weights, *i.e.*, the Full Roadster and the Light Roadster, to suit the different weights of riders—the light roadster being suitable for riders up to twelve stone, and the full roadster for heavier riders up to sixteen stone.

In the past the Rover has earned for itself the well-merited title of the best touring machine ever made, and, coupled with this the fact that we have during the past season been the most successful manufacturers of racing bicycles, it follows as a matter of course that in our '96 pattern Gentleman's Rover there will be embodied all the essential details which give strength, reliability, speed, and ease of propulsion.

When desired, crests or monograms, in gold or one colour, can be painted on this machine at an extra charge of £1 1s.

**Price,**

Including leather chain cover,

**£30.**

"THE GENTLEMANS ROVER"

## Specification.

**Saddle.**—Brooks's B90, with nickel-plated springs.
**Frame.**—As described on page 10 (above illustration showing the highest frame).
**Bottom Bracket.**—" Rover " dust-proof.
**Tread.**— 5¾in. wide.
**Gear.**—"Rover" interchangeable (see 11), the standard being 60in.; nine teeth on back wheel and nineteen teeth on crank-axle chain wheel.
**Cranks.**—" Rover " pattern, square ; 6½in. long (see page 11).
**Pedals.**—" Rover " pattern, with dust-proof capped ends, either rubber or rat-trap, 4in. or 4¼in. wide, to take boots.
**Chain.**—Best " Rover " block.
**Handle-bar.**—"Rover" rational shape, ⅝in. best weldless steel tube; special cork or felt handles.
**Wheels.**—30in. front, 28in. back ; hollow rims.

**Spokes.**—Tangent double-butted, of the highest quality.
**Tyres.**—1¾in. front and 2in. back, Dunlop or Clincher detachable.
**Forks.**—Best weldless steel tube ; detachable footrests and lamp bracket.
**Brake.**—" Rover " detachable, fitted with rubber brake block and improved connection.
**Guards.**— Best corrugated steel ; detachable without removing wheels.
**Steering.**—Special ball bearings, dust-proof, with new " Rover " steering lock (see page 11).
**Bearings.**—All cones, cups, and bearings are made of special diamond cast steel ; specially hardened.
**Finish.**—Specially finished and lined, or black enamel hand polished when ordered ; bright parts plated on copper.

*Fig. 67*

98

# The Ladies' Imperial Rover.

THE bicycle illustrated below is our new model for 1896, fitted with 30in. front and 28in. back wheel, and medium height frame. We make this in three sizes.

We have introduced this as our new best model, finding that many lady cyclists like the curved better than the straight tube frame, as there is more clearance for mounting and dismounting, and it is also a prettier shaped frame; but we also make the Ladies' Imperial Rover with a double straight tube frame (as on page 21) for those who prefer it, and also in three heights of frame.

**Price £30.**

In the production of this bicycle we have spared no expense or trouble, and place before our lady *clientèle* the most perfect bicycle it is possible to produce to suit their requirements, and we believe the result will be eminently satisfactory.

The weights have been kept down to the lowest possible point combined with strength, and are as follow: 27½ lbs. with the small frame; 28½ lbs. with the medium frame; and 30 lbs. with the high frame.

The Ladies' Imperial Rover is fitted with the " Rover " patent detachable dress and mud-guard illustrated on page 13, the " Rover " steering lock, and all the other " Rover " specialities.

To the external appearance, as well as to the internal details of this bicycle, we have devoted the most careful attention, and are prepared to finish it in the following colours: White, cream, silver grey, dark grey, sage green, olive green, blue, and chocolate, with lines to match, to order, at an extra cost of 20/-

We can also paint crests or monograms, in gold or one colour, on the bicycle when desired at a charge of £1 1s.

LADY'S "IMPERIAL ROVER"

## Specification.

**Saddle.**—Brooks's B10 special.

**Frame.**—Double curved tubes, as illustrated, or with double straight tubes as shown on page 21. Made in three sizes.

**Tread.**—5in. wide.

**Gear.**—" Rover " interchangeable; 56in.; eight teeth on back, sixteen teeth on front chain wheel.

**Cranks.**—" Rover " pattern, square; 6in. long (see page 11).

**Pedals.**—" Rover " special ladies' rat-trap (small teeth on one side of plates only); dust-proof; capped ends.

**Chain.**—Best " Rover " block.

**Handle-bar.**—" Rover " rational shape; ⅞in. best weldless steel tube; cork handles.

**Wheels.**—28in. front and 26in. back for 18in. and 21in. seat-tube frame, 30in. front and 28in. back for 24in. seat-tube frame; hollow rims.

**Spokes.**—" Rover " double-butted tangent.

**Tyres.**—1¾in. Dunlop or Clincher detachable.

**Forks.**—Best weldless steel tube; detachable foot-rests and lamp bracket.

**Brake.**—" Rover " detachable, fitted with rubber block and improved connections.

**Guards.**—Best corrugated steel mud-guards; rear guard laced with silk cord for the protection of the dress; " Rover " chain cover; rear half of back guard made detachable, to facilitate cleaning and adjustment.

**Steering.**—Improved ball; large socket tube; dust-proof top and bottom.

**Steering Lock.**—Special " Rover " pattern, designed expressly for this machine (see page 11).

**Bearings.**—All cones, cups, and bearings are made of special diamond cast steel, specially hardened.

**Finish.**—Best black enamel, hand polished; bright parts heavily plated on copper; or specially finished in colours to order as above.

*Fig. 68*

99

# Imperial Rover Path Racer.

**Price,**

including inter-
changeable gear,

**£27 10s.**

THE most successful path-racing bicycle in 1895; during the past season over 1,000 prizes and races have been won in Great Britain alone on this machine; all improvements gained by our experience during the past year have been incorporated in this, our new pattern for 1896.

The illustration shows the machine with 28in. and 30in. wheels; we, however, make our path racer with two 28in. wheels to order.

The weight of the standard pattern is 21 lbs.; any deviation from this will of necessity alter the weight.

## Specification.

**Saddle.**—Brooks's B11.

**Frame.**—As described on page 10 (above illustration shows the smaller size frame).

**Width of Tread.**—4½ inches.

**Gear.**—" Rover " interchangeable (see page 11); 73in.; eight teeth on back, twenty-one on front chain wheel.

**Cranks.**—" Rover " racer, square ; 6¼in. long.

**Pedals** —" Rover " special rat-trap, dust-proof capped ends ; screwed into cranks (see page 12).

**Chain.**—Best " Rover " block.

**Handle-bar.**—Special "Rover " drop; ⅞ best weldless steel tube ; cork handles.

**Wheels.**—30in. front and 28in. back ; hollow rims.

**Spokes.**—Special tangent; double-butted for strength at rims and hubs.

**Tyres.**—1⅜in. Dunlop, Palmer, or Clincher detachable

**Forks.**—Best weldless steel tube ; double fork crown.

**Steering.** – Special ball bearings ; dust-proof.

**Bearings.**—All cones, cups, and bearings are made of special diamond cast steel, specially hardened.

**Finish.**—Best black enamel ; bright parts plated on copper.

*N.B.—This machine is also supplied with two 28in. wheels where required.*

*Fig. 69*

# Imperial Rover Road Racer.

**Price,**
including
interchangeable
gear,

**£27 10s.**

IF anything, this bicycle can be said to have met with even greater success than our Path Racer. Many wonderful record rides have been accomplished on it during the past year, and it has also been foremost in all the important road races.

The only alterations for 1896 are in small details ; the weight remains the same, *i.e.*, 24¼lbs., with tyres, all other portions of machine as specification herewith. Any deviation from these details will alter the weight.

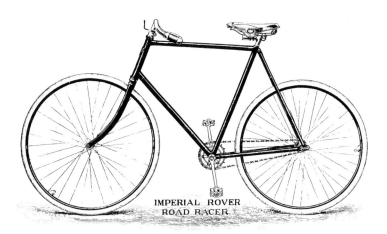

## Specification.

**Saddle.**—Brooks's B 10.

**Frame.**—As described on page 10 (above illustration shows medium-sized frame).

**Width of Tread.**—5in., with gear case clearance.

**Gear.**—" Rover " interchangeable (see page 11); 63in. ; eight teeth on back, eighteen on front chain wheel.

**Cranks.**—" Rover " pattern, square ; 6½in. (see page 11).

**Pedals.**—" Rover " special rat-trap ; dust-proof capped ends (see 12).

**Chain.**—Best " Rover " block.

**Handle-bar.**—" Rover " medium drop ; 1⅝in. best weldless steel tube ; cork handles.

**Wheels.**—30in. front, 28in. back ; hollow rims.

**Spokes.**—Special tangent; double-butted for strength at rims and hubs.

**Tyres.**—1⅜in. Dunlop and Clincher detachable.

**Forks.**—Best weldless steel tube ; double fork crown.

**Steering.**—Special ball bearings, dust-proof, with new " Rover " steering lock (see page 11).

**Bearings.**—All cones, cups, and bearings are made of special diamond cast steel, specially hardened.

**Finish.**—Best black enamel ; bright parts plated on copper.

*Fig. 70*

101

*Rover and Soldier. The badge is pre-1895 but the steering lock and chainwheel were not catalogued until 1896. The position of the rifle would make it almost impossible to ride.*

*Ladies' Popular Rover 1895, 1896 or 1897. In 1898 the pedal fitting changed and in 1899 a different fork-crown was illustrated.*

# 1897

The *Rover Light Roadster* was unchanged. The *Rover Roadster* (Fig. 71) was lighter than the 1896 model and 10s dearer. The *Royal Rover* had hollow rims, a Brooks B10 saddle, and $1^{1}/_{2}$" and $1^{5}/_{8}$" Dunlop front and rear tyres or "to order"; it weighed 28 pounds and cost £24. The *New Popular Rover* (Fig. 72) reappeared with a page of its own. The *New Light Popular Rover* was identical with it, except that it had no brake or mudguards and was fitted with lighter tyres and saddle; it weighed 29 pounds and cost £16 10s. The *Ladies' Royal Rover* in the first edition of the catalogue was identical with the 1896 version but was £4 dearer; in the second edition the specification was unchanged but the model was loop-framed (Fig. 73). There was a similar change with the *Ladies' Popular Rover* (figs. 74 and 75). The *Gentleman's Rover* had minor changes; as a light roadster it weighed 30-32 pounds (for riders up to 13 stones) and as a full roadster 36 pounds (for riders up to 18 stones). The former had a Brooks B92 saddle, the latter a B90; tyres were $1^{3}/_{4}$" front and 2" back for the full roadster, $1^{5}/_{8}$" front and $1^{3}/_{4}$" back for the light - make to order; the guards were not listed as corrugated. The *Ladies' Imperial Rover* had this new frame (Fig. 76). There is a sign of the times in the references to American fittings (not recommended) and American tires (not guaranteed). The Society Boom, that strange period when the aristocracy and the upper classes played at cycling, led to shortages of machines and equipment; the American business-men seized their opportunity and exported whatever they could lay their hands on. Some of it was good but unfortunately a lot was junk, and the prejudice engendered against American machines and accessories lasted for many years. The *Imperial Rover Path Racer* (Fig. 77) had a slightly changed specification; the weight and price were unchanged. The *Imperial Rover Road Racer* weighed $24^{1}/_{2}$ pounds as a road racer and $26^{1}/_{2}$ pounds if equipped as a special light roadster with a gearcase. It still cost £27 10s but there were more options. An extra chainwheel was supplied free to raise the gear to 73"; the square Rover cranks were $6^{1}/_{2}$" for $22^{1}/_{2}$" and 24" frames, 7" for 26" frames; wheels were 28" for $22^{1}/_{2}$" frames, 30" front and 28" back for 24" and higher frames. The system of frame-measuring should be remembered - 1" should be added to give the correct size according to the accepted method. The *Rover Cob* (Fig. 78) had been introduced in 1895 but appeared in the catalogue for the first time.

# The Rover Roadster.

**Price,**

including leather
chain cover,

**£27.**

THIS machine is built on the same lines as the Rover Light Roadster, shown on the previous page, but is constructed to carry heavier weights, and, as will be seen from the specification below, the tyres, saddle, pedals, etc., are of a heavier and stronger description than those used on the Rover Light Roadster. We specially recommend this machine for rough roads and heavy weights. The success that it has met with in the past gives us every confidence to again recommend it as a bicycle that, with ordinary care, will stand anything that it is likely to be called upon to bear.

It was on a Rover Roadster that Mr. Robert Louis Jefferson accomplished his now famous ride from London to Irkutsk, the capital of Siberia; 2,000 to 3,000 miles of this journey was made across country where no roads exist, the route being simply cart tracks, consequently the strain on the bicycle was enormous, and we were pleased to learn from Mr. Jefferson that not only did the machine stand the rough usage satisfactorily, but he had no trouble with it in any way. The bearings were not adjusted during the whole of the ride, nor did any of the nuts or other parts of the machine require attention.

**WEIGHT, complete as per specification below, 36 lbs.**

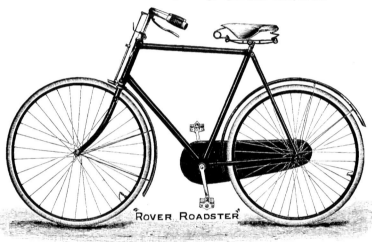

## Specification.

**Saddle.**—Brooks's B90

**Frame.**—22¼in., 24in., or 26in. seat tube, measuring from top of crank bracket to seat lug.

**Gear.**—"Rover" interchangeable, 60in.

**Cranks.**—Square, 6½in., special "Rover" pattern for 22¼in. and 24in. frames; 7in. for 26in. and higher.

**Pedals.**—3¾in., 4in., 4¼in., or 4½in., to order, fitted with rubber blocks, dust caps to ends.

**Chain.**—New and improved "Rover" roller, ¼in.

**Handle-bar.**—"Rover" rational, with Cooper's ribbed felt handles.

**Wheels.**—28in. wheels for 22¼in. frame; 30in. front, 28in. back, for 24in. and higher frames; hollow rims.

**Spokes.**—Tangent, double-butted, of the highest quality.

**Tyres.**—1¾in. front, 2in. back; full roadster, Dunlop, or other tyres to order.

**Forks.**—Best weldless steel tube; double crown plates, "Rover" pattern; detachable footrests and lamp bracket.

**Brake.**—"Rover" detachable, with rubber block and improved connections.

**Guards.**—Best steel, specially designed for easy removal; "Rover" leather case, aluminium fittings, celluloid front.

**Steering.**—Special ball bearings top and bottom, dust-proof, with "Rover" steering lock.

**Bearings.**—All cups, cones, and balls of special diamond cast steel, separately and specially hardened.

**Finish.**—Best black enamel; bright parts plated on copper.

*For List of Extras and Telegraphic Code, see page 24.*

"The Rover has set the fashion to the world."—The Cyclist.

*Fig. 71*

105

# The New Popular Rover.

**Price**

**£17**

net cash.

THIS machine was introduced by us five years ago, to meet the demand for a really sound, substantial, and reliable bicycle at a low price, and the enormous demand we have had for it proves that it has become a great favourite with those cyclists who cannot afford the luxury of a more expensive mount. We guarantee this machine, and have no hesitation in saying it is the best value for money on the market at the present time.

It will be seen that we have slightly increased the price, but we have done this to enable us to fit a better quality chain and saddle and hollow rims, which we are quite sure will find favour with our numerous clients, who will undoubtedly appreciate these improvements in detail.

**WEIGHT, to specification below, 36 lbs.**

"NEW POPULAR ROVER."

## Specification.

**Saddle.**—B302 Brooks.

**Frame.**—22½in. and 24in. seat tube, measuring from top of crank bracket to seat lug.

**Gear.**—60in.

**Cranks.**—6½in. square, "Rover" pattern.

**Pedals.**—"Rover" rubber.

**Chain.**—Best "Rover" block, ⅛in.

**Handle-bars.**—"Rover" medium drop, weldless steel tube, cork handles.

**Wheels.**—30in. front, 28in. back; hollow rims.

**Spokes.**—Tangent, best quality.

**Tyres.**—1⅜in. front, 1¾in. back; Dunlop or others to order.

**Forks.**—Special toughened steel; plate crown.

**Brake.**—"Rover" detachable, with rubber block and improved connections.

**Guards.**—Best steel, detachable.

**Steering.**—Special ball bearings top and bottom, dust-proof, with "Rover" steering lock.

**Bearings.**—All cups, cones, and balls, of special diamond cast steel, separately and specially hardened.

**Finish.**—Best black enamel; bright parts plated on copper.

*For List of Extras and Telegraphic Code, see page 24.*

" The Rover is the pioneer of the present-day cycle." – Vide Cycling Press.

*Fig. 72*

# The Ladies' Royal Rover.

**Price,**

**£24.**

THE past season has shown the Lady's Royal Rover to be a great success, and had we been in a position to deliver, we could have sold many thousands more than we were able to supply. We recommend with confidence the Royal Rover to those riders who do not care to pay the price of the Lady's Imperial, but who, at the same time, require a thoroughly serviceable and reliable mount. The standard patterns, as will be seen from the illustration below, are 19-in. and 21-in. seat tubes, but we also make 23-in. seat tubes at an extra cost of 20/-.

WEIGHT, to specification below, 32-lbs.

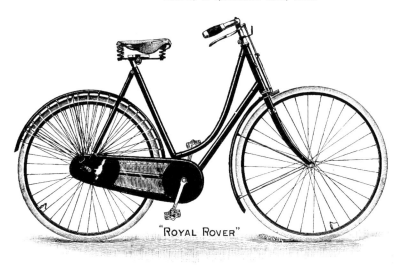

"ROYAL ROVER"

## Specification.

**Saddle.**—B302 Brooks.

**Frame.**—As illustrated.     19-in. and 21-in. seat tubes, measuring from top of crank-bracket to seat lug, also made with a 23-in. seat tube to order at an extra cost of 20/-.

**Gear.**—59-in.

**Cranks.**—6-in. square, "Rover" pattern.

**Pedals.**—Special "Rover" rat-trap or light rubber to order, thoroughly dust-proof capped ends.

**Chain.**—Best "Rover" block, ¼-in.

**Handle-bar.**—Semi-horizontal, with cork handles.

**Wheels.**—28-in. front and 26-in. back for 19-in. and 21-in. seat tubes; 30-in. front and 28-in. back for 23-in. seat tube; hollow rims.

**Spokes.**—Tangent, of best quality steel.

**Tyres.**—1½-in. Ladies' Dunlop tyres, or others to order.

**Forks.**—Specially toughened steel; double plate crown; detachable footrests.

**Brake.**—"Rover" detachable, with rubber block and improved connections.

**Guards.**—Best steel mudguards; rear guard laced (as illustrated above) for the protection of the dress; leather chain cover, celluloid front.

**Steering.**—Special ball bearings top and bottom, dust-proof, with "Rover" steering lock.

**Bearings.**—All cups, cones, and balls of special diamond cast steel, separately and specially hardened.

**Finish.**—Best black enamel, lined in one colour; bright parts plated on copper.

*For List of Extras and Telegraphic Code, see page 24.*

"**The Rover has set the fashion to the world.**"—**The Cyclist.**

*Fig. 73*

# The Ladies' Popular Rover.

**Price**
**£17**
net cash.

AS will be seen from the illustration, this machine is of the same design as the Ladies' Royal, but in order to give a range of prices to suit all pockets, we have, by using less expensive accessories and reducing the cost of labour, been able to offer this machine at the specially low price of £17; at the same time none of the wearing parts or bearings of the machine are reduced in efficiency, and when we point out that we are using a better chain and fitting hollow rims in place of solid as formerly, we are convinced that our clients will admit that the slight increase of price is warranted. We make the Ladies' Popular Rover with 23in. seat tube at an extra charge of 20/- net.

We guarantee this machine for twelve months against defective workmanship or material, and can honestly say that no better machine at the price can be purchased.

WEIGHT, to specification below, 32 lbs.

## Specification.

**Saddle.**—B302 Brooks.

**Frame.**—As illustrated. 19in. and 21in. seat tube, measuring from top of crank bracket to seat lug, also 23in. seat tube at an extra charge of 20/-

**Gear.**—59in.

**Cranks.**—6in. square, "Rover" pattern.

**Pedals.**—Special "Rover" rat-trap, or light rubber to order, thoroughly dust-proof capped ends.

**Chain**—Best "Rover" block, ¼in.

**Handle-bar.**—Semi-horizontal, with cork handles, celluloid tips.

**Wheels.**—28in. front and 26in. back for 19in. and 21in. seat tubes; 30in. front and 28in. back for 23in. seat tube.

**Spokes.**—Tangent, of best quality steel.

**Tyres**—1½in. Dunlop, or others to order.

**Forks.**—Specially toughened steel; double plate crown; detachable footrests.

**Brake.**—"Rover" detachable, with rubber block and improved connections.

**Guards.**—Best steel mudguards; rear guard laced as illustrated above for the protection of the dress, leather chain cover.

**Steering.**—Special ball bearings top and bottom, dust-proof, with "Rover" steering lock.

**Bearings.**—All cups, cones, and balls of special diamond cast steel, separately and specially hardened.

**Finish.**—Best black enamel; bright parts plated on copper.

*For List of Extras and Telegraphic Code, see page 24.*

"The Rover is the pioneer of the present-day cycle."—Vide Cycling Press.

*Fig. 74*

# The Ladies' Popular Rover.

Price,
£17,
net cash.

A S will be seen from the illustration, this machine is of the same design as the Ladies' Royal, but in order to give a range of prices to suit all pockets, we have, by using less expensive accessories, and reducing the cost of labour, been able to offer this machine at the specially low price of £17; at the same time none of the wearing parts or bearings of the machine are reduced in efficiency, and when we point out that we are using a better chain and fitting hollow rims in place of solid as formerly, we are convinced that our clients will admit that the slight increase of price is warranted. We make the Ladies' Popular Rover with 23-in. seat tube at an extra charge of 20/- net.

We guarantee this machine for twelve months against defective workmanship or material, and can honestly say that no better machine at the price can be purchased.

WEIGHT, to specification below, 32-lbs.

"POPULAR ROVER"

## Specification.

Saddle.—B302 Brooks.
Frame.—As illustrated. 19-in. and 21-in. seat tube measuring from top of crank bracket to seat lug, also 23-in. seat tube at an extra charge of 20/-.
Gear.—59-in.
Cranks.—6-in. square, "Rover" pattern.
Pedals.—Special "Rover" rat-trap, or light rubber to order, thoroughly dust-proof capped ends.
Chain.—Best "Rover" block, ⅜-in.
Handle-bar.—Semi-horizontal, with cork handles, celluloid tips.
Wheels.—28-in. front and 26-in. back for 19-in. and 21-in. seat tubes; 30-in. front and 28-in. back for 23-in. seat tube.
Spokes.—Tangent, of best quality steel.

Tyres.—1⅜-in. Ladies' Dunlop tyres, or others to order.
Forks.—Specially toughened steel; double plate crown; detachable footrests.
Brake.—"Rover" detachable, with rubber block and improved connections.
Guards.—Best steel mudguards; rear guard laced as illustrated above for the protection of the dress, leather chain cover.
Steering.—Special ball bearings top and bottom, dust-proof, with "Rover" steering lock.
Bearings.—All cups, cones, and balls of special diamond cast steel, separately and specially hardened.
Finish.—Best black enamel, bright parts plated on copper.

*For List of Extras and Telegraphic Code, see page 24.*
**"The Rover is the pioneer of the present-day Cycle."—Vide Cycling Press.**

*Fig. 75*

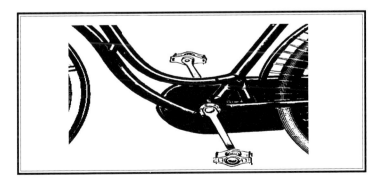

*Fig. 76*

109

# The Imperial Rover Path Racer.

THE reputation which this machine made for itself in the early part of 1894 and during season 1895 has been more than maintained by the wonderful performances achieved upon it during season 1896. In illustration of which we may mention The world's mile record made by J. Platt-Betts.

The numerous victories of Harry S. Large, including the Birmingham Club's Shield, the Appleby Cup, the Sydney Trophy, and the Surrey Cup.

E. H. Ainsworth's notable performances in winning the Essex Warwick Challenge Vase (won outright), the special Warwick Vase presented by the Countess of Warwick, the five miles N.C.U. Midland Centre Championship; five to twenty-five miles and fifty-five miles to hundred miles Scottish records, also five and hundred miles Class B Championship of Scotland, by R. C. Crawford.

The 2,000 Frs. Grand Prix at Ostend, by E. E. Parlby.

The numerous victories achieved by Messrs. Lewis, Megson, and Payne, the representatives of the Australian League, and

The following N.C.U. Centre Championships :

 One Mile N.C.U. Midland Centre Championship.
 One Mile N.C.U. North Yorks and South Durham Championship.
 One Mile N.C.U. Cornwall Centre Championship.
 Ten miles N.C.U. Sunderland Centre Championship.
 Five Miles N.C.U. Midland Centre Championship.
 Twenty-five miles N.C.U. Northampton Centre Championship.

**Price**

**£27 10s.**

WEIGHT, to specification below, 21-lbs.

"IMPERIAL PATH RACER."

## Specification.

**Saddle.**—Brooks's B 11.

**Frame.**—22½-in., 24-in., 26-in.. seat tubes, measuring from top of crank bracket to seat lug.

**Width of Tread.**—4½-in.

**Gear.**—Special "Rover" interchangeable, standard 84-in. ; extra chain wheel to raise or lower gearing supplied free of charge to order.

**Cranks.**—Square, 7-in., special "Rover" pattern ; 6½-in. or 7½-in. to order.

**Pedals.**—Special "Rover" rat-trap, 3¾-in., larger sizes to order ; special dust-proof capped ends.

**Chain.**—New and improved "Rover" roller, ½-in.

**Handle-bar.**—Special "Rover" drop or forward extension to order, cork handles, celluloid ends

**Wheels.**—28-in. wheels for 22½-in. frame ; 30-in. front, 28-in. back, for 24-in. and higher frames ; hollow rims ; (28-in. wheels can be fitted to 24-in. frames to order).

**Spokes.**—Special tangent, double-butted, of the highest quality.

**Tyres.**—1⅜-in. Dunlop or others to order.

**Forks.**—Best weldless steel tube ; double crown plates, "Rover" pattern.

**Steering.**—Special ball bearings top and bottom, thoroughly dust-proof.

**Bearings.**—All cups, cones, and balls of special diamond cast steel, separately and specially hardened.

**Finish.**—Best black enamel ; all bright parts plated on copper.

*For List of Extras and Telegraphic Code, see page 24.*

"The Rover has set the fashion to the world."—The Cyclist.

*Fig. 77*

*Imperial Rover Path Racer 1897*
*Fitted with touring saddle, back*
*brake, mudguards and wheels. The*
*original wooden racing wheels had*
*been kept.*
*Graaf-Reinett Museum, Northern*
*Cape, South Africa.*

# The Rover Cob.

**Price,**

including Rover
gear case.

**£30.**

I T will be remembered that we introduced this machine towards the close of season 1895 to meet the demand for a bicycle that could be mounted or dismounted without using the step, and our anticipations in regard to its success have been fully realised. It has met with universal satisfaction, and we have supplied a great number of "Rovers" built on these lines to gentlemen who would probably never have cycled on the ordinary bicycle. We have received many letters congratulating us upon the design, and expressing the satisfaction and safety that is felt when riding within such easy reach of the ground, and not a few riders of this machine are over seventy-five years of age.

The weight of the Rover Cob can be reduced materially to suit the requirements of lighter riders by fitting smaller tyres, lighter saddle, and pedals than those shown in the specification at foot.

WEIGHT, as full roadster, 36-lbs. ; as light roadster, 32-lbs.

## Specification.

**Saddle.**—Roadster, Brooks's B90 ; light roadster, B92.

**Frame.**—21-in., 22½-in. or 24-in. seat tubes, measuring from top of crank bracket to seat lug.

**Gear.**—" Rover " interchangeable, 60-in.

**Cranks.**—Square, 6-in., special " Rover " pattern.

**Pedals.**—3¾-in., 4-in., 4¼-in. or 4½-in. to order, fitted with rubber blocks as full roadster, or rat-trap bars as light roadster, dust caps to ends.

**Chain.**—New and improved "Rover" roller, ½-in.

**Handle-bar.**—"Rover" rational, with Cooper's ribbed felt handles.

**Wheels.**—28-in. front, 26-in. back ; hollow rims.

**Spokes.**—Tangent, double butted, of the highest quality.

**Tyres.**—1¾-in. front and 2-in. back for full roadster. 1⅝-in. front and 1¾-in. back for light roadster ; Dunlop or other tyres to order.

**Forks.**—Best weldless steel tube, double crown plates, "Rover" pattern, detachable footrests and lamp bracket.

**Brake.**—"Rover" detachable, with rubber block and improved connections.

**Guards.**—Best steel, specially designed for easy removal. "Rover" gear case.

**Steering.**—Special ball bearings top and bottom, dust-proof, with " Rover " steering lock.

**Bearings.**—All cups, cones, and balls of special diamond cast steel, separately and specially hardened.

**Finish.**—Special black enamel, lined in two colours all bright parts plated on copper.

*For List of Extras and Telegraphic Code, see page 24.*

**The Rover has set the fashion to the world."—The Cyclist.**

*Fig. 78*

112

# 1898

The *Imperial Rover Roadster* (Fig. 79) replaced the 1897 *Gentleman's Rover* (the full-roadster version) and the *Rover Roadster*. The *Imperial Rover Light Roadster* (Fig. 80) replaced the light-roadster version of the *Gentleman's Rover* and the *Rover Light Roadster*. It will be noted that according to the catalogue this model was available in 1896; but by now it should be apparent that the firm's policy on model-naming seems to have been designed to confuse the customer. The *Lady's Imperial Rover* (no longer *Ladies'*) had an unchanged frame but the specification was different (Fig. 81). The *Rover Cob* became the *Imperial Rover Cob*, and the specification changed; note that the unusual method of frame-measuring used in 1897 had changed to the customary one in 1898. The *Royal Rover Cob* (Fig. 82) was a cheaper (£26 10s) version of the *Imperial Rover Cob*. The *New Popular Rover* looked much as before but the specification had changed (Fig. 83). The *Lady's Royal Rover* (Fig. 84) was offered with a loop-frame; the straight-tubed model was abandoned. Although the catalogue said that there were no other changes, a Middlemore M73 saddle replaced the Brooks. It was said to be on a "straight seat rod", but the illustration (similar to that for the 1897 version) showed clearly the 7 pin used. The *Lady's Popular Rover* copied the Royal in dropping the straight-tubed version and in replacing the Brooks B302 saddle with an M73 (also alleged to be on a "straight seat rod" despite the illustration). It was otherwise apparently identical with the 1897 model. The *Imperial Path Racer* had minor alterations. There was another reminder that the system of frame-measurement had changed. The B11 saddle was on a 7 pin for 23½" and 25" frames, a straight pin for 27" and higher; 28" wheels could be fitted to 25" frames to order; the weight increased from 21 to 22 pounds; and the forward extension was not offered. The *Imperial Rover Road Racer* was practically unchanged. The weight had risen to 25 pounds and the B10 saddle-pin copied that on the path racer. The *Royal Rover Road Racer* (Fig. 85) had replaced the *Royal Rover*.

A word of warning is necessary here. A study of the Rover catalogues of the mid-nineties suggests strongly that the compilers had strange ideas about describing ladies' bicycles. Their K frames are now called loop frames; their loop frames were what are now called double loop frames; and their straight frames were what are now called K frames. Further comment seems unnecessary.

IMPERIAL ROVER ROADSTER

The

# Imperial Rover

## Roadster

Fig. 79

114

# The
## Imperial Rover
### Roadster

HIS machine takes the place of the Gentleman's Rover Roadster and the Rover Roadster shown in our price list of last season, and in it we combine all the best points of those two machines. It is specially recommended for heavy weights, and is a perfect touring bicycle. It is specially constructed to stand the strain of hard wear and weight-carrying, and we may mention that it was on a similar machine to this that Mr. R. L. Jefferson accomplished the unprecedented performance of riding from London to Irkutsk, the capital of Siberia, a distance of over 6,000 miles, without having to once adjust any of the bearings, or touch any part of the machine in any way. Mr. Budgett Meakin also used this bicycle in his celebrated ride through the countries of Northern Africa (Morocco, Algiers, Tunis, etc.)

PRICE

£30

WEIGHT, to specification below, (25in. frame) ⸱ 35 lbs.

## SPECIFICATION:

SADDLE - - Brooks's B 90, plated springs, 7 seat rod for 23½in. and 25in. frames; straight seat rod for 27in. frames and higher,

FRAME - - 23½in., 25in., 27in., or 29in., measuring from centre of crank spindle to top of seat lug.

GEAR - - - "Rover" interchangeable, standard 60in. Other gears to order.

CRANKS - - Special "Rover" pattern, square, 6½in. for 23½in. and 25in. frames, 7in. for higher frames.

PEDALS - - 4in. rubber, best "Rover" pattern, thoroughly dust-proof. Other sizes to order.

CHAIN - - Improved "Rover" roller, ½in.

HANDLE-BAR - "Rover" upturned (as illustrated) or "Rover" rational (at right-angles to steering tube); felt handles.

WHEELS - - 28in. for 23½in. frames, 30in. front and 28in. back for 25in. frames and higher; hollow rims.

SPOKES - - Tangent, double-butted, of the highest possible quality.

TYRES - - 1¾in. roadster Dunlop. Other tyres to order.

FORKS - - Best weldless steel tubes, with double crown-plates, "Rover" pattern; special taper steering tube; detachable foot-rests and lamp-bracket.

BRAKE - - Improved "Rover" detachable, with rubber block.

GUARDS - - Best steel, with strengthened edges, specially designed for easy removal; stays thickly plated on copper.

GEAR-CASE - Special "Rover" pattern, easily detachable.

STEERING - Special ball bearings top and bottom; improved "Rover" steering lock.

BEARINGS - - All cups, cones, and balls, of special diamond cast steel, separately and specially hardened.

FINISH - - Best black enamel, lined in two colours, all bright parts plated on copper.

FOR LIST OF EXTRAS, AND TELEGRAPHIC CODE, SEE PAGE 36.

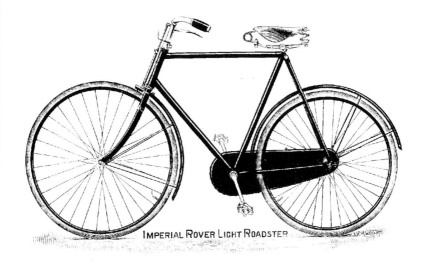

IMPERIAL ROVER LIGHT ROADSTER

The

# Imperial Rover
## Light Roadster

*Fig. 80*

116

*The* ─────

# Imperial Rover
# Light Roadster

HIS machine is introduced to take the place of the Light Gentleman's Rover and the Rover Light Roadster of last year. It is a specially high-grade bicycle, suitable for riders up to thirteen stone weight, and as a touring machine for medium weights is unrivalled. Messrs. Fraser, Lunn, and Lowe, the "Three Musketeers of the Wheel," selected three machines of this pattern when they started from England, in May, '96, on their tour round the world; at the time of compiling this list they had reached Shanghai without having any trouble whatever, although they had cycled over the worst roads in the world—through Southern Russia, Persia, India, etc.

It was also on this bicycle that Mr. William Snell, of Hamilton, Victoria, rode from Menzies to Adelaide, across the West Australian deserts, 1,600 miles, and the same machine was used by Mr. A. Richardson in his memorable journey from Coolgardie to Adelaide, a distance of 1,600 miles.

PRICE

£30

WEIGHT, to specification below (25in. frame) ⸰ 32 lbs.

## SPECIFICATION:

| | |
|---|---|
| SADDLE | Brooks's B 93, plated springs; 7 seat rod for 23½in. and 25in. frames, straight seat rod for 27in. frames and higher. |
| FRAME | 23½in., 25in., 27in., or 29in., measuring from centre of crank spindle to top of seat lug. |
| GEAR | "Rover" interchangeable, standard 63in. Other gears to order. |
| CRANKS | Special "Rover" pattern, square, 6½in. for 23½in. and 25in. frames, 7in. for higher frames. |
| PEDALS | 3¾in. rat-trap, best "Rover" pattern, thoroughly dust-proof. Other sizes to order. |
| CHAIN | Improved "Rover" roller, ½in. |
| HANDLE-BAR | "Rover" upturned (as illustrated), or "Rover" rational (at right-angles to steering tube), felt handles. |
| WHEELS | 28in. for 23½in. frames, 30in. front and 28in. back for 25in. frames and higher; hollow rims. |
| SPOKES | Tangent, double-butted, of the highest possible quality. |
| TYRES | 1⅝in. front, 1¾in. back, light roadster Dunlop. Other tyres to order. |
| FORKS | Best weldless steel tube with double crown-plates, "Rover" pattern, special taper steering tube; detachable foot-rests and lamp-bracket. |
| BRAKE | Improved "Rover" detachable, with rubber block. |
| GUARDS | Best steel, with strengthened edges, specially designed for easy removal; stays thickly plated on copper. |
| GEAR-CASE | Special "Rover" pattern, easily detachable. |
| STEERING | Special ball bearings top and bottom, improved "Rover" steering lock. |
| BEARINGS | All cups, cones, and balls, of special diamond cast steel, separately and specially hardened. |
| FINISH | Best black enamel, lined in two colours, all bright parts plated on copper. |

FOR LIST OF EXTRAS, AND TELEGRAPHIC CODE, SEE PAGE 36.

*Fig. 80a*

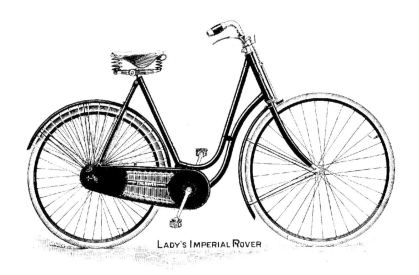

LADY'S IMPERIAL ROVER

The

## Lady's Imperial Rover

*Fig. 81*

118

The ___

# Lady's Imperial Rover

HIS machine has given such great satisfaction during the past season that we have decided to continue making the same shape frame; but by specially lightening all parts where permissible we have succeeded in reducing the weight for the 20in. and 22in. frames, to the specifications given below, to 28lbs. net. This weight is "actual," not "reputed."

"Graphis" in the *Irish Cyclist* of October 13th, 1897, writes of the Lady's Imperial Rover as follows:

"As regards this matter of weights, my own investigations of this year—carried out in a strictly scientific manner, and in an entirely sceptical spirit—which means that I insisted on seeing all the machines I tested weighed in reliable scales before my eyes—I have come to the conclusion that the Imperial Rover is about the lightest full-size Lady's machine of the year. I believe the Rover people make no particular claim to special lightness, but they seem to have got it all the same. In spite of the many advertised featherweight machines, I did not come across a single Lady's machine that weighed, with brake, mud-guards, gear-case, and comfortable saddle, less than 30lbs., and the one that touched this bottom mark was an Imperial Rover, with a very high frame and two 28in. wheels. I may remark that most of the high-grade machines I saw weighed were about 33lbs. The second-grades were in many cases 35 or 36lbs."

**PRICE**

**£30**

WEIGHT, to specification below (20in. and 22in. frames) - 28 lbs.
" " " (24in. frames and higher) - 30 lbs.

*SPECIFICATION:*

| | |
|---|---|
| SADDLE | Brooks's B 93 L, plated springs; straight seat rod. |
| FRAME | 20in., 22in., 24in., or 26in., measuring from centre of crank spindle to top of seat lug. |
| GEAR | "Rover" interchangeable, standard 59½in. Other gears to order. |
| CRANKS | Special "Rover" pattern, square; 6in. for 20in. and 22in. frames, 6½in. for higher frames. |
| PEDALS | New and improved "Rover" oval pattern, with light rubber strips, thoroughly dust-proof. |
| CHAIN | Improved "Rover" roller, ½in. |
| HANDLE-BAR | "Rover" upturned (as illustration), or "Rover" rational (at right-angles to steering tube), cork handles, celluloid tips. |
| WHEELS | 28in. front, 26in. back, for 20in. and 22in. frames; 28in. wheels for 24in. frames and higher; hollow rims. |
| SPOKES | Tangent, double-butted, of the highest possible quality. |
| TYRES | 1½in. Lady's Dunlop. Other tyres to order. |
| FORKS | Best weldless steel tube with double crown-plates, "Rover" pattern, special taper steering tube, detachable lamp-bracket, foot-rests to order. |
| BRAKE | Improved "Rover" detachable, with rubber block. |
| GUARDS | Best steel, with strengthened edges, laced over back wheel for protection of the dress; rear portion of back guard detachable without interfering with back wheel or chain; special "Rover" chain cover, real calf, aluminium fittings, celluloid front, fancy stitched; mud-guard stays thickly plated on copper. |
| STEERING | Special ball bearings top and bottom, improved "Rover" steering lock. |
| BEARINGS | All cups, cones, and balls, of special diamond cast steel, separately and specially hardened. |
| FINISH | Best black enamel, lined in two colours, all bright parts plated on copper. |

FOR LIST OF EXTRAS AND TELEGRAPHIC CODE, SEE PAGE 36.

*Fig. 81a*

MR. J. K. STARLEY

MOUNTING THE "ROVER COB."

Fig. 82
120

*The*

# Imperial Rover Cob

E have much pleasure in stating that since we introduced this specially useful bicycle for the use of middle-aged, nervous, or stout riders, who prefer mounting from the ground instead of using the step, it has met with a steadily increasing demand, and the following are a few of the distinguished patrons that have purchased this machine from us, all of whom express themselves highly pleased with its easy running and great safety :

PRICE

£30

Lord Raglan ; Lord Avonmore ; Field-Marsh. Viscount Wolseley ; Admiral Maxse ; James Clarke, Esq. (*Christian World*) ; J. A. Christie, Esq. (Director London and Midland Bank) ; Rev. J. Adams ; Justin McCarthy, Esq., M.P. ; Val Prinsep, Esq., R.A. ; Colin Hunter, Esq., A.R.A. ; Rev. James Fraser ; Thomas Hardy, Esq.

WEIGHT, to specification below (23½in. frame) ⁓ 35 lbs.

## SPECIFICATION :

| | |
|---|---|
| SADDLE | - Brooks's B 90, plated springs ; straight seat rod. |
| FRAME | - 21½in., 23½in., or 25in., measuring from centre of crank spindle to top of seat lug. |
| GEAR | - "Rover" interchangeable, standard 60in. Other gears to order. |
| CRANKS | - Special "Rover" pattern, square, 6in. |
| PEDALS | - 4in. rubber, best "Rover" pattern, thoroughly dust-proof. |
| CHAIN | - Improved "Rover" roller, ½in. |
| HANDLE-BAR | - "Rover" rational, felt handles. |
| WHEELS | - 28in. front, 26in. back ; hollow rims. |
| SPOKES | - Tangent, double-butted, of the highest possible quality. |
| TYRES | - 1¾in. roadster Dunlop. Other tyres to order. |
| FORKS | - Best weldless steel tube, with double crown-plates, "Rover" pattern, special taper steering tube ; detachable foot-rests and lamp-bracket. |
| BRAKE | - Improved "Rover" detachable, with rubber block. |
| GUARDS | - Best steel, with strengthened edges, specially designed for easy removal ; stays thickly plated on copper. |
| GEAR-CASE | - Special "Rover" pattern, easily detachable. |
| STEERING | - Special ball bearings top and bottom, improved "Rover" steering lock. |
| BEARINGS | - All cups, cones, and balls, of special diamond cast steel, separately and specially hardened. |
| FINISH | - Best black enamel, lined in two colours, all bright parts plated on copper. |

We also make the "Imperial Rover Cob" in a lighter form, 32 lbs in weight, by using the following parts instead of those mentioned in specification above : Saddle, Brooks's B 93 ; rat-trap pedals ; 1⅜in. and 1¾in. tyres.

For List of Extras, and Telegraphic Code, see page 36.

*The* ◤

# New Popular Rover

THIS machine has now been before the public for six years, during which time it has made countless friends, and is universally regarded as the best bicycle at the price and weight that has ever been offered to the public. Fitted, as it is, with best saddle, chain, etc., it stands unrivalled, and we thoroughly recommend it for hard wear and general use.

PRICE

## £17

nct cash.

WEIGHT, to specification below (25in. frame) ⁓ 32 lbs.

### SPECIFICATION:

| | |
|---|---|
| SADDLE | Middlemore's M 33; 7 seat rod for 23½in. and 25in. frames, straight seat rod for 27in. frames. |
| FRAME | 23½in., 25in., or 27in., measuring from centre of crank spindle to top of seat lug. |
| GEAR | Fixed, 60in. |
| CRANKS | "Rover" pattern, square, 6½in. for 23½in. and 25in. frames, 7in. for 27in. frames. |
| PEDALS | 4in. rubber, "Rover" pattern. |
| CHAIN | Best quality "Rover" block, ¼in. |
| HANDLE-BAR | "Rover" rational (as illustrated). |
| WHEELS | 28in. for 23½in. frames, 30in. front and 28in. back for 25in. frames and higher; hollow rims. |
| SPOKES | Tangent, double-butted. |
| TYRES | 1⅜in. front, 1¾in. back, light roadster Dunlop. Other tyres to order. |
| FORKS | Best toughened steel tube, with double crown-plates, "Rover" pattern. |
| BRAKE | Improved "Rover" detachable, with rubber block. |
| GUARDS | Best steel, detachable. |
| STEERING | Special ball bearings top and bottom, improved "Rover" steering lock. |
| BEARINGS | All cups, cones, and balls, of special diamond cast steel, separately and specially hardened. |
| FINISH | Best black enamel, bright parts plated on copper. |

This machine can be supplied without guards and brake, as a Road Racing or Club Bicycle, fitted with rat-trap pedals, modified drop handle-bar, and Middlemore's M 61 saddle, to order, and at a corresponding reduction in price.

FOR LIST OF EXTRAS, AND TELEGRAPHIC CODE, SEE PAGE 36.

*Fig. 83*

The ◢

# Lady's Royal Rover

 INCE the commencement of season 1897, we have altered the pattern of this bicycle to our new Rover "K" frame (Figure 74); we have also considerably lightened various parts of this machine, and are now offering it to the public at the weight hereunder mentioned.

PRICE

**£24**

For those requiring a thoroughly reliable bicycle, and who do not care to pay the price of the Lady's Imperial Rover, we can thoroughly recommend it.

WEIGHT, to specification below (20in. frame)    ╴    30 lbs.

## SPECIFICATION:

| | |
|---|---|
| SADDLE - - | Middlemore's 873 ; straight seat rod. |
| FRAME - | 20in., 22in., or 24in., measuring from centre of crank spindle to top of seat lug. |
| GEAR - - | Fixed, 59in. |
| CRANKS - | "Rover" pattern, square, 6in. for 20in. and 22in. frames, 6½in. for higher frames. |
| PEDALS | New and improved "Rover," oval pattern, with light rubber strips, thoroughly dust-proof. |
| CHAIN - | Best quality "Rover" block, ¼in. |
| HANDLE-BAR | "Rover" rational (as illustrated). |
| WHEELS - - | 28in. front and 26in. back for 20in. and 22in. frames, 28in. wheels for 24in. frames ; hollow rims. |
| SPOKES - | Tangent, double-butted. |
| TYRES - | 1½in. Lady's Dunlop.   Other tyres to order. |
| FORKS - | Best toughened steel tube, with double crown-plates, "Rover" pattern ; detachable lamp-bracket. |
| BRAKE - | Improved "Rover" detachable, with rubber block. |
| GUARDS - | Best steel, with strengthened edges, rear guard laced (as illustrated) for the protection of the dress. |
| GEAR-CASE - | Leather with celluloid front. |
| STEERING - | Special ball bearings top and bottom; improved "Rover" steering lock. |
| BEARINGS - | All cups, cones, and balls, of special diamond cast steel, separately and specially hardened. |
| FINISH - | Best black enamel, lined in two colours, bright parts plated on copper. |

FOR LIST OF EXTRAS, AND TELEGRAPHIC CODE, SEE PAGE 36.

*Fig. 84*

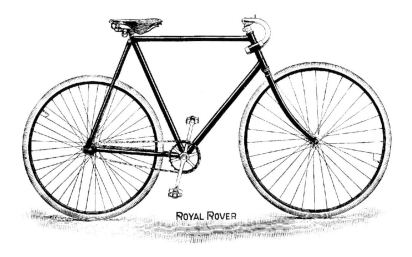

ROYAL ROVER

*The* 

*Royal Rover*

*Road Racer*

*Fig. 85*

124

The ▬

# Royal Rover
## Road Racer

E have greatly improved this machine since last season, and have reduced the weight to 27 lbs. We can thoroughly recommend it as a very serviceable mount for those who require a high-class road racing bicycle at a moderate price. We guarantee it to be equal to any bicycle offered at the same price and weight, while in design, appearance, and finish, it leaves nothing to be desired.

PRICE

£24

WEIGHT, to specification below (23½in. frame)  ⁃  27 lbs.

## SPECIFICATION:

| | |
|---|---|
| SADDLE - | Middlemore's 861; 7 seat rod for 23½in. and 25in. frames, straight seat rod for 27in. frames. |
| FRAME - | 23½in., 25in., or 27in., measuring from centre of crank spindle to top of seat lug. |
| GEAR - | Fixed, 66in. |
| CRANKS - | "Rover" pattern, square, 6½in.; 7in. for 27in. frames. |
| PEDALS - | 3¾in. rat-trap, "Rover" pattern, thoroughly dust-proof. Other sizes to order. |
| CHAIN - | Best quality "Rover" block, ¼in. |
| HANDLE-BAR | "Rover" special drop (as illustrated). |
| WHEELS - | 28in. for 23½in. frames, 30in. front and 28in. back for 25in. frames and higher; hollow rims. |
| SPOKES - | Tangent, double-butted. |
| TYRES - | 1½in. front, 1⅝in. back, road racing Dunlop. Other tyres to order. |
| FORKS - | Best toughened steel tube with double crown-plates, "Rover" pattern. |
| STEERING - | Special ball bearings top and bottom; improved "Rover" steering lock. |
| BEARINGS - | All cups, cones, and balls, of special diamond cast steel, separately and specially hardened. |
| FINISH - | Best black enamel; bright parts plated on copper. |

FOR LIST OF EXTRAS, AND TELEGRAPHIC CODE, SEE PAGE 36.

Fig. 85a

125

The 1898 catalogue gave illustrations of all the component parts of the Rover cycles. We show here the gents' and the ladies' frames, the chainwheels and cranks, the forks, the pedals, the seat-pins, the detachable foot-rest, the handlebars, a brake-lever and the head-badge. The underslung down-tubes and the mitred tube-bridges on the ladies' models should be noted. These down-tubes remained in use for three or four more years only, but the mitred tube-bridges were used almost until production ended. The mitring is helpful in identifying Rovers.

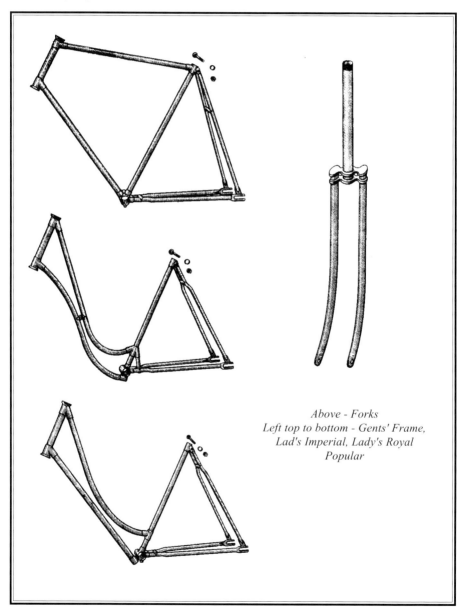

*Above - Forks*
*Left top to bottom - Gents' Frame,*
*Lad's Imperial, Lady's Royal*
*Popular*

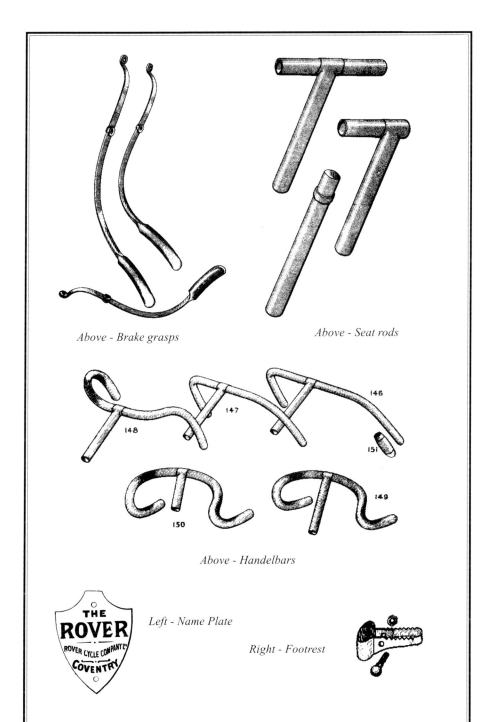

*Above - Brake grasps*

*Above - Seat rods*

146

147

148

151

149

150

*Above - Handelbars*

*Left - Name Plate*

THE
ROVER
ROVER CYCLE COMPANY L?
COVENTRY

*Right - Footrest*

*Above - Right Crank Centre*

*Right - Chain Wheel Ring*

*Left - Solid Chain Wheel and Crank*

*Below upper left - Racer Pedal*
*Below lower left - Roadster Pedal*
*Below Right - Lady's Pedal*

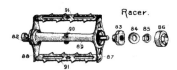

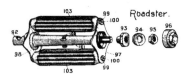

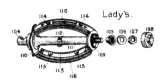

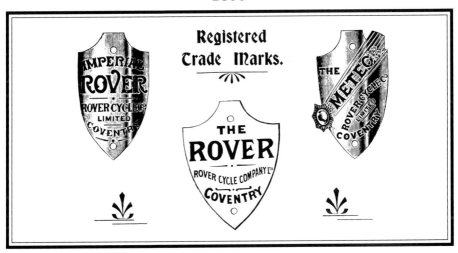

Three badges (shown here) were used on Rover cycles from 1899. The *Imperial Rover* (Fig. 86) was available as a light or a full roadster. The *Lady's Imperial Rover* (Fig. 87) had reverted to a straight-tubed frame. The *Lady's Rover* (Fig. 88) returned after a three-years interval. It replaced the *Lady's Popular Rover* and the *Lady's Royal Rover*. The *Imperial Rover Cob* (Fig. 89) had some alterations and was greatly reduced in weight and price. The *Rover Light Roadster* (Fig. 90) reappeared after a year's absence. The *Imperial Rover Path Racer* was unchanged except for a drop in price to £20, as was the *Imperial Rover Road Racer*. The *Rover Road Racer* (Fig. 91) appeared in place of the *Royal Rover Road Racer*. The trade-name Meteor reappeared. The *Meteor Light Roadster*, the *Lady's Meteor*, the *Meteor Road Racer* and the *Meteor Cob* (Figs. 92-95) were introduced as cheap bicycles guaranteed to be of reasonable quality.

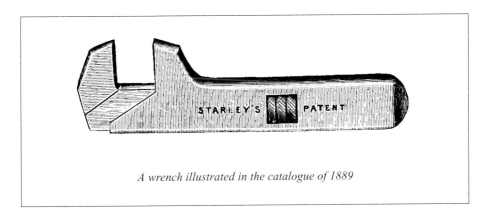

*A wrench illustrated in the catalogue of 1889*

# THE IMPERIAL ROVER

## LIGHT ROADSTER AND ROADSTER.

---

WEIGHT : *Light Roadster, 32 lbs. ;*
*Full Roadster, 35 lbs.*

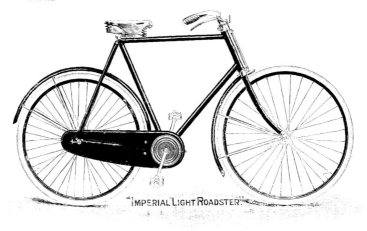

"IMPERIAL LIGHT ROADSTER"

**PRICES** (for Great Britain only) £22 nett cash ; Extended Purchase, £25.

## SPECIFICATION.

**Saddle.**—Brooks's B93, plated springs, other saddles to order. 7-seat rod with closed ends ; small hole in seat rod two inches from bottom marks the point above which it must not be raised.

**Frame.**—23½in., 25in., 27in., or 29in., measuring from centre of crank spindle to top of seat lug.

**Gear and Chain.**—" Rover " detachable chain wheels ; highest quality ½in. pitch roller chain ; gear 66in. Other gears to order.

**Cranks.**—Special " Rover " pattern, square, 6½in. for 23½in. and 25in. frames, 7in. for 27in. frames and higher. Other sizes to order.

**Pedals.**—Special " Rover " pattern, 3¾in. rat-trap. Other sizes to order.

**Handle-bar.** — Special " Rover " pattern as illustrated ; felt handles ; small hole two inches from the bottom of the stem of the handle-bar marks the point above which the handle-bar must not be raised.

**Wheels.**—28in. for 23½in. frames, 30in. front and 28in. back for 25in. frames and higher ; hollow rims.

**Spokes.**—Patent turned, double-butted, of the highest possible quality ; heavily plated.

**Tyres.**—1⅝in. light roadster Dunlops. Other tyres to order.

**Forks.**—Best weldless steel tubes with new and improved fork crown ; special taper gauge steering tube ; new pattern detachable footrests (registered) and lamp bracket ; fork ends heavily plated on copper.

**Brake.**—" Rover " detachable with rubber block ; back wheel " Rover " (band brake) to order.

**Guards.**— Best steel mudguards, with strengthened edges specially designed for easy removal ; stays heavily plated.

**Gear Case.** – Carter detachable, special " Rover " pattern, with circular disc, heavily plated on copper.

**Steering.**—Special " Rover," ball bearings top and bottom, with improved " Rover " steering lock.

**Bearings.** – All cups, cones, and balls of special diamond cast steel separately and specially hardened.

**Finish.**—Two coats of finest quality black enamel on one of priming, lined in two colours, all bright parts heavily plated on copper.

THE ROVER ROADSTER. This machine is also supplied for riders over thirteen stones with P90 saddle, rubber pedals, and 1⅞in. tyres to order.

Fig. 86

# The Lady's Imperial Rover.

## DOUBLE STRAIGHT TUBES.

WEIGHT to specification below:
28 lbs. (20in. and 22in. frames);
30 lbs. (24in. frames and higher.)

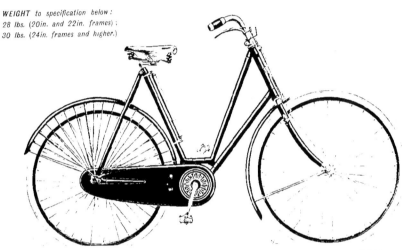

PRICES (for Great Britain only) £22 nett cash; Extended Purchase, £25.

## SPECIFICATION.

**Saddle.**—Brooks's B93, L-plated springs, 7-seat rod with closed ends; the small hole two inches from the bottom of seat rod marks the point above which the seat rod must not be raised.

**Frame.**—20in., 22in., 24in., or 26in., measuring from centre of crank spindle to top of seat lug.

**Gear and Chain.**—"Rover" interchangeable; standard 60in. Other gears to order.

**Cranks.**—Special "Rover" pattern, square, 6in. for 20in. and 22in. frames, 6½in. for higher frames.

**Pedals.**—New and improved "Rover," oval pattern, with light rubber strips, or "Rover" square pattern to order.

**Handle-bar.**—"Rover" upturned (as illustrated), cork handles, celluloid tips; the small hole two inches from the bottom of the stem of the handle-bar marks the point above which the handle-bar must not be raised.

**Wheels.**—28in. front, 26in. back, for 20in. and 22in. frames, 30in. front and 28in. back for 24in. frames and higher; 28in. wheels to order; hollow rims.

**Spokes.**—Patent turned double butted, of the highest possible quality; heavily plated.

**Tyres.**—1⅜in. Dunlops. Other tyres to order.

**Forks.**—Best weldless steel tubes with new and improved fork crown; special taper gauge steering tube; new pattern detachable footrests (registered) and lamp bracket; fork ends heavily plated on copper.

**Brake.**—Improved "Rover" detachable with rubber block; back wheel brake to order.

**Guards.**—Best steel with strengthened edges, laced over back wheel for the protection of the dress, easily detachable; special "Rover" chain cover, real calf; aluminium fittings; celluloid front, fancy stitched, or "Rover" special metal case with circular disc, heavily plated to order; mudguard stays heavily plated on copper.

**Steering.**—Special ball bearings top and bottom; improved "Rover" steering lock.

**Bearings.**—All cups, cones, and balls of special diamond cast steel, separately and specially hardened.

**Finish.**—Coats of finest quality black enamel on one of priming, lined in two colours, all bright parts plated on copper.

*Fig. 87*

131

# THE LADY'S ROVER.

WEIGHT to specification below :
30 lbs. (20in. frame).

LADY'S "ROVER."

**PRICES** (for Great Britain only) £16 16s. nett cash ; Extended Purchase, £18 18s.

## SPECIFICATION.

**Saddle.**—Brooks's B302, 7 seat rod; the small hole two inches from he bottom of the seat-pillar marks the point above which the seat-rod must not be raised.

**Frame.**—20in., 22in., 24in., or 26in., measuring from centre of crank axle to top of seat lug.

**Gear and Chain.**—" Rover " detachable chain wheel ; ¾in. pitch roller chain ; gear 60in. Other gears to order.

**Cranks.**—" Rover" pattern, square, 6in. for 20in. and 22in. frames, 6½in. for higher frames.

**Pedals.**—New and improved " Rover," oval pattern, with light rubber strips, thoroughly dustproof.

**Handle-bar.**—" Rover" upturned (as illustrated); the small hole two inches from the bottom of the stem of the handle-bar marks the point above which the handle-bar must not be raised.

**Wheels.**—28in. front, 26in. back, for 20in. and 22in. frames, 30in. front, 28in. back, or 28in. wheels for 24in. frames and higher ; hollow rims.

**Spokes.**—Tangent, double-butted, plated centres.

**Tyres.**—1¾in. Dunlop. Other tyres to order.

**Forks.**—Best toughened steel tube with double-crown plates, " Rover" pattern ; detachable lamp bracket ; footrests ; tapered gauge steering tube ; fork ends plated.

**Brake.**—Improved " Rover " detachable with rubber block.

**Guards.**—Best steel with strengthened edges; rear guard laced (as illustrated) for the protection of the dress.

**Gear Case.**—Leather, with celluloid front.

**Steering.**—Special ball bearings top and bottom improved " Rover " steering lock.

**Bearings.**—All cups, cones, and balls of special diamond cast steel separately and specially hardened.

**Finish.**—Two coats of best black enamel on one of priming, lined in two colours, bright parts plated on copper.

*Fig. 88*
132

# IMPERIAL ROVER COB.

WEIGHT to specification below :
32 lbs. (23½in. frame).

"IMPERIAL ROVER COB."

PRICES (for Great Britain only) £22 nett cash ; Extended Purchase, £25.

## SPECIFICATION.

**Saddle.**—Brooks's B93, plated springs, 7-seat rod, with closed ends; small hole in seat rod two inches from bottom marks the point above which it must not be raised.

**Frame.**—21½in., 23½in., or 25in., measuring from centre of crank spindle to top of seat lug.

**Gear and Chain.**—"Rover" interchangeable, standard 60in. Other gears to order. Highest quality ½in. pitch roller chain.

**Cranks.**—Special "Rover" pattern square, 6in.

**Pedals.**—3¾in. rat-trap, special "Rover" pattern. Other sizes to order.

**Handle-bar.**—Special "Rover" pattern (as illustrated), felt handles ; small hole in handle-bar stem two inches from bottom marks the point above which it must not be raised.

**Wheels.**—28in. front, 26in. back ; hollow rims.

**Spokes.**—Patent turned, double-butted, of the highest possible quality ; heavily plated.

**Tyres.**—1⅜in. light roadster Dunlops. Other tyres to order.

**Forks.**—Best weldless steel tube, with new and improved fork crown; special taper gauge steering tubes ; detachable foot rest (registered) and lamp bracket ; fork ends heavily plated.

**Brake.**—Improved "Rover" detachable, with rubber block ; back wheel brakes (band or rim) to order.

**Guards.**—Best steel mudguards, with strengthened edges, specially designed for easy removal ; stays heavily plated on copper.

**Gear Case.**—Special "Rover" pattern, with circular disc, heavily plated on copper.

**Steering.**—Special "Rover" ball bearings top and bottom, with improved "Rover" steering lock.

**Bearings.**—All cups, cones, and balls of special diamond cast steel separately and specially hardened.

**Finish.**—Two coats of finest quality black enamel on one of priming, lined in two colours, all bright parts heavily plated on copper.

We also make the "Imperial Rover Cob," for heavy weights, by using the following parts instead of those mentioned in specification above : Saddle, Brooks's B90 ; rubber pedals ; 1⅜in. tyres ; weight about 35 lbs.

*Fig. 89*

# ROVER LIGHT ROADSTER.

*WEIGHT to specification below*
*33 lbs. (23½in. frame).*

"ROVER" LIGHT ROADSTER.

**PRICES** (for Great Britain only) £16 16s. nett cash ; Extended Purchase, £18 18s.

## SPECIFICATION.

**Saddle.**—Brooks's 302, 7-seat rod ; small hole two inches from the bottom of the seat rod marks the point above which it must not be raised.

**Frame.**—23½in., 25in., 27in., or 29in., measuring from centre of crank spindle to top of seat lug.

**Gear.**—"Rover" detachable chain wheels; ½in. pitch roller chain ; gear 66in. Other gears to order.

**Cranks.**—Square "Rover" pattern, 6½in. for 23½in. and 25in. frames, 7in. for 27in. frames and higher.

**Pedals.**—3¾in. "Rover" pattern rat-trap; rubber pedals to order.

**Handle-bar.**—1¾in. upturned (as illustrated) ; small hole in handle-bar stem two inches from the bottom marks the point above which the handle-bar must not be raised.

**Wheels.**—28in. wheels for 23½in. frames, 30in. and 28in. wheels for 25in. frames and higher; hollow rims; 28in. wheels to order.

**Spokes.**—Double-butted tangent ; plated centres.

**Tyres.**—1⅝in. light roadster; Clipper or Warwick, hollow rims.

**Forks.**—Best weldless steel with "Rover" double plate crown; special taper gauge steering tube ; detachable footrests and lamp bracket ; fork ends plated.

**Brake.**—Improved "Rover" detachable with rubber block.

**Guards.**—Best steel with strengthened edges.

**Gear Case.**—"Rover" metal case ; plated disc.

**Steering.**—Special ball bearings top and bottom; improved "Rover" steering lock.

**Bearings.**—All cups, cones, and balls of special diamond cast steel, separately and specially hardened.

**Finish.**—Two coats of best black enamel on one of priming, lined in two colours, bright parts plated on copper.

*Fig. 90*

134

# ROVER ROAD RACER.

WEIGHT to specification below:
27 lbs. (23½in. frame).

"ROVER" ROAD RACER.

**PRICES** (for Great Britain only) £16 16s. nett cash ; Extended Purchase, £18 18s.

## SPECIFICATION.

**Saddle.**—Brooks's B10. 7-seat rod with closed ends ; the small hole two inches from the bottom of the seat rod marks the point above which the seat rod must not be raised.

**Frame.**—23½in., 25in., 27in., or 29in., measuring from centre of crank spindle to top of seat lug.

**Gear and Chain.**—" Rover " detachable chain wheels ; ½in. pitch roller chain ; gear 72in. Other gears to order.

**Cranks.**—" Rover " pattern, square, 6½in. ; 7in. for 27in. frames.

**Pedals.**—3¾in. rat-trap, " Rover " pattern, thoroughly dustproof. Other sizes to order.

**Handle-bar.**—As illustrated ; the small hole two inches from the bottom of the stem of handle-bar marks the point above which the handle-bar must not be raised.

**Wheels.**—28in. for 23½in. frames. 30in. ront and 28in. back for 25in. frames and higher ; hollow rims ; 28in. wheels to order.

**Spokes.**—Double-butted, tangent, plated centres.

**Tyres.**—1⅜in. road racing Dunlops. Other tyres to order.

**Forks.**—Best weldless steel tubes with double crown plates ; special taper gauge steering tube ; lamp bracket ; fork ends plated.

**Steering.**—Special ball bearings top and bottom ; improved " Rover " steering lock.

**Bearings.**—All cups, cones, and balls of special diamond steel, separately and specially hardened.

**Finish.**—Two coats of best black enamel on one of priming, bright parts plated on copper.

*Fig. 91*

135

# THE METEOR LIGHT ROADSTER.

WEIGHT to specification below :
33 lbs. (23½in. frame).

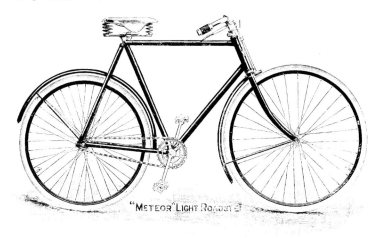

"METEOR" LIGHT ROADSTER

PRICES (for Great Britain only) £12 12s. nett cash; Extended Purchase, £15.

## SPECIFICATION.

**Saddle**—Middlemore's M33. 7 seat rod; the small hole two inches from the bottom of the seat rod marks the point above which the seat rod must not be raised.

**Frame.**—23½in., 25in., 27in., measuring from the centre of the crank spindle to the top of the seat-lug.

**Gear and Chain.**—Detachable chain wheels, best quality ¾in. block chain; gear 66in. Other gears to order.

**Cranks.**—Square, 6½in. for 23½in. and 25in. frames, 7in. for 27in. frames.

**Pedals.**—3⅝in. rat-trap, thoroughly dustproof.

**Handle-bar.**—Rational shape (as illustrated); the small hole two inches from the bottom of the stem of the handle-bar marks the point above which the handle-bar must not be raised

**Wheels.**—28in. or 23½in. frames, 30in. front and 28in. back for 25in. frames and higher; hollow rims.

**Tyres**—1⅜in. light roadster Clipper or Warwick; hollow rims.

**Forks.**—Toughened steel tube, with double crown plates tapered gauge steering tube.

**Brake**—Detachable, spoon, with rubber block.

**Guards.**—Detachable, best steel strengthened edges.

**Steering.**—Special ball bearings top and bottom and efficient steering lock.

**Bearings.**—All cups, cones, and balls of special diamond cast steel separately and specially hardened.

**Finish.**—Best black enamel, bright parts plated on copper.

If Dunlop, Palmer, Clincher, or Clipper-Reflex tyres are required, the price will be as follows:

For Great Britain only, **£13 13s.** nett cash; extended purchase **£16.**

*Fig. 92*

136

# THE LADY'S METEOR.

WEIGHT to specification below:
31 lbs. (22in. frame).

LADY'S "METEOR."

**PRICES** (for Great Britain only) £12 12s. nett cash; Extended Purchase, £15.

## SPECIFICATION.

**Saddle.** Middlemore's M73. 7-seat rod; the small hole two inches from the bottom of seat rod marks the point above which the seat-pillar must not be raised.

**Frame.** 20in., 22in., 24in., or measuring from centre of the crank spindle to the top of the seat lug.

**Gear and Chain.** Best quality block chain, ⅜in.; gear, 60in. Other gears to order.

**Cranks.** Square, 6in. for 20in. and 22in. frames, 6½in. for 24in. frames.

**Pedals.** 3½in light rubber.

**Handle-bar.** Rational shape (as illustrated); the small hole two inches from the bottom of the stem of the handle-bar marks the point above which the handle-bar must not be raised.

**Wheels.** 28in. front and 26in. back for 20in. and 22in. frames, 30in. front and 28in. back or 28in. equal wheels for 24in. frames and higher; hollow rims.

**Tyres.**—1½in. Clipper or Warwick; hollow rims.

**Forks.**—Toughened steel tube with double-crown plates; detachable lamp bracket; taper gauge steering tube.

**Brake.**—Detachable, with rubber block.

**Guards.**—Best steel, rear guard laced (as illustration) for the protection of the dress.

**Chain Cover.**—Good quality leather.

**Steering.**—Special ball bearings top and bottom; improved steering lock.

**Bearings.** All cups, cones, and balls of special diamond cast steel separately and specially hardened.

**Finish.** Best black enamel, bright parts plated on copper.

If Dunlop, Palmer, Clincher, or Clipper-Reflex tyres are required the price will be as follows:

For Great Britain only, **£13 13s.** nett cash; extended purchase, **£16.**

*Fig. 93*

137

# THE METEOR ROAD RACER.

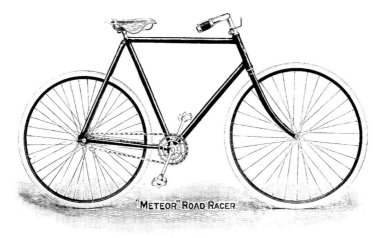

WEIGHT to specification below :
23¼ lbs. (25in. frame).

"METEOR" ROAD RACER.

**PRICES** (for Great Britain only) £12 12s nett cash ; Extended Purchase, £15.

## SPECIFICATION.

**Saddle.**—Middlemore's M61, 7-seat rod ; the small hole two inches from the bottom of the seat rod marks the point above which the seat rod must not be raised.

**Frame.**— 23½in., 25in., or 27in., measuring from the centre of the crank spindle to the top of the seat lug.

**Gear and Chain.**—Detachable chain wheels ; best quality ¼in. block chain ; gear, 72in.

**Cranks.**— Square, 6⅜in. for 23½in. and 25in. frames, 7in. for 27in. frames.

**Pedals.** - 3¾in. rat-trap.

**Handle-bar.**—Rational shape (as illustrated), or modified drop to order ; the small hole two inches from the bottom of the stem of the handle-bar marks the point above which the handle-bar must not be raised.

**Wheels.**—28in. for 23½in. frames, 6in. front and 28in back for 25in. frames and higher ; hollow rims.

**Tyres.**—1½in. road racing Clipper or Warwick ; hollow rims.

**Forks.**—Toughened steel tube, with double crown plate ; taper gauge steering tube.

**Steering.**—Special ball bearings top and bottom ; improved steering lock.

**Bearings.**—All cones, cups, and balls of special diamond cast steel separately and specially hardened.

**Finish.**—Best black enamel ; bright parts plated on copper.

If Dunlop, Palmer, Clincher, or Clipper-Reflex tyres are required, the price will be as follows :

For Great Britain only, **£13 13s.** nett cash ; for extended purchase, **£16.**

*Fig. 94*

138

# METEOR COB.

## Specially designed for mounting and dismounting without the use of step.

---

*WEIGHT to specification below;*
*35 bs. 21½in. frame).*

**PRICES** (for Great Britain only) £12 12s. nett cash ; Extended Purchase, £15.

## SPECIFICATION.

**Saddle.**—Middlemore's M33, 7-seat rod ; the small hole two inches from the bottom of the seat-pillar marks the point above which the seat-pillar must not be raised.

**Frame.**—21½in., 23½in., or 25in., measuring from the centre of the crank spindle to the top of the seat-lug.

**Gear and Chain.**—Detachable chain wheels; best quality ½in. block chain; gear 60in.

**Cranks.**—" Rover " pattern, square. 6in.

**Pedals.**—3¾in. rat-trap, thoroughly dustproof. Rubber pedals to order.

**Handle-bar.**—Rational shape (as illustrated); the small hole two inches from the bottom of the stem of the handle bar marks the point above which the handle-bar must not be raised.

**Wheels.** - 28in. front, 26in. back; hollow rims.

**Tyres.**—1¾in. Clipper or Warwick; hollow rims.

**Forks.** - Toughened steel tube, with double crown plates; taper gauge steering tube.

**Brake** —Detachable spoon with rubber block.

**Guards.**—Detachable, best steel, strengthened edges, specially designed for easy removal.

**Steering.**—Special ball bearings top and bottom; improved " Rover " steering lock.

**Bearings.**—All cups, cones, and balls of special diamond cast steel separately and specially hardened.

**Finish.** - Best black enamel, bright parts plated on copper.

If Dunlop, Palmer, Clincher, or Clipper-Reflex tyres are required, the price will be as follows :

**£13 13s.** nett cash ; extended purchase, **£16.**

*Fig. 95*

*Ladies Rover 1899. The down-tube fitting under the bottom bracket was introduced in 1898, but the curved tube had no bridge to the down tube (see p. 126). However, the pedals were 1905 and the handlebars 1905 pattern; they were clearly added later.*

# PART 4 - BICYCLES FROM 1900-1925
## The Imperial Range
### 1900

This year was the last in which a 30" front wheel was part of any standard specification on any Rover bicycle.

The *Imperial Rover* was again offered as either full or light roadster, the price dropping to £20. The full roadster weighed 34 pounds, the light remained at 32 – both weights were for 22" frames; 24", 26" and 28" were also available. The pedals were Rover 4" with rubber blocks and tyres were $1^5/_8$" light roadster Dunlops, still on Westwood rims. Plated pump-clips were fitted to the seat-tube, and a pump was supplied. There was a change in the gearcase cover, as explained later. The *Lady's Imperial Rover* was offered at £20 for either double straight or double curved tubes, the specification almost unchanged. The 1898 oval pedals were replaced by a conventional type. The *Imperial Rover Cob* was reduced to £20, the $23^1/_2$" frame weighing 32 pounds. It was fitted with pump-clips on the seat-tube, a Bluemel's Featherweight pump and Rover 4" rubber pedals. Each Imperial model could be fitted with a free-wheel, two brakes and plated rims, or rims plated and enamelled over, for an extra £2. The standard specification for each gave the brake as a plunger with rubber block, but all except the *Cob* were fitted with the rim brake.

The *Imperial Rover Path Racer* (Fig. 96) had the ungainly dropped top-tube that was to become fashionable. The *Imperial Rover Road Racer* showed a slight downward tilt of the top-tube, contrasting with the slight upward tilt of 1899. Frame sizes were 22", 24", 26" and 28", with 28" wheels (Westwood rims) for 22" and 24" frames, 30" and 28" wheels for 26" frames and higher. The weight was 25 pounds for a 22" frame, and the price dropped to £19.

*A weathered Rover enamel sign from 1896-98.*

# IMPERIAL ROVER PATH RACER.

WEIGHT, to specification:
22in. frame, 22 lbs.

## SPECIFICATION.

**Saddle**—Brooks's B11; 7 seat rod, with closed ends; the small hole two inches from bottom marks the point above which the seat-pillar must not be raised.

**Frame**—22in., 24in., 26in., and 28in., measuring from centre of crank spindle to top of seat lug.

**Gear and Chain**—"Rover" interchangeable, standard 84in. Other gears to order. Highest quality ⅜in. pitch roller chain.

**Cranks**—Special "Rover" pattern, 6½in. for 22in. and 24in. frames.

**Pedals**—3¾in. rat-trap, best "Rover" pattern, thoroughly dust-proof.

**Handle-bar**—Special "Rover" drop (as illustrated); the small hole two inches from bottom marks the point above which it must not be raised.

**Wheels**—26in. for 22in. frames, 28in. for 24in. frames and higher.

**Spokes**—Patent turned, double-butted, of the highest possible quality; heavily plated.

**Tyres**—1¾in. path racing Dunlop. Westwood rims.

**Forks**—Best weldless taper gauge steel tubes, with new and improved box crown; special taper gauge steering tube.

**Steering**—Special ball bearings top and bottom.

**Bearings**—All cups, cones, and balls of special diamond cast steel, separately and specially hardened.

**Finish**—Two coats of finest quality black enamel on one or priming, all bright parts heavily plated on copper.

**Price** (for Great Britain only) ... £19 net cash.

*Fig. 96*

# 1901

The catalogue showed the handlebars available, the new rim-brake, the roller free-wheel that had been in use and the ratchet pattern that was to replace it (see Fittings). The *Imperial Rover* had minor changes. Rims were 28" plated Westwoods, tyres were $1^1/_2$" light roadster Dunlops and a front pull-up brake, operated by an inverted lever, replaced the plunger. The *Imperial Light Roadster* could be fitted with Grose's leather gearcase with celluloid panels to reduce the weight from 32 to $30^1/_2$ pounds. The *Imperial Rover Roadster* was supplied for riders over 13 stones with B90 saddle and $1^3/_4$" tyres. Only one *Lady's Imperial Rover* was offered; fashion had triumphed over engineering science and the straight-tubed model had disappeared. The Westwood rims were plated, the tyres were $1^1/_2$" Dunlops and the frame was gold-lined. With Grose's celluloid-panelled gearcase the weight went down from 30 to 29 pounds. The *Imperial Rover Cob* (Fig. 97) had abandoned the rising top-tube. It is difficult to see what is left of the original conception of the low-built bicycle depicted in the 1898 illustration of J.K. Starley with one foot on the ground; one would have to have very long legs to do that with a 26" frame. All these *Imperial* models had the option of a fixed wheel and front rim brake or a free-wheel and two brakes. On 9 March 1901 an advertisement (Fig. 98) for an *Imperial Rover* with "Parallel X Frame" appeared in *Cycling*. There was an editorial note that J.K. Starley would be using the design in 1901. There must have been some delays in production, as the model did not appear in the 1901 catalogue until the sixth edition, without details of the specification, at £24. An *Imperial Rover Road Racer* with dropped handlebar was also shown. The catalogue said "We do not consider this frame equal to our ordinary diamond frame bicycle, as the elasticity in the latter gives life to the machine which the former does not possess. We understand, however, that some riders consider the X or stayed frame bicycle is more rigid and a better hill-climber, and on this account they favour it. It will be noticed that the bottom backbone tube and the top stay tube are made parallel. This is important, as, when they are made to converge at the crank bracket, forming an apex at that point, there is a great tendency to break either one or the other of the tubes near the junction, but by taking them parallel the strain is more equally distributed, and we can therefore recommend this shape with confidence as superior to any other design." The assertion that the bottom tubes had to be parallel if the frame were to be mechanically correct must have amused or annoyed makers like Raleigh, Referee, Centaur and the Cycle Components Co., who were producing different versions of the fashionable frame. Many firms, incidentally, were paying royalties to G.L Morris of Referee, who in 1899 patented as many versions of cross frames as he could think of without duplicating Bowden's 1894 patent that was being used by Raleigh. In 1901 *Cycling* carried out what it said was an exhaustive examination of the claims made for cross frames, and came to the conclusion that there was very little difference between them and the conventional diamond frames as far as weight and strength were concerned.

The *Imperial Rover Path Racer* had 28" x 1³/₈" rims only and the price rose to £19. The *Imperial Rover Road Racer* was unchanged.

# IMPERIAL ROVER COB.

### Specially designed for mounting and dismounting without step.

#### SPECIFICATION.

**Saddle**—Brooks's B93, plated springs; 7 seat rod, with closed ends; small hole in seat rod two inches from bottom marks the point above which it must not be raised.

**Frame**—22in., 24in., or 26in., measuring from centre of crank spindle to top of seat lug.

**Pump Clips**—Heavily plated on copper; featherweight pump.

**Gear and Chain**—"Rover" detachable chain wheels; highest quality ½in. pitch roller chain; gear, 60in.

**Cranks**—Special "Rover" pattern, square, 6½in.

**Pedals**—Special "Rover" pattern, ½in. best quality, square rubber.

**Handle-bar**—Special "Rover" pattern (as illustrated); felt handles; small hole in handle-bar stem two inches from bottom marks the point above which it must not be raised.

**Wheels**—28in.; Westwood rims, heavily plated on copper.

**Spokes**—Patent turned, double butted, of the highest possible quality; heavily plated on copper.

**Tyres**—1⅝in. light roadster Dunlop.

**Forks**—Best weldless taper gauge steel tube, with new and improved box crown; special taper gauge steering tubes; detachable footrests to order; lamp bracket; fork ends heavily plated on copper.

**Brake**—"Rover" front rim (as illustrated).

**Guards**—Best steel mudguards, with strengthened edges, specially designed for easy removal; stays heavily plated on copper.

**Gear Case**—"Carter Rover" detachable, with circular disc, heavily plated on copper.

**Steering**—Special "Rover," ball bearings top and bottom, with improved "Rover" steering lock (see illustrations page 27).

**Bearings**—All cups, cones, and balls of special diamond cast steel, separately and specially hardened (see illustrations page 28).

**Finish**—Two coats of finest enamel on one of priming, lined burnished gold, all bright parts heavily plated on copper.

WEIGHT, to specification:
22in. frame, 32 lbs : with Grose's leather case and celluloid panels, 30½ lbs.

**PRICES** (for Great Britain only) :

Fixed wheel and front rim brake ... ... **£20** net cash.

Free-wheel and two brakes ... ... **£22** net cash.

*Fig. 97*

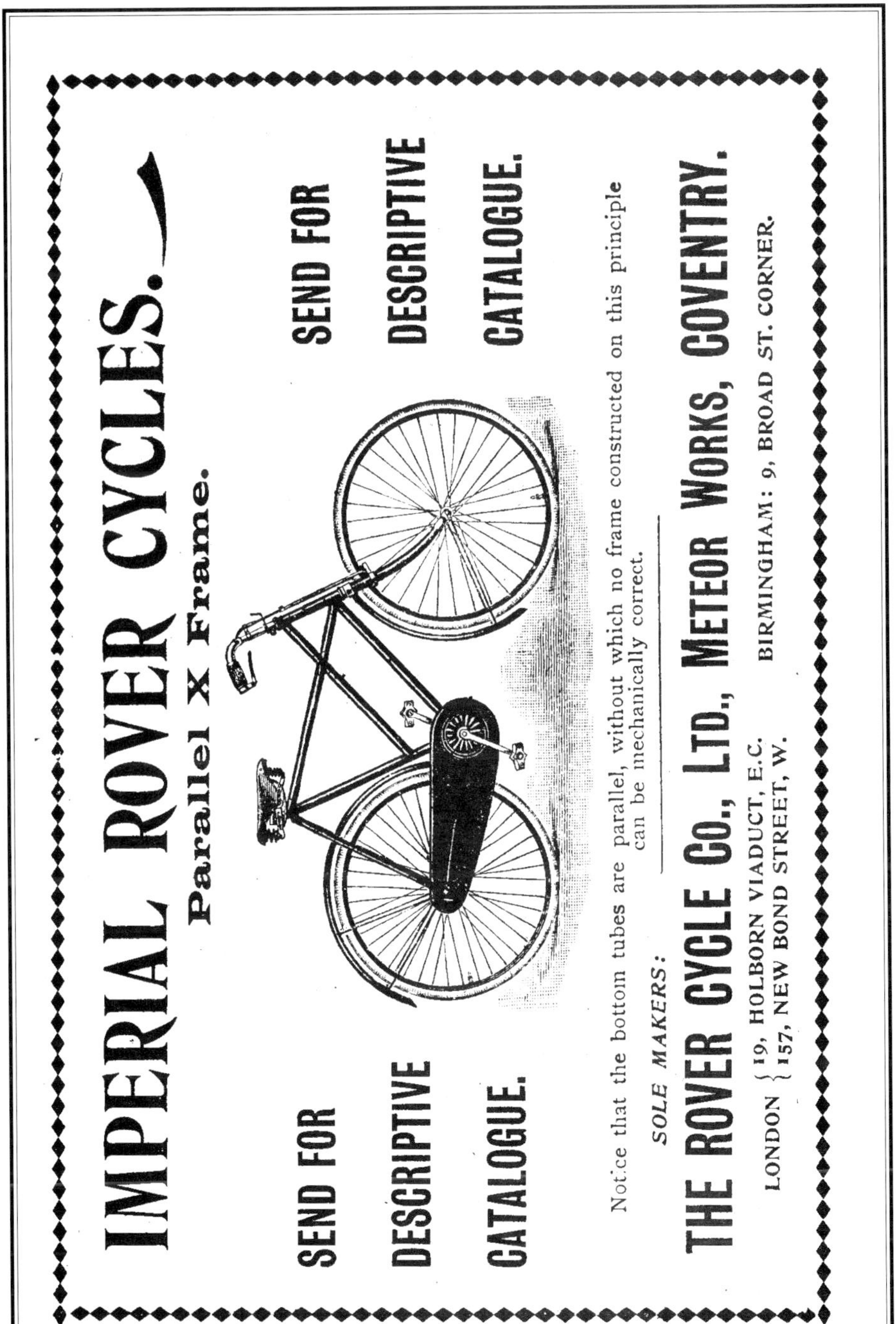
IMPERIAL ROVER CYCLES.
Parallel X Frame.
SEND FOR
DESCRIPTIVE
CATALOGUE.
SEND FOR
DESCRIPTIVE
CATALOGUE.
Notice that the bottom tubes are parallel, without which no frame constructed on this principle can be mechanically correct.
SOLE MAKERS:
THE ROVER CYCLE CO., LTD., METEOR WORKS, COVENTRY.
LONDON { 19, HOLBORN VIADUCT, E.C.
157, NEW BOND STREET, W.
BIRMINGHAM: 9, BROAD ST. CORNER.

*Fig. 98*

The catalogue showed an optional diagonal stay, recommended for tall and heavy riders, which was fitted free to *Imperials* and *Rovers* but cost extra if specified on *Meteor-Rovers* (shown here). Unfortunately our catalogue is unpriced so the 1903 prices have to be compared with those of 1901. A Rover ratchet free-wheel and two rim-brakes were standard fitments on all Imperial models except the path racer, as was a Hans Renold $1/2$" pitch roller chain which replaced the previous "highest quality" one. A Brooks B10 saddle was provided on all models except the Path Racer, which had a B11. The *Cob* had disappeared, possibly because it was no longer possible to pretend that it was any easier to mount than the *Imperial*. On all models, where fitted, the "heavily plated" pump-clips had enamelled bands. The *Imperial Rover Light Roadster* and the *Imperial Rover Roadster* were unchanged. The *Lady's Imperial Rover* could be obtained with a Revod gearcase (instead of Grose's) and light fittings at a weight of 28 pounds; the frame with double straight tubes could be obtained specially. The *Special Imperial Rover Light Roadster* was a new model for riders up to 11 stones, available in 22", 24", 26" and 28" – the 24" weighed 28 pounds. The specification was similar to that for the other *Imperial Roadsters* except that it had 26" x $1^3/_8$" light Dunlops and no gearcase.

The *Imperial Rover Path Racer* was largely unchanged but the downward tilt of the top-tube was less pronounced, it had a special handlebar-fitting (not illustrated in the catalogue) and the Renold chain was specified. The *Imperial Rover Road Racer* (Fig. 99) was fitted with a free-wheel and two brakes.

# THE IMPERIAL ROVER ROAD RACER.

**WEIGHT, to specification:**
24in. frame. 26 lbs.

**Saddle**—Brooks's B10; 7 seat rod, with closed ends; small hole in seat rod two inches from bottom marks the point above which it must not be raised.

**Frame**—22in., 24in., 26in., or 28in., measuring from centre of crank spindle to top of seat lug.

**Gear and Chain**—"Rover" interchangeable, 7⅞in. standard; Hans Renold's best quality ⅜in. pitch roller chain.

**Cranks**—Special "Rover" pattern, square, 6¾in. or 22in. and 24in. frames, 7in. for higher frames.

**Pedals**—3¾in. rat-trap, best "Rover" pattern, thoroughly dustproof.

**Handle-bar** — Special drop "Rover" (as illustrated); cork handles; small hole in handle-bar stem two inches from bottom marks the point above which it must not be raised.

**Wheels**—28in.; Westwood rims, plated tracks.

**Spokes**—Patent turned, double-butted, of the highest possible quality, heavily plated on copper.

**Tyres**—1⅜in. road-racing Dunlop.

**Forks**—Best weldless taper gauge steel tube, with new and improved box crown; special taper gauge steering tube; lamp bracket.

**Brakes**—Front pull-up rim brake, with inverted grasp; back wheel rim brake on slot end tubes as illustrated).

**Free-wheel**—"Rover" ball bearing frictionless free-wheel (as illustrated on page 26).

**Steering**—Special ball bearings top and bottom; improved "Rover" steering lock (see illustration page 27).

**Bearings**—All cups, cones, and balls of special diamond cast steel, separately and specially hardened (see illustration page 28).

**Finish**—Two coats of finest quality black enamel on one of priming, all bright parts heavily plated on copper. Lined burnished gold.

**Valise, oilcan, and spanners**

For special illustrations of parts see pages 24 to 29 inclusive.

**PRICES** (for Great Britain and Ireland only):

Nett cash     ..     ..     ..     ..     ..     ..     £20     0     0

Exchange, gradual payments, or credit ..     ..     25     0     0

*Fig. 99*

147

# 1903

All *Imperial* models except the path racer had plated rims with red-edged black centres and gold-lined frames. A Rover two-speed was offered. The *Imperial Rover* (Fig. 100) was listed as a *Light Roadster* only, although this may have been an administrative hiccup rather than a change of policy. The pump was illustrated for the first time. The *Special Imperial Rover Light Roadster* had a Brooks Featherweight saddle, celluloid mudguards and the new rims but was otherwise unchanged; the price was as for the *Imperial Rover*. The weight, however, had been reduced; a 24" minus pump and valise weighed 24$^1$/$_2$ pounds.

The *Lady's Imperial Rover* (Fig. 101) was no longer obtainable with double straight tubes. The *Imperial Rover* and the *Lady's Imperial Rover* had celluloid handles; the other *Imperial* models had cork. All these models cost £18 8s, or £22 fitted with two-speed or three-speed gear (makes unspecified) to order.

The *Imperial Rover Path Racer* was unchanged; it cost £18 18s. The *Imperial Rover Road Racer* was also apparently unchanged except for the new rims yet was said to be one pound lighter. It also cost £18 18s or £22 with two-speed or three-speed gear.

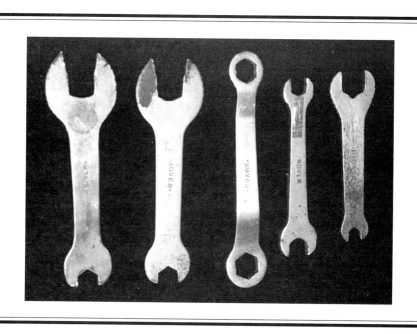

*Selection of Rover spanners.*

# THE IMPERIAL ROVER.

**WEIGHT, Light Roadster,**
24in. frame, 30 lbs. with aluminium guards and gear case.
32 lbs. with steel    „    „    „

**PRICES** (for Great Britain and Ireland only) :

| | | | | |
|---|---|---|---|---|
| Nett cash | ... | ... | ... | £18 18 0 |
| Fitted with two or three-speed gear to order ... | | | | 22 0 0 |

## SPECIFICATION.

**Saddle**—Brooks's B9 size 2, plated springs ; 7 seat rod, with closed ends ; small hole in seat rod two inches from bottom marks the point above which it must not be raised.

**Frame**—22in., 24in., 26in., or 28in., measuring from centre of crank spindle to top of seat lug.

**Pump Clips**—Heavily plated ; enamelled bands ; celluloid pump.

**Gear and Chain**—Hans Renold's best quality, pitch roller chain ; gear 72in.

**Cranks**—Special "Rover" pattern, square ; 6½in. for 22in. and 24in. frames ; 7in. for 26in. frames and higher.

**Pedals**—Special "Rover" pattern, 4in. best quality square block felt.

**Handle-bar**—14in. up-turned, Bluemel's best quality celluloid handles ; small hole two inches from bottom of handle-bar marks the point above which it must not be raised.

**Wheels**—28in. Westwood rims, black enamelled centres, edged red, plated tracks.

**Spokes**—Patent turned, double-butted, of the highest possible quality, heavily plated on copper.

**Tyres**—1½in. light roadster Dunlops.

**Forks**—Best toughened steel sides, with "Rover" new and improved box crown ; special taper gauge steering tube, detachable lamp bracket ; fork ends heavilyplated on copper.

**Brakes**—Front pull-up rim ; back rim actuated by concealed wire ; inverted levers.

**Free-wheel**—"Rover" ball bearing frictionless clutch.

**Guards**—Best steel mudguards, with strengthened edges, specially designed for easy removal ; stays heavily plated on copper.

**Gear Case**—Best metal, with celluloid panels and plated circular disc.

**Steering**—Special "Rover" ball bearings top and bottom, with improved "Rover" steering lock.

**Bearings**—All cups, cones, and balls of special diamond cast steel, separately and specially hardened.

**Finish**—Two coats of finest quality black enamel on one of priming, lined burnished gold ; all bright parts heavily-plated on copper.

### Valise, Oilcan, Spanners, and Pump.

All parts guaranteed interchangeable and true to gauge.

For special illustrations of parts see pages 25 to 32 inclusive.

*Fig. 100*

# THE LADY'S IMPERIAL ROVER. DOUBLE CURVED TUBES.

**WEIGHT, to specification:**

22in. frame, 28 lbs. with aluminium guards and gear case.

30 lbs. with steel   "   "   "

## SPECIFICATION.

**Saddle**—Brooks's B13L, plated springs; 7 seat rod, with closed ends; small hole two inches from bottom marks the point above which it must not be raised.

**Frame**—22in., 24in., or 26in., measuring from centre of crank spindle to top of seat lug.

**Pump Clips**—Heavily plated; enamelled bands; celluloid pump.

**Gear and Chain**—Hans Renold's best quality ½in. pitch roller chain; gear 60in.

**Cranks**—Special "Rover" pattern, square; 6½in.

**Pedals**—New and improved "Rover" pattern, best quality felt.

**Handle-bar**—⅞in. up-turned celluloid handles; small hole in handle-bar stem two inches from bottom marks the point above which it must not be raised.

**Wheels**—28in., Westwood rims, black enamelled centres, edged red, plated tracks.

**Spokes**—Patent turned, double-butted, of the highest possible quality, heavily plated on copper.

**Tyres**—1⅜in. Dunlop lady's.

**Forks**—Best toughened steel sides, with "Rover" new and improved box crown; special taper gauge steering tube; lamp bracket; fork ends heavily plated on copper.

**Brakes**—Front pull-up rim, back rim actuated by concealed wire; inverted levers.

**Free-wheel**—"Rover" ball bearing frictionless clutch.

**Guards**—Best steel, with strengthened edges, laced over back wheel for protection of the dress, easily detachable by means of adjustable clip; mudguard stays heavily plated on copper.

**Gear Case**—Best metal, with celluloid panels and plated circular disc.

**Steering**—Special ball bearings top and bottom; improved "Rover" steering lock.

**Bearings**—All cups, cones, and balls of special diamond cast steel, separately and specially hardened (see illustration, page 31).

**Finish**—Two coats of finest quality black enamel on one of priming, lined burnished gold; all bright parts heavily plated on copper.

## Valise, Oilcan, Spanners, and Pump.

All parts guaranteed interchangeable and true to gauge.

**PRICES** (for Great Britain and Ireland only):

| | | | | | |
|---|---|---|---|---|---|
| Nett cash | ... | ... | ... | ... | £18 18 0 |
| Fitted with two or three-speed gear to order | ... | | | | 22 0 0 |

**For special illustrations of parts see pages 25 to 32 inclusive.**

*Fig. 101*

150

# 1904

All models except the racer had Rover square cranks with rounded edges. The *Imperial Rover Roadster* replaced the *Imperial Rover*. It had a B15 saddle with plated springs, the eccentric bracket (see Fittings section), divided rubber pedals and a new gearcase (Fig. 102). The transparent sections of the gearcase were made of celluloid. The S*pecial Imperial Rover Light Roadster* was replaced by the *Imperial Rover Light Roadster* – the specification was unchanged except for a reversion to steel mudguards. The *Lady's Imperial Rover* had a B14L saddle with plated springs, the eccentric bracket, divided rubber pedals and the new gearcase. In addition to the 22", 24" and 26" frames with 28" wheels a 20" frame was available with 26" wheels – all still with $1^3/8$" Dunlop ladies tyres. The *Imperial Rover Path* and *Road Racer* replaced the two former models. It was apparently identical with the 1903 path racer but the price had dropped to £12 12s.

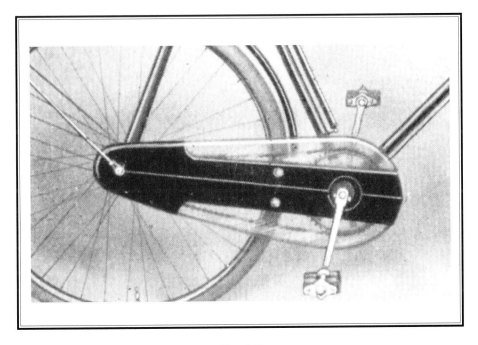

*Fig. 102*

*Gentleman's Imperial Rover c1904. The gearcase and pump are 1904 but the front brake fitting is 1903.*

# 1905

The warning about not raising the seat-pillar and handlebar stem too high was omitted, as was the instruction on how to discover the frame size. As Rovers had apparently been the only firm ever to measure frames by using the top of the bracket as a measuring-point their warning had perhaps been necessary while they re-educated any customers they had led astray. Items detailed in the catalogue included the gearcase end and a "new" pedal. There was no explanation of how the pedal differed from the divided pedal offered in 1904, and the two models fitted with rubber pedals (the *Imperial Rover Roadster* and the *Ladies' Imperial Rover*) had "new and improved Rover pattern, best quality rubbers", 4" and $3^1/_2$" wide respectively. The Sturmey-Archer three-speed gear was also illustrated and was named in the specifications for the first time.

The *Imperial Rover Roadster* and the *Ladies' Imperial Rover* (the plural was used for 1905) had the eccentric bracket, the new gearcase, and enamelled saddle-springs. Together with the *Imperial Rover Light Roadster* (now minus the 28" frame) they had frames and rims lined in Brunswick green. All three models cost £15 15s, a Rover two-speed being £2 2s extra and a Sturmey-Archer three-speed £3 3s (See Variable Gears). The *Imperial Road Racer* had lost even its combined existence; only the *Imperial Rover Path Racer* was offered at £12 12s. This was available in 22" and 24" (or to order) with 7" (or to order) cranks, and the handlebar had about a 3" extension (unless otherwise ordered) with a "new and improved fastening" that was not described. The machine could be supplied fitted as a road racer at the same price. As before, the rims were 26" for 22" frames and 28" for 24" and above. The 26" rims were Actual Boston Fairbank Laminated, or steel to order. Sprint tyres could be ordered instead of the $1^3/_8$" path-racing ones offered.

# 1906

This year saw the company's name changed from Rover Cycle Company to Rover Company Limited, reflecting the growing emphaisis on the production of motorcars and motorcycles.

The three *Imperial* road machines increased to £16 16s, £18 18s and £19 19s for single-speed, two-speed and three-speed models respectively; but whereas the Sturmey-Archer gear was offered on all three models the two-speeds were Griffin or Fagan for the *Imperial Rover Roadster* and the *Imperial Rover Lady's*, and the *Imperial Rover Light Roadster* offered the Rover two-speed as a third option. The illustration of the Sturmey-Archer gear shows that the control wire had been moved to the offside and a step fitted on the nearside. It should be remembered that the step was used by gentlemen mounting their machines; the absence of that facility in the 1905 gear had perhaps militated against acceptance of that gear. Other changes common to the three were plated saddle-springs and the abandonment of the inverted brake-levers. The *Imperial Rover Roadster* used the new system of braking; the Rover oil-bath case is also shown. The *Imperial Rover Light Roadster* had a Brooks B32/1 saddle and 1¹/₂" Dunlop tyres with extra-thick tread that was "puncture-resisting and non-slipping". Other tyres could be specified on all models.

The *Imperial Rover Path Racer* had a Brooks B17 Champion saddle with enamelled springs. This was the first appearance on a *Rover* as a standard fitment of the saddle that Brooks advertised for many years as "man's favourite saddle". As before, the path racer could be fitted as a road racer at no extra cost.

## 1907

Specifications were unchanged but the prices of the road machines dropped to £14 14s, £16 15s and £16 16s according to the gearing. The Fagan and Rover two-speed gears disappeared and the Hub replaced them.

## 1908

The *Imperial Rover Roadster* and the *Imperial Rover Lady's* had a detachable all-metal gearcase as a standard fitment but the oil-bath version was available if preferred. Any other standard two-speed gear could be specified instead of the Hub or Griffin, and the Armstrong-Triplex three-speed could replace the Sturmey-Archer. The *Imperial Rover Path Racer* had Dunlop sprint tyres on wood rims but could be fitted with road-racing tyres for the same price. Whether this was different from the previous offer to fit the model as a road racer it is impossible to tell. The path racer was naturally brakeless; presumably by 1905, when the offer was first made, a reputable firm would have fitted at least one brake to a machine intended for racing on the public highway.

## 1909

The *Imperial Rover Roadster*, the *Imperial Rover Light Roadster* and the *Lady's Imperial Rover* (another change of position for *"Lady's"*) were practically identical except that the Brunswick green lining on frames and rims was replaced by gold. The price went down to £14. A specially light version (26¹/₂ pounds) of the *Lady's Imperial Rover* was offered at £14. It was available in 22" and 24" only, with 28" wheels, and had a transparent celluloid gearcase. The only speed-gear offered was the Armstrong-Triplex at £1 15s extra; it had the gear-lever working in a slot in the top tube.This was the first time that the weight of any Imperial had been given since 1904.

The *Imperial Rover Path Racer* dropped in price from £12 12s to £8 8s; it could be fitted as a road racer for the same price.

# 1910

The catalogue illustrated the tapered head-tubes, the brakework, and the pressed-steel carrier that had replaced the tubular version introduced in 1905 (see Fittings section). The *Imperial Rover Roadster* had a Brooks B302 saddle with plated springs and 1½" Rover A or Dunlop tyres. The *Special Imperial Rover Light Roadster* replaced the *Imperial Rover Light Roadster*; it was available in 24" or 26" with 7" cranks, B10 saddle with plated springs, 28" x 1⅜" aluminium rims with "bright tracks" lined to match the frame, Rover A or Dunlop tyres with exposed sides, aluminium mudguards and gold frame-lining. It weighed 27½ pounds. The *Lady's Imperial Rover* had 1½" (instead of 1⅜") Rover A or Dunlop tyres. All three models had the rear brake working under the chainstays. They cost £11 11s with two brakes but could be fitted with a coaster and front brake only for the same price. The Armstrong-Triplex three-speed cost £1 10s extra.

The *Imperial Rover Path Racer* was unchanged but the price rose slightly to £8 10s; the weight was given as 21 pounds. The *Imperial Rover Road Racer* reappeared as a separate machine. Like the *Path Racer*, it had a slightly dropped top-tube but the handlebar had a shallow drop and no extension. It was fitted with steel mudguards and cost £11 5s with two brakes (as on the roadsters), coaster hub and front brake (no charge) or Armstrong-Triplex (£1 10s extra). The 26" wheels had enamelled centres and plated tracks, with tyres as on the new *Special*.

# 1911

Among the specialities illustrated were the Rover oval-to-round front fork and the back brake (shown in the Fittings section).

The *Imperial Rover Roadster* was advertised as 24" or 26" with other sizes to order. Its specification included a 1909-pattern rear brake, a B90/1 saddle with plated springs, 7" cranks, 4" felt pedals, 28" Roman rims lined to match the frame, a reflector (then known as a reflex light), and a new open-centred gearcase which the catalogue described as a detachable oil bath. This case was decorated with a Rover shield in the disc. It was probably embossed. The front mudguard was extended in front of the fork-crown. The frame-lining was two gold lines and a green centre line. Only Dunlop tyres were specified, the Rover A having ended its brief appearance. The *Lady's Imperial Rover* had a B85L saddle with plated springs, Roman rims and 3¼" felt pedals; frame and rims were lined like the roadster's. The rear brake was unchanged from the 1910 version. Both these

*1911: C B Kingsbury, 10, 25 and 50 mile Champion of England.*

155

models cost £14 with either two brakes or a coaster hub and front brake, an Armstrong-Triplex three-speed being £1 7s 6d extra. The Sturmey-Archer three-speed could be fitted if required. The *Special Imperial Rover Light Roadster* was replaced by the *Imperial Rover Special*. This had a 24" or 26" frame, 28" Roman rims, a B84 saddle with plated springs, a Renold $^1/_2$" roller chain, 7" cranks, Rover $3^3/_4$" rat-trap pedals, $1^3/_8$" Dunlop tyres with exposed sides, new-pattern pump-clips, Bluemel's pump, aluminium mudguards and a reflector. Frame and wheels were lined gold with a green centre-line. The 1909-pattern rear brake was fitted and cost £13.

The *Imperial Rover Path Racer* increased in price to £9 10s with an unchanged specification, except that 1" Constrictor tyres were named. The separate *Imperial Rover Road Racer* disappeared; the *Path Racer* could be supplied to order as a road racer fitted with North Road handlebar, free-wheel, mudguards and two brakes at £12.

## 1912

The *Imperial Rover Roadster* had steel instead of Roman rims and $^5/_{16}$" balls in the back hub. The *Lady's Imperial Rover* similarly had $^5/_{16}$" balls and the standard 60" gear was increased to 63". On each model there was the usual offer of coaster hub and front brake at the same price; an Armstrong-Triplex three-speed gear or a three-speed coaster hub and front brake cost £1 2s 6d extra. A Sturmey-Archer three-speed or Tricoaster hub could be fitted if required. The *Imperial Rover Special (Special Imperial Rover Light Roadster)* had disappeared.

The *Imperial Rover Path Racer* (weighing 21 pounds) was unchanged except for the $^5/_{16}$" balls and 1" Dunlops instead of Constrictors. Fitted for road racing as before it cost £12.

## 1913

This year saw the formation of the New Rover Cycle Company Limited – and the provision of brazed-on pump-clips.

The *Imperial Rover Roadster* was once more offered in 22", 24", 26" and 28", with $6^1/_2$" cranks for the 22" and 7" for the other sizes. A B95 saddle with plated springs replaced the B90, and rubber pedals were fitted. The *Lady's Imperial Rover* had a B302L saddle with plated springs, 28" steel rims, rubber pedals, and no plating on the fork-ends or the ends of the mudguard stays. The price for both models went down to £10 10s (single gear or with coaster hub and front brake). The Armstrong-Triplex gear (with top-tube control) cost £1 extra, and a Sturmey-Archer gear could be fitted if desired. Three-speed coaster hubs cost 7s 6d extra. The gearcase was no longer described as an oil-bath.

The *Imperial Rover Path Racer* dropped in price to £8 5s; no road-racing machine was offered.

# 1914

The *Imperial Rover Roadster* had only 7" cranks but was otherwise unchanged. The *Lady's Imperial Rover* had a new frame (Fig. 103) similar to the one that had been used on the cheaper models since 1897. There was no mention of the central top-tube control for the Armstrong-Triplex gear, and the offer of the coaster hubs for 7s 6d was withdrawn.

The *Imperial Rover Path Racer* was unchanged.

# Lady's Imperial Rover

### SPECIFICATION.

**Frame**—22-in., 24-in., or 26-in.

**Forks**—Box crown, oval to round sides, 3½-in. curve; lamp bracket.

**Handle-bar**—Upturned, celluloid handles.

**Saddle**—Brooks' 302L. plated springs.

**Tool-bag**—Brooks' No. 9060/1, with ticket holder, cleaning cloth, and tools.

**Chain and Gear**—Best quality Renold ½-in. pitch roller; gear 63-in.

**Cranks**—"Rover" pattern, 6½-in

**Pedals**—3¼-in. "Rover" pattern, best quality rubber.

**Pump**—Dover Pump, new pattern pump clips.

**Wheels**—28-in., lined to match frame, steel rims.

**Tyres**—1½-in. Dunlops.

**Spokes**—Double-butted, of the highest possible quality, enamelled black, plated centres.

**Guards**—Best steel, with strengthened edges; extension to front guard, laced over back wheel, for the protection of the dress; mudguard stays enamelled.

**Brakes**—Front and back rim, outside levers.

**Gear Case**—Rover detachable, open front.

**Free-wheel**—"Rover" ball-bearing, frictionless.

**Steering**—Special ball-bearings top and bottom; "Rover" steering lock.

**Bearings**—All cups, cones, and balls of special steel.

**Finish**—Finest quality black enamel, fine gold lines, with centre line green, all bright parts heavily plated on copper.

### Reflex Rear Light, Oilcan, Spanners, and Pump.

*All parts guaranteed interchangeable and true to gauge.*

---

**PRICE** (for Great Britain and Ireland only):

| | £ | s | d |
|---|---|---|---|
| **Nett Cash** to above specification ... ... ... | £10 | 10 | 0 |
| With Coaster Hub and Front Brake only ... ... ... | 10 | 10 | 0 |
| With Sturmey-Archer or Armstrong-Triplex Three-Speed Gear ... ... ... ... ... | 11 | 10 | 0 |

*Fig. 103*

# 1915

A new-pattern domed fork-crown was introduced, and the *Imperial Rover Roadster* was unchanged except that only 7" cranks were offered and a fully covered detachable gearcase was fitted; the Rover shield had disappeared from the disc. The *Lady's Imperial Rover* also had the new case. Both models cost £10 10s complete with Sturmey-Archer three-speed gear; no variation was offered.

The *Imperial Rover Path Racer* was reduced to £7 10s.

# 1916

The price for the two road machines rose to £12 12s. They were both single-speed and the only variation offered was the familiar coaster hub and front brake instead of two brakes. There was no further mention of the Rover free-wheel.

The *Imperial Rover Path Racer* was unchanged.

# 1917

The price for the two road machines rose to £14 5s and the offer of a coaster hub was withdrawn. The *Imperial Rover Path Racer* was also withdrawn.

# 1918–1919

The authors have not found any catalogues for either of these years. The following is a copy of the *Cycling* report on the Rovers at the December 1919 Olympia Cycle Show:

"The *Imperial Rover* is seen as the leading production, combining first-class material, scientific construction and first rate fittings. The standard equipment including a gearcase, Brooks's saddle and Dunlop tyres. With a beautiful finish, this model is listed at £20 10s. The *Royal Rover* is also fitted with Dunlop tyres and Brooks's saddle, and will represent the Rover next highest grade at the respective prices of £18 15s and £19 10s for gent's and lady's models. The *All-Weather Rover* appears as a machine eminently adapted to the winter rider's needs. Aluminium rims are fitted and the all-black finish is relieved by green and bronze lines. The price is £20 10s for lady's or gent's pattern. The *Rover Roadster* is seen equipped with Warwick tyres as a standard fitting, the prices of the diamond-framed model being £16 and the lady's pattern £16 15s. A cheap model is seen in the *Model A*, the prices of which are £13 13s for the racing and gent's patterns and £13 17s 6d for the lady's model. The famous *Imperial Rover Path Racer* is attracting the attention of speedmen, while the *Road Racer* is seen with road equipment at £15."

# 1920

The prices of the road machines remained at £20 10s, the *Imperial Rover Roadster* having a Brooks B302 saddle and an open-centre gearcase (as in 1914). The *Imperial Rover Path Racer* was listed with the 1912–16 specification and priced at £15.

# 1921–1922

All models were unchanged according to the catalogues. But the following extracts from the report on the 1920 Olympia Cycle Show, taken from *Cycling* of 2 December 1920, gives a picture that does not agree entirely with that obtained from the catalogues:

"Among the constructional features to be noted are the domed fork-crown and the oval-to-round section blades. 'Clean' handlebars with neat brakework and brazed-on pump-pegs add to the appearance. Chief of the roadster models is the *Imperial,* with first-class equipment, inclusive of Brooks 302 saddle, Dunlop tyres, and a detachable gearcase. Single-geared, this is priced at £20 10s. The *R.I.C. Rover*, a sturdy machine made for heavy riders, has a Brooks B90 (size 3) saddle and $1^3/_4$" Dunlop Magnum tyres, and costs £19 5s. The *Royal Rover* has first-class equipment with a Brooks spirally-sprung saddle, Dunlop tyres and Rover metal gearcase, the price being £18 15s for the gent's model and 5s extra for the lady's. An attractive mount for the winter rider is the *All-Weather*, priced in lady's and gent's models at £20 10s. It is a fully-protected roadster with all-black finish relieved by two-colour lining, and has a Brooks B75 saddle, Dunlop tyres and a metal gearcase. A standard mount is seen in the *Roadster* at £16, while Juvenile models are staged, the respective prices being £13 and £13 10s for boy's and girl's models. The *Rover Road Racer* has an Eadie coaster hub and 26" x $1^3/_8$" Cambridge, and is equipped with mudguards. The *Imperial Path Racer* has a Brooks B17 Champion saddle and Dunlop sprint tyres on laminated wood rims in the price of £15. The *Rover Model A* group of machines is staged, including a roadster and a fully equipped *Road Racer* at £13 13s and a lady's model at £13 17s 6d."

Comparison of that report with the accounts in the various model-ranges reinforces our warning that although the catalogues may usually be relied on as expressions of intent it is important never to claim that "It must be so because it is in the catalogue!"

# 1923

A new-style catalogue was introduced; the *Imperial Rover Path Racer* model is shown here (Fig. 104).

# Imperial Rover Path Racer

Weight 21-lbs.

## *Specification*

| | | |
|---|---|---|
| Frame | ... ... | 22-in. or 24-in. |
| Saddle | ... ... | Brooks' B17 Champion, enamelled springs. |
| Chain and Gear | | Very best quality chain. |
| Cranks | ... ... | 6½-in. or 7-in. Special "Rover" pattern, square. |
| Pedals | ... ... | Rat trap, square "Rover" pattern. |
| Wheels | ... ... | 26-in. laminated wood rims. |
| Tyres | ... ... | 1-in. Dunlops. |
| Finish | ... ... | Finest quality black enamel, all bright parts heavily plated on copper. |

### Tools and Pump

## Price : £15 0 0

*Fig. 104*

*Above: Imperial Path Racer, 1906.*

*1911. B Scheider*
*Champion of Australia*
*Holder of the Dunlop Bath Gold Cup.*

## 1924

Mr H. B. Light, mentioned earlier, wrote that the manufacture of Rover cycles ended in 1923 and although Rovers were mentioned after that date there was apparently no evidence to contradict him. Shortly before this book was printed, however, catalogues for 1924 and 1925 were found. The *Imperial Rover Roadster* cost £15 15s, the price increase perhaps to cover the return of the Brooks B90/1 saddle with enamelled springs and Brooks tool-bag. Cranks were $6\frac{1}{2}$" on 22" frames, 7" on 24" and higher. A Hans Renold chain replaced the "very best quality" of 1923, and the brakes had brazed lugs "throughout". The detachable chainwheel was not offered. The finish was black with gold lines - no mention was made of the green lines of 1923. The old-pattern gearcase with the shield chainwheel disc reappeared on this and *Royal* models. The bicycle was available as an All-Weather Model (i.e. with no plated parts but with gold lining) at no extra cost. An ordinary free-wheel hub could be fitted instead of the standard BSA three-speed (which had a normal gear of 68") at the reduced price of £15 12s. The specification of the *Lady's Imperial Rover* was identical except that 7" cranks were not offered, there was no mention of a reduction for a free-wheel instead of a speed gear, and a Brooks B302 saddle with enamelled springs was fitted. The *Imperial Path Racer* had disappeared.

## 1925

There was one change in this range: the *Imperial Path Racer* was announced as "An Old Favourite Reintroduced", priced £9 10s.

# The Rover Range
## 1900

The four *Rover* models catalogued in 1900 are shown here. It will be noted that the gearcase shown in Fig. 108 is not the type described in the specification. The cost of the free-wheel and special brake mentioned was as follows:

Free-wheels, 15s

Back wheel rim, band or block brake, £1 10s

Front wheel rim brake free with free-wheel on *Lady's* and *Light Roadsters*, £1 with *Road Racer*.

# ROVER LIGHT ROADSTER.

WEIGHT, to specification :
22in. frame, 33 lbs.

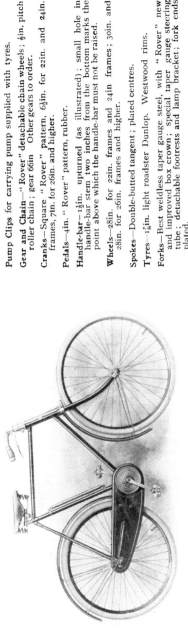

**Price** (for Great Britain only) **£16 16s.** net cash.

**Rover Roadster.**—This machine is also supplied as a roadster with larger saddle and 1¾in. tyres to order.

For cost of free-wheel and special brakes see page 9.

## SPECIFICATION.

**Saddle**—"Rover" light roadster ; **7** seat rod ; small hole two inches from bottom marks the point above which it must not be raised.

**Frame**—22in., 24in., 26in., or 28in., measuring from centre of crank spindle to top of seat lug.

**Pump Clips** for carrying pump supplied with tyres.

**Gear and Chain**—"Rover" detachable chain wheels ; ⅝in. pitch roller chain ; gear 66in   Other gears to order.

**Cranks**—Square "Rover" pattern, 6½in. for 22in. and 24in. frames, 7in. for 26in. and higher.

**Pedals**—4in. "Rover" pattern, rubber.

**Handle-bar**—1⅜in. upturned (as illustrated) ; small hole in handle-bar stem two inches from the bottom marks the point above which the handle-bar must not be raised.

**Wheels**—28in. for 22in. frames and 24in frames ; 30in. and 28in. for 26in. frames and higher.

**Spokes**—Double-butted tangent ; plated centres.

**Tyres**—1⅝in. light roadster Dunlop.  Westwood rims.

**Forks**—Best weldless taper gauge steel, with "Rover" new and improved box crown ; special taper gauge steering tube ; detachable footrests and lamp bracket ; fork ends plated.

**Brake**—Improved "Rover" detachable, with rubber block.

**Guards**—Best steel, with strengthened edges.

**Gear Case**—"Rover," metal, plated disc.

**Steering**—Special ball bearings top and bottom, improved "Rover" steering lock.

**Bearings**—All cups, cones, and balls of special diamond cast steel, separately and specially hardened.

**Finish**—Two coats of best black enamel on one of priming, lined green and straw, all bright parts heavily plated on copper.

*Fig. 105*

163

# ROVER ROAD RACER.

WEIGHT, to specification: 22in. frame, 26 lbs.

## SPECIFICATION.

**Saddle**—"Rover" road racer; 7 seat rod; small hole two inches from bottom marks the point above which the seat rod must not be raised.

**Frame**—22in., 24in., 26in., and 28in, measuring from centre of crank spindle to top of seat lug.

**Gear and Chain**—"Rover" detachable chain wheels; ⅜in. pitch roller chain; gear 72in.

**Cranks**—"Rover" pattern, square, 6¾in.; 7in. for 26in. frames and higher.

**Pedals**—3¾in. "Rover" rat-trap, thoroughly dustproof.

**Handle-bar**—As illustrated; small hole two inches from bottom marks the point above which it must not be raised.

**Wheels**—28in. for 22in. and 24in. frames; 30in. and 28in. for 26in. frames and higher.

**Spokes**—Double-butted tangent; plated centres.

**Tyres**—1½in. road-racing Dunlop. Westwood rims.

**Forks**—Best weldless taper gauge steel tubes with new and improved box crown; special taper gauge steering tube; lamp bracket; fork ends plated.

**Steering**—Special ball bearings top and bottom; improved "Rover" steering lock.

**Bearings**—All cups, cones, and balls of special diamond cast steel, separately and specially hardened.

**Finish**—Two coats of best black enamel on one of priming, all bright parts heavily plated on copper.

𝔓rice (for Great Britain only) £15 15s. net cash.

*Fig. 106*

164

# ROVER PATH RACER.

WEIGHT, to specification: 23½in. frame, 23 lbs.

## SPECIFICATION.

**Saddle**—"Rover" racer; **7** seat rod, with closed ends; the small hole two inches from bottom marks the point above which it must not be raised.

**Frame**—22in., 24in., 26in., or 28in., measuring from centre of crank spindle to top of seat lug.

**Gear and Chain**—"Rover" interchangeable, standard 84in. Other gears to order. ⅜in. pitch roller chain.

**Cranks**—Special "Rover" pattern, square, 6¾in. for 22in. and 24in., 7in. for 26in. frames and higher.

**Pedals**—3¾in., rat-trap, best "Rover" pattern, thoroughly dustproof.

**Handle-bar**—Special "Rover" drop (as illustrated); the small hole two inches from bottom marks the point above which it must not be raised.

**Wheels**—28in. wheels for 22in. and 24in. frames; 30in. front and 28in. back for 26in. frames and higher; 28in. wheels to order.

**Spokes**—Tangent, double-butted; plated centres.

**Tyres**—1⅜in. path racing Dunlop. Westwood rims.

**Forks**—Best weldless taper gauge steel tubes, with new and improved box crown; special taper gauge steering tube.

**Steering**—Special ball bearings top and bottom.

**Bearings**—All cups, cones, and balls of special diamond cast steel, separately and specially hardened.

**Finish**—Two coats of best black enamel on one of priming, all bright parts heavily plated on copper.

**Price** (for Great Britain only) £15 15s. net cash.

Fig. 107

165

# THE LADY'S ROVER.

## SPECIFICATION.

**Saddle**—Lady's "Rover"; 7 seat rod; small hole two inches from bottom marks point above which it must not be raised.

**Frame**—20in., 22in., 24in., or 26in., measuring from centre of crank axle to top of seat lug.

**Pump Clips** for carrying pump supplied with tyres.

**Gear and Chain**—"Rover" detachable chain wheel; ½in. pitch roller chain; gear 60in.

**Cranks**—"Rover" pattern, square, 6in. for 20in. and 22in. frames, 6¾in. for higher frames.

**Pedals**—New and improved "Rover" rubber block pattern, thoroughly dustproof.

**Handle-bar**—"Rover" upturned (as illustrated); small hole two inches from bottom marks the point above which it must not be raised.

**Wheels**—28in. for 20in. and 22in. frames, 30in. front and 28n. back for 24in. frames and higher. 28in. to order.

**Spokes**—Tangent, double-butted; plated centres.

**Tyres**—1⅜in. Dunlop. Westwood rims.

**Forks**—Best weldless taper gauge steel tube, with new and improved box crown; detachable footrests and lamp bracket.

**Brake**—Improved "Rover" detachable, with rubber block.

**Guards**—Best steel, with strengthened edges; rear guard laced (as illustrated) for the protection of the dress.

**Gear Case**—"Rover," metal, with plated disc.

**Steering**—Special ball bearings top and bottom, improved "Rover" steering lock.

**Bearings**—All cups, cones, and balls of special diamond cast steel, separately and specially hardened.

**Finish**—Two coats of best black enamel on one of priming, lined green and straw, bright parts plated on copper.

**WEIGHT,** to specification : 22in. frame, 30 lbs.

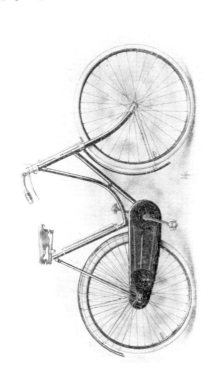

**Price** (for Great Britain only) £16 16s. net cash.

For cost of free-wheel and special brake see page 9.

*Fig. 108*

166

# 1901

The *Rover Light Roadster* had minor changes: it had only 28" rims, $1\frac{1}{2}$" light roadster Dunlop tyres, the new front Rover rim-brake (see Fittings) and a Brooks B302 saddle; footrests could be supplied to order. It could be supplied as the *Rover Roadster* with a larger saddle and $1\frac{3}{4}$" tyres. The *Lady's Rover* had only $6\frac{1}{2}$" cranks, only 28" Westwood rims, $1\frac{1}{2}$" Dunlop tyres and new rim-brake. Both models cost £15 15s with fixed wheel and front brake; with free-wheel and two rim-brakes they cost £16 16s. The *Rover Road Racer* had only 28" Westwood rims, $1\frac{3}{8}$" road-racing Dunlop tyres, $6\frac{1}{2}$" cranks for 22" and 24" frames and 7" for 26" and 28"; it cost £14 14s. The *Rover Path Racer* was dropped.

# 1902

Our 1902 catalogue contained no prices but they were probably unaltered from those of 1901. The *Rover Light Roadster* was no longer offered as a full roadster, and footrests were not available. On this model and the *Lady's Rover* a free-wheel was standard equipment but a fixed wheel was available at the same price. The *Rover Road Racer* had a 77" gear.

# 1903

The 24" *Rover Light Roadster* was announced as weighing 32 pounds (one pound less than the 1902 24" machine). Its gear was raised to 72" and it was fitted with a detachable lamp-bracket. The 20" *Lady's Rover* was withdrawn, as were the 6" cranks. Both these models had celluloid pumps. The *Rover Light Roadster Special* (Fig. 109) was a new model. The 24" frame weighed only half a pound more than the 1902 22" *Rover Road Racer* (withdrawn this year) although it was fitted with steel mudguards. The frame finishes were green and gold bronze lining; wheels had plated tracks and black-enamelled centres edged green.

# 1904

This year saw the introduction of the Royal range and more renaming of models. The *Rover Roadster* specification was similar to that of the 1903 *Rover Light Roadster* except that it had a Brooks B20 saddle, no 28" model and a steel gearcase without a plated disc; it was lined in two unspecified colours; the price was £12 12s.

The *Lady's Rover* had an identical specification (even to the saddle) but the 22" model weighed 32 pounds (two more than the 1903 model). It also cost £12 12s. The *Rover Light Roadster Special* had become the *Rover Light Roadster*, also at £12 12s. The 24" model weighed 27 pounds without pump, valise and contents. This was the first reference to omitting accessories when weighing; although the implication is that they were usually left on it is impossible to be sure. The 28" frame had disappeared and a detachable lamp-bracket was fitted. The finish was similar to that on the other models; all three machines had plated unlined rims. From 1904 onwards there was no plating on the fork-ends.

# ROVER LIGHT ROADSTER.
## SPECIAL.

WEIGHT, to specification 24in. frame. 26 lbs.

## SPECIFICATION.

**Saddle**—Brooks's B11 ; 7 seat rod ; small hole two inches from bottom marks the point above which the seat rod must not be raised.

**Frame**—22in., 24in., 26in., and 28in., measuring from centre of crank spindle to top of seat lug.

**Gear and Chain**—" Rover" detachable chain wheels; ⅜in. pitch roller chain ; gear 72in.

**Cranks**—" Rover" pattern, square ; 6½in. for 22in. and 24in. frames ; 7in. for 26in. and higher.

**Pedals**—3¾in. " Rover" rat-trap; thoroughly dust-proof.

**Handle=bar**—As illustrated ; small hole two inches from bottom marks the point above which it must not be raised, cork handles.

**Wheels**—28in. ; Westwood rims, plated tracks, black enamelled centres, edged green.

**Spokes**—Double-butted tangent, heavily plated on copper.

**Tyres**—1⅜in. road-racing Dunlop.

**Forks**—Best toughened steel sides, with " Rover" new and improved box crown ; special taper gauge steering tube ; detachable lamp bracket ; fork ends plated.

**Brakes**—Front pull-up rim, back wheel rim, inverted levers.

**Free=wheel**—" Rover" ball bearing frictionless clutch.

**Guards**—Best steel, with strengthened edges, specially designed for easy removal.

**Steering**—Special ball bearings top and bottom ; improved " Rover" steering lock.

**Bearings**—All cups, cones, and balls of special diamond cast steel, separately and specially hardened.

**Finish**—Two coats of best black enamel on one of priming, lined green and gold bronze; all bright parts heavily plated on copper.

### Valise, Oilcan, Spanners, and Pump,

All parts guaranteed interchangeable and true to gauge.

**PRICE** (for Great Britain and Ireland only) :

Nett cash    ...    ...    ...    **£15 15 0**

For special illustrations of parts see pages 25 to 32 inclusive.

*Fig. 109*

# 1905

See the 1905 *Imperial* range for comment on safety measures and frame measuring. The prices of all models dropped to £10 10s, or £12 12s with Rover two-speed gear, £13 13s with Sturmey-Archer three-speed gear. Frames were red-lined. A Brooks B18 saddle was fitted on each model.

# 1906

The *Rover Roadster* and the *Rover Light Roadster* were available with 28" frames; their saddles were B75. The *Rover Roadster* and the *Lady's Rover* had oil-bath gearcases as extras; the latter was available also in 20" with 26" wheels. The Griffin and Fagan two-speed gears could be specified; prices were as in 1905.

*Rover fitted with optional stay 1905/6: M Knight*

# 1907

Prices of all models dropped to £8 8s, or £9 18s with Hub or Griffin two-speed gear and £10 10s with Sturmey-Archer three-speed gear. The *Rover Roadster* lost its gearcase and was fitted with a "large and comfortable" Rover saddle; the tyres were anonymous pneumatics. The *Lady's Rover* had a leather gearcase with two celluloid panels. Outside levers replaced the inverted ones that had been in use (see the comment in the 1906 Imperial range).

# 1908

The *Rover Roadster* and the *Rover Lady's* had B75 saddles with plated springs, Bluemel's pumps and Dunlop tyres; they were otherwise unchanged. The *Rover Light Roadster* had a B18 saddle, Bluemel's pump and Dunlops.

The *Rover Road Racer* (Fig. 110) was introduced.

# The Rover Road Racer.

## SPECIALLY DESIGNED FRAME, SLOPING TOP TUBE

## SPECIFICATION.

SADDLE.—" Brooks B18."

FRAME.—22in., 24in., 26in., or 28in.

CHAIN AND GEAR.—½in. pitch roller chain ; gear 72in.

CRANKS.—" Rover " pattern ; 6½in. for 22in. and 24in. frames ; 7in. for 26in. frames and higher.

PEDALS.—3⅛in. rat-trap.

HANDLE-BAR.—Road racing. Bluemel's handles.

WHEELS.—28in., Westwood rims, plated tracks ; 26in. wheels for 22in. frames.

TYRES.—1⅜in. Dunlop ; narrow rims.

FORKS.—Box crown, tapered sides, 3½in. curve ; detachable lamp-bracket.

BRAKES.—Front and back rim, inverted levers.

FREE-WHEEL.—" Rover " ball-bearing frictionless.

STEERING.—Special ball bearings top and bottom.

MUDGUARDS.

BEARINGS.—All cups, cones, and balls or special steel, separately and specially hardened.

FINISH.—Best black enamel, bright parts plated on copper.

Valise, oilcan, spanners, and Bluemel's pump.

*All parts guaranteed interchangeable and true to gauge.*

## PRICE.

(FOR GREAT BRITAIN AND IRELAND ONLY.)

| | | |
|---|---|---|
| Nett Cash .. .. .. .. .. .. .. .. | £8 | 8 | 0 |
| With " Hub," " Griffin," or other Standard Two-speed Gear .. | £9 | 18 | 0 |
| With Sturmey-Archer or Armstrong-Triplex Three-speed Gear | £10 | 10 | 0 |

*Fig. 110*

## 1909

The lining to frame and wheels changed from red to green on the *Rover Roadster,* the *Lady's Rover* and the *Rover Light Roadster.* Pumps were simply celluloid, although of course they may have been Bluemel's. The only change-speed gear offered was the Armstrong-Triplex; it cost £1 15s extra.

## 1910

The *Rover Light Roadster* disappeared. Prices dropped; the *Rover Roadster,* the *Lady's Rover* and the *Rover Road Racer* were £6 10s with two brakes or coaster hub and front brake, £8 with Armstrong-Triplex three-speed gear. Brooks's saddles also disappeared, all models were fitted with Rover saddles with enamelled springs.

The *Rover Road Racer* was fitted with 1³/₈" Rover B tyres instead of Dunlops. A new model, the *Special Rover Road Racer,* was similar to the other racer but had 26" laminated wood rims, 1¹/₄" Rover Speed tyres and a coaster hub; it cost £7 10s.

## 1911

The *Rover Roadster* rose in price to £8 10s (free-wheel or coaster hub and front brake) or £9 17s 6d with Armstrong-Triplex three-speed hub - or Sturmey-Archer three-speed hub if preferred. It had a B75 saddle with plated springs, Dunlop 1¹/₂" tyres, a new gearcase with the Rover shield decorating the disc. This was similar to the new case used on the *Imperials,* except that those were open-centred. An extension to the front mudguard was shown for the first time. No deviation from this specification was permitted. The prices of the *Lady's Rover* were similar. A Brooks B75L with plated springs replaced the Rover saddle, and a gearcase similar to that on the roadster was fitted. The finish on both machines included three fine lines and panel (box) lining.

The *Rover Road Racer* cost £7 10s, the Armstrong-Triplex three-speed gear being £1 7s 6d extra. It had a B10 saddle with plated springs, Dunlop 1³/₈" tyres with exposed sides, and a new chainwheel. The standard specification included a front rim-brake with short pull-up lever and a New Departure coaster hub, but two rim-brakes were offered as an alternative. The *Special Rover Road Racer* had a B10 saddle with plated springs, 1¹/₄" Clipper Speed tyres and a New Departure coaster hub also cost £7 10s.

## 1912

The *Rover Roadster* and the *Lady's Rover* were fitted with the new fork. The remarks about the *Imperial Rover Roadster* and the *Lady's Imperial Rover* apply to these two models, except that the gear of the *Lady's Rover* was increased from 60" to 63". An *All-Black Rover* was offered at £8 10s.

The *Rover Road Racer* had a horizontal top tube, and a New Departure coaster hub was specified. The 1911 short pull-up lever and the offer of a free-wheel and two brakes were withdrawn. The *Special Rover Road Racer* also had a horizontal top tube.

## 1913

Prices dropped again. The *Rover Roadster* and the *Lady's Rover* were £6 17s 6d with free-wheel and two brakes or with coaster hub and front brake only, or £7 17s 6d with either Armstrong-Triplex (central top-tube control) or Sturmey-Archer three-speed gears. A three-speed coaster hub was 7s 6d extra. Rover saddles with plated springs once more replaced Brooks, and 1½" Warwick tyres replaced Dunlops. No gearcase was fitted to the *Rover Roadster*; the *Lady's Rover* had a leather case with celluloid panels.

The *Rover Road Racer* dropped in price to £5 15s and reverted to the sloping top tube and was fitted with an Eadie or New Departure coaster hub and a front rim-brake operated by an inverted lever. It was fitted with Dunlop Cambridge tyres. The saddle was a Rover with plated springs. The *Special Rover Road Racer* had a similar (perhaps identical) frame and offered either make of coaster hub; it cost £5 19s 6d.

## 1914

The *Rover Roadster* had a Brampton chain but was otherwise unchanged; the price dropped to £6 10s with free-wheel, £6 12s 6d with coaster hub and front brake only, and £7 10s with Sturmey-Archer or Armstrong-Triplex three-speed gear. The *Rover Lady's* had a Brampton chain; prices were £6 15s, £6 17s 6d and £7 15s respectively.

The *Rover Road Racer* had a Brampton chain; only the Eadie coaster hub was offered. The *Special Rover Road Racer* had a Rover saddle with plated springs, and only the Eadie coaster was offered. The price for both machines was £5 19s 6d. All models except the lady's had the extension to the front mudguard which had been introduced in 1911.

## 1915

The *Rover Roadster* was finished with fine green and red lines, panel lining. Prices were £6 15s, £6 17s 6d and £7 15s for the usual three types, but only the Sturmey-Archer three-speed gear was offered. The *Lady's Rover* had the extension to the front mudguard and a leather gearcase without celluloid panels but with a plated disc over the chainwheel. It was lined like the *Roadster* and its prices were £6 19s 6d, £7 2s and £7 19s 6d respectively.

The *Rover Road Racer* and the *Special Rover Road Racer* had the new lining. The former could have a free-wheel and two rim-brakes at no extra charge, the latter a front rim-brake at a cost of 4s 6d.

## 1916

The *Rover Roadster* and the *Lady's Rover* cost £8 8s and £8 12s 6d respectively, or £8 10s 6d and £8 15s respectively with coaster hub and front rim-brake. No three-speed was offered. Either bicycle could be finished all-black for 5s extra. The plated disc disappeared from the latter's gearcase. There was no further mention of the Rover free-wheel.

The *Rover Road Racer* could be fitted with upturned bar, or free-wheel and two rim-brakes, without increase in the new charge of £7 10s. The *Special Rover Road Racer* could have a front rim-brake for an extra 5s 6d. No oil-can was supplied free with any model, probably as a result of shortage of steel.

## 1917

Prices rose to £10 10s and £10 15s respectively for the *Rover Roadster* and the *Lady's Rover*. These were single-speed models and no additions or changes were offered. A further probable effect of the war was the withdrawal of both racers.

## 1918-1919

We have not found any catalogues for either of these years. See the *Imperial* range for the *"Cycling"* report on the *Rovers* at the December 1919 Olympia Cycle Show.

## 1920

The *Rover Roadster* had a 22", 24", 26" or 28" frame, a Rover saddle, 7" Rover cranks, 1½" Dunlop Warwick tyres, 28" steel Westwood rims with enamelled centres and plated tracks, front and back lever-operated brakes and a "frictionless" free-wheel. It was finished in black enamel with fine green and red lines, panel lining, with bright parts plated, and was supplied with tools and pump. It cost £16, with a Sturmey-Archer or BSA three-speed £1 18s extra. The *Lady's Rover* was similar except that it had 6½" cranks, a leather gearcase and no 28" model. It cost £16 15s or £2 extra with either three-speed. The 2s difference may have been for handle-bar control, outer cable and its stop, and two extra pulley-wheels for the gear cable.

## 1921

The *Rover Roadster* and the *Lady's Rover* were all-black models but not given that name. The roadster had Rover saddle and tool-bag, Warwick tyres, no gearcase, and steel 28" x 1½" rims. The finish was lined green and red. The lady's version had a similar specification plus a Rover leather gearcase. The respective prices were £16 and £16 15s, with Sturmey-Archer or BSA three-speed gears £2 10s or £2 12s 6d extra respectively.

## 1922

There were no changes.

# ROVER ROAD RACER

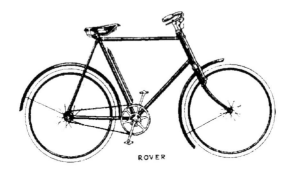

## S P E C I F I C A T I O N

FRAME.—22-in. or 24-in.

WHEELS.—26-in. only, steel rims, enamelled centres, plated tracks.

TYRES.—1½-in. Warwicks.

SADDLE.—"Rover."

TOOL BAG.—"Rover."

CRANKS.—"Rover" pattern 7-in.

CHAIN WHEEL.—Detachable.

BRAKES.—Coaster hub and front rim brake.

FINISH.—Best black enamel, green and red lines, bright parts plated.

TOOLS AND PUMP.

Price, with Wood Rims and Clipper Speed Tyres, £11 5 0.

This Machine may be supplied with dropped bar, or free wheel and two rim brakes if required, without extra charge.

P R I C E
£10 5 0
NET CASH

*Fig. 111*

### 1923

A cheaper new-style catalogue was produced. The *Rover Roadster* cost £9 10s with Sturmey-Archer or BSA three-speed gear £1 5s extra. As an All-Weather (all-black) model it had no plated parts but retained the usual lining. The *Lady's Rover* was similar except that the respective prices were £9 19s 6d and £1 7s. The *Rover Road Racer* (Fig. 111) returned for the last time.

### 1924

The *Rover Roadster* dropped in price to £9, with BSA three-speed gear £1 3s extra. The catalogue illustration shows a chainwheel similar to that fitted in 1923, but it was not advertised as detachable. It had a Coventry chain, brazed brake-lugs "throughout", $6^1/_2$" cranks for 22" frame and 7" for 24" and higher. The *Lady's Rover* had a similar specification apart from $3^1/_2$" divided-rubber pedals, and a leather gearcase with celluloid panels (not shown in the catalogue illustration). It was reduced to £9 5s with BSA three-speed gear £1 5s extra. The *Rover Road Racer* disappeared.

### 1925

The *Rover* models were no longer listed.

# Meteor-Rovers

### 1900

There were seven *Meteor* models, all labelled *Meteor-Rover*. The firm may have hoped that the old name Meteor would have been remembered as a trail-blazer for Starley and Sutton; if so, they were clearly wrong. The *Meteor-Rover Light Roadster* was similar to the 1899 model except that it had 4" rubber pedals, upturned handlebar and Westwood rims; a free-wheel and an extra brake were obtainable at extra cost. The *Lady's Meteor-Rover* had the same differences from the 1899 specification. The *Meteor-Rover Road Racer* (Fig. 112), the *Meteor-Rover No. 2 Light Roadster* (Fig. 113), the *Meteor-Rover No. 2 Road Racer* (Fig. 114), the *Lady's Meteor-Rover No. 2* (Fig 115) and the *Meteor-Rover Cob* (Fig 116) were new models. These No. 2 models were apparently cheaper versions of the *Meteor-Rovers,* probably with identical frames but inferior accessories. This year saw the last appearance in the catalogues of the 30" front wheel.

*1911: Ben Jones. South African Champion. Used the same Rover bicycle for seven years.*

175

# THE METEOR - ROVER.

**ROAD RACER.**

**WEIGHT**, to specification :
25in. frame, 27 lbs.

## SPECIFICATION.

**Saddle**—Middlemore's **M61** ; **7** seat rod ; small hole two inches from bottom marks the point above which it must not be raised.

**Frame**—23½in., 25in., and 27in., measuring from the centre of crank spindle to top of seat lug.

**Gear and Chain**—Detachable chain wheels ; ½in. roller chain ; gear 72in.

**Cranks**—Square, 6¾in. for 23½in. and 25in. frames, 7in. for 27in. and higher.

**Pedals**—3¾in. rat-trap.

**Handle-bar**—As illustrated ; the small hole two inches from bottom marks the point above which it must not be raised.

**Wheels**—28in. for 23½in. frames, 30in. front and 28in. back for 25in. frames and higher ; hollow rims.

**Tyres**—1⅜in. road racing Reflex-Clipper. Westwood hollow rims.

**Forks**—Toughened steel tube, with double crown plate ; taper gauge steering tube.

**Steering**—Special ball bearings top and bottom, improved steering lock.

**Bearings**—All cups, cones, and balls of special diamond cast steel, separately and specially hardened.

**Finish**—Best black enamel, bright parts plated on copper.

**Price** (for Great Britain only) £11 11s. net cash.

For cost of free-wheel and special brake see page 9.

*Fig. 112*

# THE METEOR-ROVER No. 2.

## LIGHT ROADSTER.

WEIGHT, to specification :
23¾in. frame 33 lbs.

### SPECIFICATION.

**Saddle**—"Meteor" light roadster; 7 seat rod; small hole two inches from bottom marks the point above which it must not be raised.

**Frame**—23¾in., 25in., and 27in., measuring from the centre of the crank spindle to top of seat lug.

**Gear and Chain**—Detachable plated chain wheels; ⅜in. block chain; gear ⅚6in.

**Cranks**—Square, 6½in. for 23¾in. and 25in., 7in. for 27in. frames and higher.

**Pedals**—4in. rubber pedals.

**Handle-bar**—Upturned (as illustrated); the small hole two inches from bottom marks point above which it must not be raised.

**Wheels**—28in. for 23¾in. frames, 30in. front and 28in. back for 25in. frames and higher.

**Tyres**—1⅝in. light roadster Clipper on Westwood rims.

**Forks**—Toughened steel tube, with double crown plates; tapered gauge steering tube.

**Brake**—Detachable, with rubber block.

**Guards**—Detachable, best steel strengthened edges.

**Steering**—Special ball bearings top and bottom, and efficient steering lock.

**Bearings**—All cups, cones, and balls of special diamond cast steel, separately and specially hardened.

**Finish**—Best black enamel, bright parts plated.

**Price** (for Great Britain only) £10 10s. net cash.

Extended Purchase ... £12 12s.

For cost of free-wheel and extra brakes see page 9

*Fig. 113*

177

ROAD RACER.

WEIGHT, as per specification: 23½in. frame, 27 lbs.

## SPECIFICATION.

**Saddle**—"Meteor" road racer; 7 seat rod; the small hole two inches from bottom marks the point above which it should not be raised.

**Frame**—23½in., 25in., and 27in., measuring from centre of crank spindle to top of seat lug.

**Chain and Gear**—Detachable plated chain wheels; ½in. block chain.

**Cranks**—Square, 6½in. for 23½in. and 25in. frames, 7in. for 27in. frames.

**Pedals**—⅝in. rat-trap.

**Handle-bar**—Modified drop (as illustrated) the small hole two inches from bottom marks the point above which it must not be raised.

**Wheels**—28in. for 23½in. frame, 30in. front and 28in. back for 25in. frames and higher.

**Tyres**—1½in. road-racing Clipper on Westwood rims

**Forks**—Toughened steel tube with double-crown plates; taper gauge steering tube

**Steering**—Special ball bearings top and bottom, and efficient steering lock.

**Bearings**—All cups, cones, and balls of special diamond cast steel, separately and specially hardened.

**Finish**—Best black enamel, bright parts plated.

**Price** (for Great Britain only) £10 10s net cash.

Extended Purchase ... £12 12s.

For cost of free wheel and extra brakes see page 9.

*Fig. 114*

# THE LADY'S METEOR-ROVER No. 2.

**WEIGHT, as** per specification: frame, 31 lbs.

## SPECIFICATION.

**Saddle**—Lady's "Meteor"; **7** seat rod; the small hole two inches from bottom marks the point above which it must not be raised.

**Frame**—20in., 22in., and 24in., measuring from centre of crank spindle to top of seat lug.

**Gear and Chain**—Block chain, ¼in.; gear 60in.

**Cranks**—Square, 6in. for 20in. and 22in. frames, 6½in. for 24in. frames.

**Pedals**—3¾in. rubber.

**Handle-bar** Upturned (as illustrated); the small hole two inches from bottom marks the point above which it must not be raised.

**Wheels**—28in. or 20in. and 22in. frames, 30in. front and 28in. back for 24in. frames.

**Tyres**—⅜in. Clippers on Westwood rims.

**Forks**—Toughened steel tube, with double crown plates; detachable lamp bracket; taper gauge steering tube.

**Brake**—Detachable, with rubber block.

**Guards**—Best steel; rear guard laced (as illustration) for the protection of the dress.

**Chain Cover**—Leather, with celluloid panel.

**Steering**—Special ball bearings top and bottom, and efficient steering lock.

**Bearings**—All cups, cones, and balls of special diamond cast steel, separately and specially hardened.

**Finish**—Best black enamel, bright parts plated.

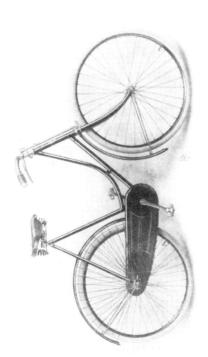

**ℙrice** (for Great Britain only) £10 10s. net cash.
Extended Purchase ... £12 12s.

For cost of free-wheel and special brake see page 9.

*Fig.115*

179

# THE METEOR-ROVER COB.

## Specially designed for mounting and dismounting without step.

**WEIGHT,** to specification :
21½in. frame, 32 lbs.

### SPECIFICATION

**Saddle**—Middlemore's M33; **7** seat rod; the small hole two inches from bottom marks the point above which it must not be raised.

**Frame**—21½in., 23½in., and 25in., measuring from centre of crank spindle to top of seat lug.

**Gear and Chain**—Detachable chain wheels; ⅝in. pitch roller chain; gear 60in.

**Cranks**—" Rover" pattern, square, 6in.

**Pedals**—4in. rubber, thoroughly dustproof.

**Handle-bar**—Upturned (as illustrated). The small hole **two** inches from bottom marks the point above which it must not be raised.

**Wheels**—28in. front and 26in. back.

**Tyres**—1⅝in. Reflex-Clipper. Westwood hollow rims.

**Forks**—Toughened steel tube, with double crown plates ; taper gauge steering tube.

**Brake**—Detachable spoon, with rubber block.

**Guards**—Detachable, best steel, strengthened edges, specially designed for easy removal

**Steering**—Special ball bearings top and bottom, improved " Rover" steering lock.

**Bearings**—All cups, cones, and balls of special diamond cast steel, separately and specially hardened.

**Finish**—Best black enamel, bright parts plated on copper.

**Price** (for Great Britain only) £12 12s. net cash.

For cost of free wheel and extra brakes see page 9.

*Fig.116*

180

# 1901

The *Meteor-Rover Light Roadster* had 22", 24" and 26" frames, with 28" x $1^1/_2$" wheels and Dunlop tyres. It had a new brake (shown in the Fittings section) and for an extra two guineas the buyer got a free-wheel, two rim-brakes and plated rims. The *Lady's Meteor-Rover* had 28" x $1^1/_2$" wheels with Dunlop tyres, the new front brake, and a new chain-cover of leather with double celluloid panels. Again, an extra two guineas obtained a free-wheel, rim-brakes and plated rims. A maroon cord dress-guard was fitted; this was the first time that a colour had been specified. The *Meteor-Rover Cob* had 22", 24" and 26" frames; the top tube had become horizontal. Wheels were 28" front and 26" back, with $1^1/_2$" Dunlop tyres. These three models had a black-enamel finish lined red and straw. The *Meteor-Rover Road Racer* had 28" x $1^3/_8$" rims for all frame-sizes, with Dunlop tyres, and the price had risen to 12 guineas. The *Meteor-Rover No. 2 Light Roadster* frame was 22", 24" or 26", with Clipper, Warwick or Clincher tyres fitted on 28" x $1^1/_2$" rims. Westwood rims were specified, but clearly they would have had to take beaded-edge tyres had Clinchers been fitted. The new brake was standard but an extra two guineas brought the usual changes; Dunlop tyres cost an extra guinea. The *Meteor-Rover No. 2 Road Racer* had 28" x $1^3/_8$" Westwood rims with Clipper, Warwick or Clincher tyres; Dunlops were a guinea extra. The *Lady's Meteor-Rover No. 2* had similar changes except the rim size; in addition it had the new brake and the two-guinea option for extras.

## 1902

A new fork was fitted to all Rovers, with tapered-gauge fork blades and a box crown replacing the former use of liners to strengthen the forks. Probably to avoid confusion, the *Meteor-Rover* range became the *Meteor-Rover No. 1*. Every model in the *No. 1* and *No. 2* ranges was fitted with a free-wheel, two rim-brakes and inverted levers. The *No. 1 Road Racer* had a 77" gear. The *Cob* was discontinued. At additional cost a diagonal stay to the frame could be fitted to frames for tall or heavy riders, and a back-pedalling brake (rim or band) was also obtainable at a price (see Fittings section).

## 1903

The *No. 1 Light Roadster* and *Lady's* models had Brooks B24/1 saddles, the new pull-on brakes used on the *Imperial* models, and cork grips with celluloid tips. The *No. 1 Road Racer* had a Brooks B19 saddle and oval cranks ($6^1/_2$" for 22" and 24", 7" for 26" "and higher" - although only 22", 24" and 26" frames were offered). These three models had clip-on pump-clips and plated pump, and plated rims with black centres. The 20" lady's frame was discontinued and only $6^1/_2$" cranks were offered. All *No. 1* frames were lined in two unspecified colours. The *No. 2 Light Roadster* had a Brooks B24/1 saddle, oval cranks ($6^1/_2$" for 22" and 24" frames, 7" for 26" "and higher", no higher being offered), and 4" rubber pedals. The *No. 2 Lady's* model had a Brooks B24/1L saddle and oval $6^1/_2$" cranks. Both these models had clip-on pump-clips and a plated pump. The *No. 2 Road Racer* had a Brooks B19 saddle and oval cranks (offered on the *No. 2 Light Roadster*).

## 1904

The *No. 1* and *No. 2* models were discontinued; there were only three models on offer: the *Meteor-Rover*, the *Meteor-Rover Roadster* and the *Lady's Meteor-Rover*. All had plated rims with black centres but the lining on frame and rims had gone, and a celluloid pump replaced the plated one. They were all priced at 10 guineas. The *Meteor-Rover Roadster* was one pound lighter than the 1903 light roadsters and had a Brooks B20 saddle and a 70" gear, which seem fairly minor changes - not enough to account for the price reduction. Two-speed or three-speed gears could be fitted to order and either Warwick or Dunlop tyres were available - the extra charge for Dunlops had disappeared. The *Meteor-Rover* was apparently identical with the *Roadster* but it had a 66" gear and there was no offer of a hub-gear; as the price was also 10 guineas it is hard to see why it was catalogued as a separate machine. *The Lady's Meteor-Rover* had a 20", 22", 24" or 26" frame. the 20" size reintroduced after a year's absence. It had 26" rims for 20" frames, 28" for others. Tyres were Dunlop or Warwick first grade $1^{3}/_{8}$".

## 1905

The *Meteor-Rover* disappeared; the four models offered were the *Meteor-Rover Roadster*, the *Meteor-Rover Light Roadster*, the *Ladies' Meteor-Rover* and the *Meteor-Rover Path* or *Road Racer*. The first three were eight guineas each, with a Rover two-speed two guineas extra and a Sturmey-Archer three-speed three guineas. No weights were given. The instructions on how to fit the handlebar and measure the frame were dropped, mudguards were no longer described as having strengthened edges; presumably the public took that for granted after so many years of reassurance. Rover saddles and tyres replaced Brooks and Dunlop, and rims were plated without enamelled centres or linings. The steering-lock was abandoned, but the first three models named were fitted with fork lamp-brackets; they had also lined frames but no colours were specified. The two roadsters and the racer had $3^{3}/_{4}$" rat-trap pedals, the ladies' model had $3^{1}/_{4}$" rubbers; it had also a metal chain-cover, possibly single-sided, lined in an unspecified colour, and was offered in 20", 22" and 26", with no explanation of the absence of 24". The *Meteor-Rover Path* or *Road Racer* is shown in Fig. 117.

*1911. B Busby, Quarter-Mile Southern Champion. Holder Sir Chas. Wakefield 100 Guinea Challenge Cup.*

*1905 Meteor Rover*

# THE METEOR-ROVER PATH OR ROAD RACER.

## SPECIFICATION.

**Saddle**—The "Rover."

**Frame**—22 in., 24 in.

**Gear and Chain**—Standard 84 in. $\frac{1}{2}$ in. pitch roller chain.

**Cranks**—Special "Rover" pattern, 6$\frac{1}{2}$ in.

**Pedals**—3$\frac{3}{4}$ in. rat-trap.

**Handle-bar**—Special pattern, as illustrated.

**Wheels**—26 in. for 22 in. frames, 28 in. for 24 in. frames.

**Tyres**—1$\frac{3}{4}$in. path-racing or road-racing "Rover."

**Finish**—Plain black, all bright parts plated.

**PRICE** (for Great Britain & Ireland only) :

Nett Cash     ...     ...     ...     ...     ...     **£7  15  0**

*For special illustrations of parts see pages 21 to 27 inclusive.*

*Fig.117*

# 1906

This year saw the introduction of a new head-badge; as far as we know it was also the last year in which the Meteors were to appear until their short swan-song in 1924. It seems reasonable to suppose that the decision to abandon the Meteor name was made because its association with low-priced Rover bicycles contrasted unfavourably with its use for a high-quality Rover car. At all events, it vanished for seventeen years. The prices of all models rose to £8 15s; Griffin or Fagan two-speed gears cost two guineas extra and a Sturmey-Archer three-speed three guineas. The *Meteor-Rover Light Roadster* was not offered. The *Meteor-Roadster* had rubber pedals and Clipper-Reflex tyres, and the frame was unlined; but the rims had black centres edged red. The *Meteor-Rover Lady's* (not *Ladies'* as in 1905) was available in 20", 22", 24" and 26" and the metal chain-cover was replaced by a leather version with four celluloid panels. No deviation from the standard pattern was allowed on any of these models. The *Meteor-Rover Road Racer* was fitted with a free-wheel and two rim-brakes operated by inverted levers, a 72" gear and Clipper Reflex tyres (size unspecified but probably $1^3/_8$"). Wheels were 26" for 22" frames and 28" for 24" frames. This machine could be supplied also as a path or road racer, with fixed wheel and no brakes or mudguards, for £7 15.

## 1924

As already noted, the *Model "A"s* became the *Meteors*. The *Meteor Rover Roadster* offered $6^1/_2$" cranks on a 22" frame, 7" on 24" and higher. The chainwheel had a different pattern (as shown in Fig. 111) and brazed pegs replaced pump-clips. The price dropped to £7 10s with BSA three-speed £1 3s extra. The *Lady's Meteor Roadster* is not shown as having either clips or pegs for the pump, but as one was supplied that was probably a catalogue error. The gearcase was leather with celluloid panels; but again that is not shown in the catalogue illustration. The price was £7 15s with BSA three-speed £1 5s extra. The higher price of the BSA gear was no doubt to cover the extra cost of two additional cable-pulleys, the longer cable to the handlebar control and the outer-cable and frame stop. The *Meteor Rover Light Roadster* had 22", 24" and 26" frames, 26" x $1^3/_8$" Cambridge tyres, 7" cranks, North Road upturned handlebar and 4" rat-trap pedals. The price was £7 10s with BSA three-speed £1 2s extra. The *Meteor Rover Road Racer* (Fig. 118) was a much "sportier" affair than the *Model A* version it replaced.

## 1925

The only change in this range was to the *Meteor Rover Road Racer*, which had a Continental handlebar with a deep drop instead of the shallower Shirley.

# Meteor
# Rover Road Racer

CLUBMEN, and all who desire a speedy machine for fast road work, will find the Meteor Rover Road Racer an attractive proposition. Its specification is the result of the years of experience which we have had in the production of machines of this type, and this model undoubtedly deserves great popularity.

## Specification

| | | |
|---|---|---|
| Frame | .. .. | 22 in. or 24 in. |
| Wheels | .. .. | 26 in. steel rims, enamelled centres, plated tracks. |
| Tyres | .. .. | 1⅝ in. Clipper Speed. |
| Saddle | .. .. | Rover. |
| Tool Bag | .. .. | Rover. |
| Cranks | .. .. | 7 in. |
| Chain | .. .. | Coventry. |
| Brake | .. .. | Short pull up front only. |
| Gear | .. .. | Fixed gear 75. |
| Handlebar | .. .. | Dropped, Shirley pattern. |
| Pedals | .. .. | 4 in. Rat-trap. |
| Finish | .. .. | Finest quality black enamel, lined bronze, bright parts heavily plated. |

TOOLS AND PUMP

## Price  -  -  £7  10  0

*Fig.118*

This illustration of the *New Zealand Rover Roadster* seems to have been taken from a 1925 catalogue which we have not seen. It is endorsed in ink "All sent direct 19-3-26". It resembles the *Meteor Light Roadster* with its sloping top tube. The 28" x 1½" wheels and coaster brake were presumably to meet overseas demand.

# THE ROVER COY. LTD., COVENTRY
### ENGLAND

*Specially designed model for the New Zealand market*

THE "NEW ZEALAND" ROVER ROADSTER

### SPECIFICATION :

FRAME—22in., 24in. or 26in. Sloping Top Tube (Parallel if required).
TYRES—28in. × 1⅛in. Dunlop.
BRAKE—Eadie Coaster Hub.
SADDLE—Rover Three-coil Spring.
TOOLBAG—Rover.
CHAINWHEEL—Detachable.

HANDLEBAR—Reversible.
PEDALS—Rubber.
CHAIN—Renold.
FINISH — Best Black Enamel over coslett. Lined Bronze. Bright parts plated.
TRANSFERS — Rover and special New Zealand.

## Price :   £    :    :

This Bicycle can be finished ALL BLACK and lined without extra charge.
Front rim brake can be fitted as an extra.

*Resident Representatives :*

# SEDGLEY LTD., 94 Gloucester Street, CHRISTCHURCH, N.Z.

TELE PHONE 5393 GRAMS TRADEOVRSE                    (P.O. BOX 495)

*Fig.119*

# Royal Rovers

## 1904

This range was introduced in 1904, probably to bridge the gap between the prices of the Imperials and the Rovers, and lasted until the extinction of the marque. The *Royal Rover Roadster* (Fig 119), the *Royal Rover Light Roadster* (Fig. 120) and the *Lady's Royal Rover* (Fig. 121) are shown here.

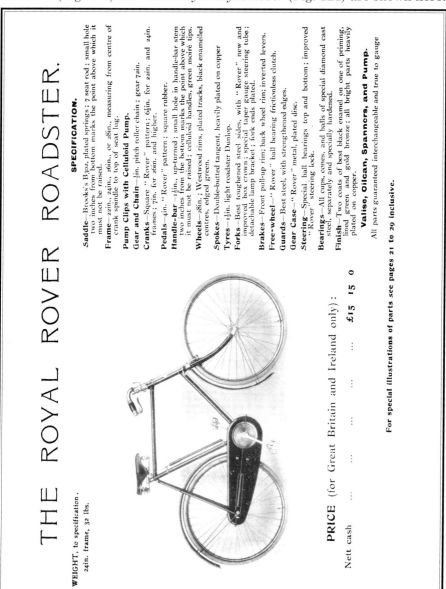

## THE ROYAL ROVER ROADSTER.

WEIGHT, to specification.
24in. frame, 32 lbs.

### SPECIFICATION.

**Saddle**—Brooks's B92z, plated springs ; 7 seat rod ; small hole two inches from bottom marks the point above which it must not be raised.

**Frame**—22in., 24in., 26in., or 28in., measuring from centre of crank spindle to top of seat lug.

**Pump Clips with Celluloid Pump.**

**Gear and Chain**—⅝in. pitch roller chain ; gear 72in.

**Cranks**—Square " Rover " pattern; 6½in. for 22in. and 24in. frames; 7in. for 26in. and higher.

**Pedals**—4in. " Rover " pattern ; square rubber.

**Handle-bar**—1¾in., up-turned ; small hole in handle-bar stem two inches from the bottom marks the point above which it must not be raised ; celluloid handles, green moiré tips.

**Wheels**—28in. ; Westwood rims, plated tracks, black enamelled centres, edged green.

**Spokes**—Double-butted tangent, heavily plated on copper

**Tyres**—1¾in. light roadster Dunlop.

**Forks**—Best toughened steel sides, with " Rover " new and improved box crown ; special taper gauge steering tube ; detachable lamp bracket ; fork ends plated.

**Brakes**—Front pull-up rim; back wheel rim; inverted levers.

**Free-wheel**—" Rover " ball bearing frictionless clutch.

**Guards**—Best steel, with strengthened edges.

**Gear Case**—" Rover " metal, plated disc.

**Steering**—Special ball bearings top and bottom ; improved " Rover " steering lock.

**Bearings**—All cups, cones, and balls of special diamond cast steel, separately and specially hardened.

**Finish**—Two coats of best black enamel on one of priming, lined green and gold bronze ; all bright parts heavily plated on copper.

**Valise, Oilcan, Spanners, and Pump.**

All parts guaranteed interchangeable and true to gauge

For special illustrations of parts see pages 21 to 29 inclusive.

**PRICE** (for Great Britain and Ireland only) :

Nett cash ... ... ... **£15 15 0**

*Fig.119*

# THE ROYAL ROVER LIGHT ROADSTER.

**WEIGHT**, to specification:
24in. frame (without pump, valise and contents), 26 lbs.

## SPECIFICATION.

**Saddle**—Brooks's B11, plated springs; 7 seat rod; small hole two inches from bottom marks the point above which the seat rod must not be raised.

**Frame**—22in., 24in., 26in., and 28in., measuring from centre of crank spindle to top of seat lug.

**Gear and Chain**—"Rover" detachable chain wheels; ⅛in. pitch roller chain; gear 72in.

**Cranks**—"Rover" pattern, square; 6½in. for 22in. and 24in. frames; 7in. for 26in. and higher.

**Pedals**—3¾in. "Rover" rat-trap; thoroughly dust-proof.

**Handle-bar**—As illustrated; small hole two inches from bottom marks the point above which it must not be raised, cork handles.

**Wheels**—28in.; Westwood rims, plated tracks, black enamelled centres, edged green.

**Spokes**—Double-butted tangent, heavily plated on copper.

**Tyres**—1⅜in. road-racing Dunlop.

**Forks**—Best toughened steel sides, with "Rover" new and improved box crown; special taper gauge steering tube; detachable lamp bracket; fork ends plated.

**Brakes**—Front pull-up tire, back wheel tire, inverted lever; "Rover" ball bearing frictionless clutch.

**e-wheel**—"Rover" ball bearing frictionless clutch.

**ards**—Best celluloid, specially designed for easy removal.

**ering**—Special ball bearings top and bottom; improved "Rover" steering lock.

**irings**—All cups, cones, and balls of special diamond cast steel, separately and specially hardened.

**Finish**—Two coats of best black enamel on one of priming, lined green and gold bronze; all bright parts heavily plated on copper.

### Valise, Oilcan, Spanners, and Pump.

All parts guaranteed interchangeable and true to gauge.

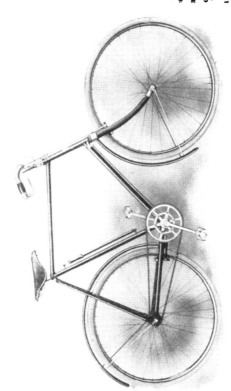

**PRICE** (for Great Britain and Ireland only) :

Nett cash ... ... ... ... **£15 15 0**

For special illustrations of parts see pages 21 to 29 inclusive.

*Fig. 120*

# THE LADY'S ROYAL ROVER.

**WEIGHT**, to specification : 22in. frame, 32 lbs.

## SPECIFICATION.

**Saddle**—Brooks's B302L, plated springs ; 7 seat rod ; small hole two inches from bottom marks point above which it must not be raised.

**Frame**—20-in., 22in., 24in., or 26in., measuring from centre ot crank spindle to top of seat lug.

### Pump Clips with Celluloid Pump.

**Gear and Chain**—⅜in. pitch roller chain ; gear 60in.

**Cranks**—"Rover" pattern, square, 6½in.

**Pedals**—New and improved "Rover" pattern rubber.

**Handle-bar**—"Rover" upturned ; small hole two inches from bottom marks the point above which it must not be raised ; celluloid handles, green moiré tips.

**Wheels**—26in. tor 20in. frames, others 28in., Westwood rims, plated tracks, black enamelled centres, edged green.

**Spokes**—Tangent, double-butted ; heavily plated on copper.

**Tyres**—1⅜in. Dunlop.

**Forks**—Best toughened steel sides, with "Rover" new and improved box crown ; detachable lamp bracket ; fork ends plated.

**Brakes**—Front pull-up rim ; back wheel rim ; inverted levers.

**Free-wheel**—"Rover" ball bearing frictionless clutch.

**Guards**—Best steel, with strengthened edges ; rear guard laced for the protection of the dress.

**Gear Case**—"Rover" metal, with plated disc.

**Steering**—Special ball bearings top and bottom ; improved 'Rover' steering lock.

**Bearings**—All cups, cones, and balls of special diamond cast steel, separately and specially hardened.

**Finish**—Two coats of best black enamel on one of priming, lined green and gold bronze ; bright parts plated on copper.

### Valise, Oilcan, Spanners, and Pump.

All parts guaranteed interchangeable and true to gauge.

**PRICE** (for Great Britain and Ireland only) :

Nett cash ... ... ... **£15 15 0**

For special illustrations of parts see pages 21 to 29 inclusive.

*Fig. 121*

# 1905

Prices of all models dropped to £12 12s. A Rover two-speed was £2 2s extra, a Sturmey-Archer three-speed £3 3s extra. Instructions on how to measure the frame and how to fit saddle and handlebar safely disappeared. No weights were given. The cranks were no longer said to have rounded edges. The *Royal Rover Roadster* had a Brooks B75 saddle, the *Royal Rover Light Roadster* a Brooks B11 and the *Ladies' Royal Rover* a Brooks B75; all had enamelled springs. (Note another minor change - from *Lady's* to *Ladies'*.)

# 1906

Instead of the Rover gear, a Fagan or Griffin two-speed could be supplied at the same price, except on the lady's model. The *Royal Rover Roadster* had a Brooks B302 saddle, the *Royal Rover Light Roadster* a Brooks B13 and the *Royal Rover Lady's* (yet another change) a Brooks B302L; all had plated springs. The Rover oilbath gearcase could be fitted, at an unspecified extra cost, on the *Royal Rover Roadster* and the lady's model. Tyres for the *Royal Rover Roadster*, the *Royal Rover Light Roadster* and the *Royal Rover Lady's* were respectively $1^1/_2$" roadster Dunlops, $1^1/_2$" light Dunlops and $1^1/_2$" Dunlops.

# 1907

Prices dropped to £10 10s, or £12 with a Hub or Griffin two-speed or £12 12s with a Sturmey-Archer three-speed. Roller-lever brakes were fitted. The linings on the rims changed from green to gold bronze. The *Royal Rover Lady's* and the *Royal Rover Roadster* lost the plated disc on the gearcase, and the gear of the latter machine went down to 70".

# 1908

The choice of two-speed gear was extended to "other standard" version, and the Armstrong-Triplex was offered as an alternative to the Sturmey-Archer three-speed. Bluemel's celluloid grips were fitted, as was a Bluemel's pump. The lady's handlebar was $2^1/_2$" upturned instead of $1^1/_2$", and $1^3/_8$" Dunlops were fitted to that model and the *Light Roadster*. The latter had a Brooks B18 saddle.

# 1909

Two-speed gears were no longer offered, and only the Armstrong-Triplex three-speed was available, at £1 15s extra instead of the previous £2 2s. The *Royal Rover Road Racer* (Fig. 122) was introduced. On the other three models the rims were lined to match the frames. The offer of the oil-bath case was withdrawn. The celluloid grips and the pump were not specified as Bluemel's. The *Light Roadster* had Rover rat-traps and its gear went down to 70".

# Royal Rover Road Racer.

## SPECIFICATION.

**SADDLE.**—Brooks' B 18, plated springs.

**FRAME.**—22in., 24in., or 26in.

**CHAIN AND GEAR.**—½in. pitch roller ; gear 84in.

**CRANKS.**—"Rover" pattern ; 6½in. for 22in. and 24in., 7in. for 26in. frames and higher.

**PEDALS.**—3¾in., rat-trap.

**HANDLE-BAR.**—Road racing.

**WHEELS.**—26in. for 22in., 28in. for 24in. frames and higher, black enamelled centres, plated tracks.

**SPOKES.**—Double butted, heavily plated.

**TYRES.**—1⅝in. road racing. Dunlops.

**FORKS.**—Box crown, tapered sides, 3½in. curve ; lamp-bracket ; fork-ends plated.

**BRAKES.**—Front and back rim, inverted levers.

**FREE-WHEEL.** — "Rover" ball-bearing frictionless.

**GUARDS.**—Best steel, with strengthened edges.

**STEERING.**—Special ball bearings top and bottom.

**BEARINGS.**—All cups, cones, and balls of special steel, separately and specially hardened.

**FINISH.**—Best black enamel, bright parts plated.

### Valise, oilcan, spanners, and pump.

ALL PARTS GUARANTEED INTERCHANGEABLE AND TRUE TO GAUGE.

## PRICE.

(FOR GREAT BRITAIN AND IRELAND ONLY.)

| | |
|---|---|
| NETT CASH .. .. .. .. .. .. .. .. | £10 10 0 |
| With Armstrong-Triplex Three-speed Gear .. .. .. | £12 5 0 |

*Fig. 122*

# 1910

The *Racer* and the *Light Roadster* were not listed. The *Royal Rover Roadster* had a Brooks B75 saddle with plated springs, a Rover chain, 7" cranks for 24" and higher frames, $1^1/_2$" Rover A or Dunlop tyres, "celluloid handles" on the brakes (presumably on the brake-levers), and unplated fork-ends. There was no mention of the finish to the spokes. The price of both models was £8 15s with either two rim-brakes or a coaster hub and front brakes; an Armstrong-Triplex three-speed gear was £1 10s extra, and on the gent's model it had the central control in the top tube. The 20" frame was dropped from the lady's specification and only 28" wheels were offered. There was a note in the catalogue that the bicycles were made at the Meteor Works in Coventry and that anyone interested could visit to watch them being made.

# 1911

There were many minor changes in the 1911 *Royals*, as can be seen in the illustrations (Figs. 123 and 124); the increase in prices will also be noted. The new roller-lever system was much neater than the previous one. It is interesting that although the gent's model had the extension to the front mudguard it was apparently not thought necessary to afford the ladies similar protection. Perhaps they were not expected to ride in the rain.

# 1912

The cost of fitting an Armstrong-Triplex three-speed, or three-speed coaster and front rim brake, dropped from £1 7s 6d to £1 2s 6d. Both models had $^5/_{16}$" balls in the back hub, and the lady's model had a 63" gear. The frame-lining was green and bronze, there was no mention of the fine green lines; the rim linings matched. The make of chain was not given. A Sturmey-Archer three-speed or Tricoaster hub could be fitted if required; the price was not stated.

# 1913

Prices fell. The *Royal Rover Roadster* cost £8 10s with two rim-brakes or coaster hub and front brake, £9 10s with Armstrong-Triplex three-speed gear, and £9 17s 6d with three-speed coaster hub and front brake; the Sturmey-Archer three-speed could be fitted if required at an unlisted price but there was no mention of the S-A Tricoaster. A Brooks saddle with plated springs replaced the B95, and a Brooks 3594/1 toolbag was fitted. There was a closed Rover gearcase, and there was no mention of $^5/_{16}$" balls. Changes in the lady's model were similar (with a B75L saddle).

ESTABLISHED 1898.

Being the OFFICIAL ORGAN of the
SOUTHERN COUNTIES CYCLING UNION.

EDITED BY J. H. STAPLEY.

Vol. XIV. No. 159.          AUGUST 1st, 1911.          Subscription 1/- per annum.

# CATFORD HILL CLIMB.

## THE "ROVER" AGAIN SUCCESSFUL.

# Royal Rover Roadster.

## Specification.

**Frame**—22 in., 24 in., 26 in., or 28 in.

**Forks**—Box crown, tapered sides, 3½ in. curve ; lamp-bracket.

**Handle-bar**—1½ in. upturned, celluloid handles

**Saddle**—Brooks' B 95, plated springs.

**Tool-bag**—Brooks' No. 9060/1, with cleaning cloth.

**Chain & Gear**—½ in. pitch roller ; gear 70 in.

**Cranks**—"Rover" pattern ; 6½ in. for 22 in., 7 in. for 24 in. frames and higher.

**Pedals**—4 in. "Rover" pattern, rubber.

**Wheels**—28 in., black enamelled centres, lined to match frame, plated tracks.

**Tyres**—1½ in. Dunlops.

**Guards**—Best steel, with strengthened edges. Extension to front guard.

**Brakes**—Front and back rim, outside levers, with celluloid handles.

**Gear Case**—"Rover" metal, open front.

**Free-wheel**—"Rover" ball-bearing frictionless

**Steering**—Special ball-bearings top and bottom, "Rover" steering lock.

**Bearings**—All cups, cones, and balls of special steel.

**Finish**—Best black enamel, two fine green lines, with inner line of bronze, all bright parts plated

**Oilcan, spanners and pump.**

*All parts guaranteed interchangeable and true to gauge.*

## PRICE

(For Great Britain and Ireland only).

| | | |
|---|---|---|
| Nett Cash ... ... ... ... ... ... ... | **£10 10 0** | |
| Fitted with Coaster Hub and Front Brake only ... ... ... | **£10 10 0** | |
| Armstrong-Triplex Three-speed Gear, with Special Central Control in top tube ... ... ... ... ... ... | **£11 17 6** | |

Sturmey-Archer 3-Speed Hub can be fitted if required.

**All parts of these bicycles are made at the Meteor Works, Coventry, and anyone interested is invited to inspect the various processes through which they pass.**

*Fig. 123*

# Lady's Royal Rover.

## Specification.

**Frame**—22 in., 24 in., or 26 in.

**Forks**—Box crown, tapered sides, 3½ in curve ; lamp-bracket.

**Handle-bar**—2½ in. upturned, celluloid handles.

**Saddle**—Brooks' B 302L, plated springs.

**Tool-bag**—Brooks' No. 9060/1, with ticket holder and cleaning cloth.

**Chain & Gear**—½ in. pitch roller ; gear 60 in.

**Cranks**—"Rover" pattern, 6½ in.

**Pedals**—3¼ in., "Rover" pattern, rubber.

**Wheels**—28 in., black enamelled centres, lined to match frame, plated tracks.

**Tyres**—1½ in. Dunlops.

**Guards**—Best steel, with strengthened edges ; rear guard laced for the protection of the dress.

**Brakes**—Front and back rim, outside levers, with celluloid handles.

**Gear Case**—"Rover" metal, open front.

**Free-wheel**—"Rover," ball-bearing frictionless

**Steering**—Special ball-bearings top and bottom "Rover" steering-lock.

**Bearings**—All cups, cones, and balls of special steel.

**Finish**—Best black enamel, two fine green lines, with inner line of bronze, bright parts plated.

**Oilcan, spanners and pump.**

*All parts guaranteed interchangeable and true to gauge.*

## PRICE

(For Great Britain and Ireland only).

| | |
|---|---|
| Nett Cash ... ... ... ... ... | **£10 10 0** |
| Fitted with Coaster Hub and Front Brake only ... ... ... | **£10 10 0** |
| With Armstrong-Triplex Three-speed Gear ... ... ... | **£11 17 6** |

Sturmey-Archer 3-Speed Hub can be fitted if required.

All parts of these bicycles are made at the Meteor Works, Coventry, and anyone interested is invited to inspect the various processes through which they pass.

*Fig. 124*

196

## 1914

Prices were unchanged, but the Sturmey-Archer three-speed was offered as an alternative to the Armstrong-Triplex; tricoaster hubs were not available. Both models had a Brampton chain and the roadster had only 7" cranks.

## 1915

A new-pattern fork-crown with domed top was introduced. The front mudguard was at last extended on the lady's machine, the price of which rose for £8 15s or £9 15s with a Sturmey-Archer three-speed gear (the only one listed for either version). The brake-levers introduced in 1911 were replaced by the more conventional pattern. The Rover shield disappeared from the gearcase, and there were no details of gear-sizes or the chain-maker.

## 1916

Prices rose by £2, making £10 10s for the roadster and £10 15s for the lady's. The only changes were the replacement of the Brooks 3594/1 toolbag by their 2557 version and the absence of any offer of a three-speed gear as an extra.

## 1917

Prices rose again by £2, making £12 10s for the roadster and £12 15s for the lady's. The coaster hub was no longer offered as an alternative to two rim-brakes.

## 1918 and 1919

Unfortunately the authors have not been able to find catalogues for these years. See Olympia Show Report in *Imperial* range.

## 1920

Prices had risen steeply, to £18 15s for the roadster and £19 for the lady's. A Sturmey-Archer or BSA three-speed gear cost £1 18s extra on the roadster and £2 on the lady's.

## 1921 and 1922

There were no changes apparent from the catalogues. See Olympia Show Report in *Imperial* range.

## 1923

A new-style catalogue was introduced. Prices were down: £12 12s for the *Royal Rover Roadster* plus £1 5s for Sturmey-Archer or BSA three-speed; £12 12s for the *Lady's Royal Rover* plus £1 7s for either of those three-speeds. Either bicycle could be supplied as an all-weather model with no plated parts but lined as standard. A detachable chainwheel was fitted. Saddle and toolbag were "best quality Rover".

## 1924

The prices of these models dropped considerably. The *Royal Rover Roadster* was two guineas cheaper at £10 10s with BSA three-speed £1 3s extra instead of £1 5s. It had a Brooks B75 saddle with enamelled springs, $6^1/_2$" cranks on 22" frame and 7" on 24" and higher, a Hans Renold chain, brazed brake-lugs "throughout" and 4" rubber pedals and a Rover tool-bag. The *Lady's Royal Rover* had a similar specification except for $3^1/_2$" divided -rubber pedals and only $6^1/_2$" cranks; the BSA three-speed gear cost £1 5s extra.

## 1925

There were no changes in this range.

# The Six Guinea Rovers

## 1908

The *Meteor-Rover* range, comprising a *Roadster*, a *Lady's* and a *Road or Path Racer*, was discontinued after 1906. Those machines were the company's cheapest models at £8 15s, compared with £10 10s, £12 12s or £16 16s for *Rovers*, *Royals* or *Imperials* respectively. In 1907 the prices of all models were reduced by £2 2s, and in 1908 the *Six Guinea Rover Lady's*, the *Six Guinea Roadster* and the *Six Guinea Rover Road Racer* were introduced. The specifications were almost identical with those of the 1906 *Meteor-Rovers*, but the inverted-levers were replaced by roller-levers and there was blue lining to the frames of the *Roadster* and the *Lady's*; the *Road Racer* had only a coaster hub for braking and had no frame-lining. This range appeared only in the 1908 catalogue.

*Half way through the sensational 100 Kilometres Race at the Olympic Games of 1908, won by C H Bartlett on a Rover. From The Racing Supplement to the Rover List.*

# Juveniles

## 1908

The *Rover Juvenile (Boy's)* (Fig. 125) and *Rover Juvenile (Girl's)* (Fig. 126) were introduced this year. They were apparently smaller versions of the adult models, although the lower prices suggest slightly inferior materials. Specifications were unalterable.

## The Rover Juvenile (Boy's).

### SPECIFICATION.

SADDLE.—The " Rover," enamelled springs.

FRAME.—18in. or 20in.

CHAIN AND GEAR.—⅜in. pitch roller chain ; gear 60in.

CRANKS.—" Rover " pattern.

PEDALS.—Square, rubber.

HANDLE-BAR.—1¼in. upturned.

WHEELS.—24in. for 18in. frame ; 26in. for 20in. frame.

TYRES.—Pneumatic.

FORKS.—Box crown, tapered sides ; detachable lamp-bracket.

BRAKES.—Front and back rim, outside levers

FREE-WHEEL.—Ball-bearing frictionless.

GUARDS.—Detachable steel, strengthened edges.

STEERING.—Special ball bearings top and bottom.

BEARINGS.—All cups, cones, and balls of special steel, separately and specially hardened.

FINISH.—Best black enamel, bright parts plated on copper.

Valise, oilcan, spanners, and Bluemel's pump.

*All parts guaranteed interchangeable and true to gauge.*

### PRICE.

(FOR GREAT BRITAIN AND IRELAND ONLY.)

Nett Cash    ..        ..        ..        ..        ..        ..        ..        ..        **£5  0  0**

NO DEVIATION FROM STANDARD PATTERN.

*Fig. 125*

# The Rover Juvenile (Girl's).

## SPECIFICATION.

SADDLE. - The " Rover," enamelled springs.

FRAME.—15in. or 20in.

CHAIN AND GEAR.—⅛in. pitch roller chain ; gear 56in.

CRANKS.—" Rover " pattern.

PEDALS.—Square, rubber.

HANDLE-BAR.—1¼in. upturned.

WHEELS.—24in. for 18in. frame, 20in. for 20in. frame.

TYRES.—Pneumatic.

FORKS.—Box crown, tapered sides, detachable lamp-bracket.

BRAKES. — Front and back rim, outside levers.

FREE-WHEEL.—Ball-bearing frictionless.

GUARDS.—Steel mudguards.

STEERING.—Special ball bearings top and bottom.

BEARINGS.—All cups, cones, and balls of special steel, separately and specially hardened.

FINISH.—Best black enamel, bright parts plated on copper.

Valise, oilcan, spanners, and pump.

*All parts guaranteed interchangeable and true to gauge.*

## PRICE

(FOR GREAT BRITAIN AND IRELAND ONLY.)

Nett Cash   ..   ..   ..   ..   ..   ..   ..   **£5 5 0**

NO DEVIATION FROM STANDARD PATTERN.

*Fig. 126*

## 1909

There was yet another of the company's name-changes. The 1908 boy's model became the *Youth's Rover*, the girl's model the *Girl's Rover*; both cost £5 5s. Dunlop tyres were specified and the lamp bracket was no longer listed as detachable – although it was not shown in either the 1908 or the 1909 illustrations it might have been either detachable or fixed. The *Girl's Rover* had a steel gearcase with two panels, probably of celluloid, and dress-guards were fitted. Tyre-size was still not given.

## 1910

Prices rose to £5 10s. Rover $1^{3}/_{8}$" tyres replaced Dunlops and were guaranteed for 12 months from the purchase date; a Rover chain was fitted; celluloid grips replaced cork according to the illustrations, although this was not mentioned in the specifications; the rims had enamelled centres and plated tracks; the *Youth's Rover* was shown with a Rover-pattern chainwheel.

## 1911

Prices rose: the *Youth's Rover* cost £6 10s, the *Girl's Rover* £6 15s. The youth's saddle was a Brooks R25, the girl's a Brooks B94; both had plated springs. Dunlop tyres were back, a Brooks 9617 tool-bag was fitted and the frame was lined in red. The new-pattern brake-levers (illustrated in the Fittings section) were shown in the catalogue illustrations but were not mentioned in the specifications. The girl's model had a steel gearcase without panels but with a Rover shield trade-mark (probably a transfer) in the centre.

## 1912

The only changes were in the forks (oval-to-round "sides" – presumably "section" was meant) and the tyres (Clipper replacing Dunlop). The make of chain was not given but it may have been a Rover.

## 1913

Prices fell to £5 5s for the youth's and £5 10s for the girl's model. Cambridge tyres replaced Clippers, and the girl's gearcase was leather with celluloid panels.

## 1914

The designer of the catalogues for 1914 to 1917 apparently decided that the prospective purchasers needed a little more information: the word "Bicycle" was added to the names. Rover saddles with plated springs and Rover toolbags replaced the Brooks equipment; Brampton chains were specified. The girl's dress-guard was fitted only between gearcase and seatstay, not to the end of the mudguard as it had been.

# 1915

There were no changes apparent from the catalogue.

# 1916

Prices rose to £5 15s for the youth's and £6 for girl's models. The leather gearcase had no celluloid panels, and no oil-can was provided.

# 1917

Prices rose again to £8 10s and £8 15s. By that time the Great War was well into its third year, and shortages of labour and materials were doubtless taking their toll.

# 1918 and 1919

Unfortunately the authors have not been able to find any catalogues for these years.

# 1920

Prices had risen steeply again, to £13 and £13 10s for the youth's and girl's models respectively. The illustrations show extensions to the front mudguards. These are not mentioned in the specifications but that may be because they had been introduced in 1918 or 1919. The girl's model had a full dress-guard as on the 1913 and earlier models and its upper down-tube had a more pronounced curve, the tube meeting the seat-tube an inch or so higher than previously.

# 1921 and 1922

There were no changes apparent from the catalogues. See the Olympia Show Report in *Cycling* in the Imperial range section.

# 1923

A new-style catalogue was introduced. Prices were down to £7 10s and £7 19s 6d for the youth's and girl's models respectively. No changes in specifications were listed but the illustrations suggest cheaper brakework, clip-on rather than brazed-on pump-pegs, and longer brake-levers.

# 1924

The *Youth's Rover* changed its name to the *Boy's Rover* and its price dropped to £6 10s. The *Girl's Rover* was £6 17 6d.

# 1925

Apart from slightly different handlebars there were no apparent changes.

*A Girl's Rover reconstructed from remnants found in a Birmingham outhouse.*

# R.I.C. Rover

## 1909

This model was available until 1916; its purpose is explained in the 1909 catalogue (Fig. 127). It was not in the 1917 catalogue; no catalogues have been found for 1918 or 1919; it was not mentioned in the *Cycling* report of the 1919 show. It was not listed in 1920.

## R.I.C. Rover.

*(Specially constructed for the Royal Irish Constabulary.)*

(AS SUPPLIED TO H.M. GOVERNMENT.)

THE enormous popularity of "ROVER" Cycles amongst members of the Royal Irish Constabulary has induced us to design a bicycle adequately suited for use on all sorts and conditions of roads, and specially built for heavy riders. The machine is not heavy, but all fitments are specially strengthened.

### SPECIFICATION.

**SADDLE.**—B 90/3.

**FRAME.**—24in., 26in., or 28in.

**CHAIN AND GEAR.**—⅛in. pitch roller, gear 70in.

**CRANKS.**—"Rover" pattern. 6½in. for 24in., 7in. for 26in. frames and higher.

**PEDALS.**—4½in. square rubber.

**HANDLE-BAR.**—1½in. upturned, celluloid handles.

**WHEELS.**—28in., black enamelled centres lined to match frame, plated tracks.

**TYRES.**—1¾in. roadster. Dunlops.

**FORKS.**—Box crown, tapered sides, 3½in. curve; lamp-bracket.

**BRAKES.**—Front and back rim, outside levers.

**FREE-WHEEL.**—Ball-bearing frictionless.

**GUARDS.**—Steel, with strengthened edges.

**STEERING.**—Special ball bearings top and bottom, "Rover" steering-lock.

**BEARINGS.**—All cups, cones, and balls of special steel, separately and specially hardened.

**FINISH.**—Best black enamel, lined green, bright parts plated.

Valise, oilcan, spanners, and pump.

ALL PARTS GUARANTEED INTERCHANGEABLE AND TRUE TO GAUGE.

### PRICE

(FOR GREAT BRITAIN AND IRELAND ONLY.)

| | | | | | | | |
|---|---|---|---|---|---|---|---|
| NETT CASH | .. | .. | .. | .. | .. | .. | £8 8 0 |
| With Armstrong-Triplex Three-speed Gear | | | .. | .. | | | £10 3 0 |

NO DEVIATION FROM STANDARD PATTERN.

*Fig. 127*

## 1910

The standard model went up to £8 15s, at which price a coaster hub and front brake were offered as an alternative. The Armstrong-Triplex three-speed gear cost 30s extra. A Brooks B95 with enamelled springs, a Rover chain and a forward extension to the front mudguard were fitted; this last was not mentioned in the specification but it was illustrated in the catalogue. Rover A tyres were available instead of Dunlops, and the offer of 6½" cranks was withdrawn. Bronze was added to the green lining.

## 1911

The price rose to £10 10s with either two rim brakes or coaster hub and front brake. The Armstrong-Triplex cost £1 7s 6d extra, and a Sturmey-Archer three-speed could be supplied at an unspecified price. The saddle was a Brooks B130 with enamelled springs. The tool-bag was a Brooks 8024. Only Dunlop tyres were fitted, and the lining was two green lines with a bronze centre line. The mudguard extension appeared in the text.

## 1912

A diagonal stay (Fig. 128) was fitted to 26" and 28" frames. The price dropped to £9 10s for the single-speed model with either two rim-brakes or a coaster hub and front brake, and to £10 12s 6d with the Armstrong-Triplex three-speed with the special top-tube control which had been available since 1909. A Sturmey-Archer three-speed or Tricoaster hub could be fitted if required. The saddle was a Brooks B90/3 with enamelled spring. The make of chain was unspecified. The Rover back hub had $5/16$" balls and the forks had "oval to round sides"; presumably "sides" really meant "section".

*Fig. 128*

## 1913

The diagonal stay was neither illustrated nor offered. Instead the 26" and 28" frames were made of specially strong material. There was another price reduction, and the standard model cost £8 15s with the usual option; with Armstrong-Triplex it was £9 15s, and with a three-speed coaster hub and front brake it was £10 2s 6d. An all-black finish, lined green and bronze, was offered at no extra charge. There was no mention of "two fine green lines with inner line of bronze" as in 1911 and 1912.

## 1914

Prices were unchanged, and so was the specification apart from the Brampton chain. A Sturmey-Archer was offered as an alternative to the Armstrong-Triplex.

## 1915

The only changes were the provision of Dunlop Magnum tyres and the dropping of the offer of coaster hub and front brake and the Armstrong-Triplex gear. It was mentioned that the G.P.O. used the *R.I.C. Rover* this year.

## 1916

The option of two rim-brakes or coaster hub and front brake was restored, but no three-speed was listed. The price was £10 10s, and there was a note that the bicycle was as supplied to the government.

## 1921

It reappeared with the price increased to £9 5s for the ungeared version. Except for the brake-levers the illustration was identical with that of the 1909 version (Fig. 127). The BSA hub-gear was listed after the Sturmey-Archer, each costing £2 10s.

# The Popular Range

## 1909

Price increases meant that the 1908 cheap Six Guinea models had to be renamed. The *Popular Rover Roadster* at £6 10s (£8 5s with Armstrong-Triplex three-speed gear) offered 7" cranks for 26" and "higher" frames (28" being the only higher one offered), Dunlop tyres, unnamed celluloid handlebar-grips and red instead of blue frame-lining. The make of pump was not specified. The *Lady's Popular Rover* at the same price had similar changes; in addition, 26" x 1³/₈" Dunlops were fitted. The *Special Popular Road Racer* at £7 7s had dropped the 28" frame and was unlined. Rims were laminated wood, aluminium lined, 26" for 22" frame, 28" for 24" and 26". Tyres were 1¹/₄" Clipper Speed. Although there was no mention of them in the specification, mudguards were shown on the illustration in the catalogue.

ESTABLISHED 1898.

SOUTHERN COUNTIES Cycling Union Gazette

Being the OFFICIAL ORGAN of the SOUTHERN COUNTIES CYCLING UNION.

EDITED BY J. H. STAPLEY.

Vol. XIV, No. 158.      JULY 1st, 1911.      Subscription 1/- per annum.

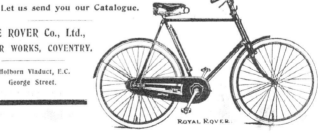

The make of pump was not specified. The *Popular Rover Road Racer* was the same except that had steel rims, and $1^3/_8$" Dunlops; it cost £6 10s. This range appeared only in the 1909 catalogue.

# The Rover Three-Speed Specials

## 1909

The *Rover Three-Speed Special* and the *Rover Three-Speed Special (Lady's)* were basically the Popular models fitted with Armstrong-Triplex three-speed gears. The gent's model had a green-enamelled frame, lined bronze, and plated rims with green-enamelled centres lined bronze. The lady's model was black-enamelled, had no frame-lining and had rims with plated tracks. There was one price - £8 8s. No deviation from the standard pattern was allowed.

## 1910

The gent's model had the central gear-control in the top tube. The lady's model was also green-enamelled. The gent's gears were 54", 71" and 93", the lady's 47", 62" and 81". The prices had increased to £8 10s and £8 15s respectively. No deviation from the standard pattern was allowed.

## 1911

Prices rose to £10 10s. The gent's model had Dunlop tyres and a metal gearcase with a shield-shaped cover over the chainwheel. The saddle was Brooks B75 with plated springs. The tool-bag was specified as Brooks 3594/1. The front mudguard was provided with a forward extension. The lady's model had frame and rims as on the gent's model, a Brooks B75L saddle with plated springs and a Brooks 3594/1 tool-bag. As usual, no deviation was allowed.

## 1912

The only change this year was that an open-fronted gearcase (see Fig. 123) replaced the closed one fitted in 1911.

## 1913-1914

The three-speed models were not listed as separate models.

## 1915

The Armstrong-Triplex gear was replaced by the Sturmey-Archer. Both models (the word "Lady's" was not used for the lady's version) had Warwick tyres, a Rover tool-bag and rims with green-enamelled centres and plated tracks. The gent's model had no gearcase, the lady's a leather Rover case with plated disc. The saddles were Rover with plated springs, and only 7" cranks were fitted to the gent's model. The prices were £7 15s for the gent's and £7 19s 6d for the lady's version.

# The Tradesman's Rover

The decision to reintroduce a purely commercial model for the first time since 1889 may have been an attempt to cater for the tradesmen who served the middle-class customers who were increasingly buying Rovers.

**1910**

## The Tradesman's Rover.

### Including Plate and Basket.

### SPECIFICATION.

**SADDLE.** — The "Rover" enamelled springs.

**FRAME.**—22 in., 24 in., 26 in., or 28 in.

**CHAIN AND GEAR.**—"Rover," ½ in. pitch roller; gear 70 in.

**CRANKS.**—"Rover" pattern; 6½ in. for 22 in., 7 in. for 24 in. frames and higher.

**PEDALS.**—4 in., square rubber.

**HANDLE-BAR.**—1½ in. upturned, celluloid handles.

**WHEELS.**—28 in., enamelled rims.

**TYRES.**—1¾ in. "Rover A" or Dunlops.

**FORKS.**—Box crown, tapered sides, 3½ in. curve; lamp-bracket.

**BRAKES.**—Front and back rim, outside levers.

**FREE-WHEEL**—Ball-bearing frictionless.

**GUARDS.**—Steel, with strengthened edges.

**STEERING.**—Special ball bearings top and bottom, "Rover" steering lock.

**BEARINGS.**—All cups, cones, and balls of special steel.

**FINISH.**—Best black enamel all over, no bright parts, frame-plate not lettered.

**Valise, oilcan, spanners, and pump.**

*All parts guaranteed interchangeable and true to gauge.*

**Rover Tyres are guaranteed for 12 months from date of purchase.**

### PRICE

(FOR GREAT BRITAIN AND IRELAND ONLY.)

**Nett Cash** ...    ...    ...    ...    ...    ... **£8 10 0**

NO DEVIATION FROM STANDARD PATTERN.

All parts of these bicycles are made at the Meteor Works, Coventry, and anyone interested can see the various processes through which they pass.

*Fig. 129*

As can be seen, a slightly different basket-carrier was fitted. Other changes were a Brooks B75 saddle with enamelled springs, a mudguard extension, only Dunlops offered, and a lamp-bracket on the front of the carrier (where it would be useful). The illustration shown that this model was a standard roadster with a clip-on carrier.

# The Tradesman's Rover.

### Including Plate and Basket.

### Specification.

**Frame**—22 in., 24 in., 26 in., or 28 in.

**Forks**—Box crown, tapered sides, 3½ in. curve; lamp-bracket on front of carrier.

**Handle-bar**—1½ in. upturned, celluloid handles

**Saddle**—Brooks' B 75, enamelled springs.

**Tool-bag**—Brooks' No. 3594/1, with cleaning cloth.

**Chain & Gear**—½ in. pitch roller; gear 70 in.

**Cranks**—"Rover" pattern; 6½ in. for 22 in., 7 in for 24 in. frames and higher.

**Pedals**—4 in., square rubber.

**Wheels**—28 in., enamelled rims.

**Tyres**—1¾ in. Dunlops.

**Guards**—Steel, with strengthened edges. Extension to front guard.

**Brakes**—Front and back rim, outside levers.

**Free-wheel**—Ball-bearing frictionless.

**Steering**—Special ball bearings top and bottom "Rover" steering lock.

**Bearings**—All cups, cones, and balls of special steel.

**Finish**—Best b'ack enamel all over, no bright parts, frame-plate not lettered.

### Oilcan, spanners and pump.

*All parts guaranteed interchangeable and true to gauge.*

## PRICE

(For Great Britain and Ireland only).

| | | | | | | | |
|---|---|---|---|---|---|---|---|
| **Nett Cash** ... | ... | ... | ... | ... | ... | ... | **£10 10 0** |
| Fitted with Coaster Hub and Front Brake only | | | | ... | | ... | **£10 10 0** |

### NO DEVIATION FROM STANDARD PATTERN.

**All parts of these bicycles are made at the Meteor Works, Coventry, and anyone interested is invited to inspect the various processes through which they pass.**

*Fig. 130*

## 1915

After its absence from the catalogues from 1912 to 1914 it reappeared as the *Rover Tradesman's Carrier*. Only 22" and 24" frames were offered, a Rover saddle and tool-bag had replaced the Brooks equipment, and the finish was black or green with enamelling in other colours extra. The name-plate was enamelled with lettering extra. The rear stand shown cost 7s 6d extra to the price of £7 7s 6d. The carrier was detachable; the illustration suggests that there were sockets for the lower stays. The 1910 and 1911 models had been offered "including plate and basket" this one was listed as "with basket, carrier and plate". However, as no prices were shown for the earlier carriers it seems likely that they were included in the cost.

## 1916

The specifications were unchanged but the price rose to £8 8s. The catalogue offered "a very excellent new stand (motor cycle pattern) for 10/- extra".

# The Rover Tradesman's Carrier
### With Basket, Carrier, and Plate.

### SPECIFICATION.

**Frame**— 22-in. or 24-in.

**Saddle**— "Rover," plated springs

**Tool-bag**— "Rover."

**Cranks**— "Rover" pattern, 7-in.

**Tyres**— 1¼-in. Dunlops.

**Wheels**— 26-in., enamelled.

**Brakes**— Front and back rim, outside levers    Or Coaster hub and front rim brake.

**Carrier**— Special detachable pattern.

**Free-wheel**— "Rover" ball-bearing, frictionless.

**Finish**— Enamelled black or green. Enamelling in other colours extra; plate in frame enamelled only, lettering extra.

### Oilcan, Spanners and Pump.

***

**PRICE** (for Great Britain and Ireland only):

**Nett Cash** to above specification    ...    **£7  17  6**

*Fig. 131*

# The All-Weather Rover

## 1911

The catalogue illustration suggests that the *All Weather Rover* was simply an all-black version of the 1911 *Royal Rover* but with minor changes. The finish was gold-lined, and it had a Brooks B302 saddle and 7838 tool-bag. Single speed coaster and front brake only £12 or Armstrong-Triplex, with central control £13 7s 6d.

## 1912

This year the name acquired a hyphen. The machine had oval-to-round fork blades, Roman rims, $5/16$" balls in the rear hub, special wide-section mud-guards, a "best quality" instead of a Rover chain, inverted levers and celluloid-covered handlebar. The price of the three-speed version was 5s lower even though the Armstrong-Triplex control in the top tube was fitted.

## 1913

A lady's model was introduced. The *All-Weather Rover* had aluminium rims, "outside" (i.e. roller) brake-levers, a Brooks B75 saddle and 3594/1 tool-bag. The free-wheel was simply ball-bearing frictionless, not Rover, and the ball-size in the rear hub was not given. The frame was lined green and bronze. The price went down to £8 10s, with £1 instead of £1 2s 6d for the Armstrong-Triplex gear; but the three-speed coaster hub was 5s extra at £9 17s 6d. However, the 30% drop in price was doubtless a reduction in profit to meet competition, and although there may have been drastic economising where it did not show it seems likely that the model was being subsidised by others in the Rover range.The *Lady's All-Weather Rover*, identical except for the loop frame, cost 5s extra. This was obviously an economy model, and the increase was occasioned by the additional lug to the seat tube, the bridge between the down and loop tubes, and the bending of the loop tube.

## 1914

Only 7" cranks were offered on the *All-Weather Rover*, and only the Sturmey-Archer or Armstrong-Triplex three-speed gears were listed; the *Lady's All-Weather Rover* followed the gent's model; the prices were still 5s higher.

## 1915

The open gearcases were replaced by closed versions, the lady's model showed a forward extension to the front mudguard, specified but not illustrated for the past two years, and a coaster hub and front brake could be provided instead of two rim-brakes. Only a Sturmey-Archer three-speed gear was available.

## 1916

No three-speed was offered. The Brooks 2557 tool-bag replaced the 3594/1, and prices rose by £2.

## 1917

No coaster hub was offered. The prices rose by £2 10s.

## 1918–1919

Unfortunately it has not been possible to find any catalogues for these years, but the 1919 show report in *Cycling* gave the price for each version as £20 10s, the specifications as in 1917.

## 1920

Specifications were unchanged. The gent's model cost £20 10s, with £1 18s extra for Sturmey-Archer or BSA three-speed gear; the lady's model was £20 10s but either gear cost 2s extra (doubtless to pay for the extra length of wire and pulleys).

## 1921 and 1922

The specifications and prices were unchanged from those of 1920.

## 1923 and 1924

All-weather versions were offered, at no extra cost, for *Imperials, Royals* and *Rovers*; but not for *Racers, Meteors, Boy's* or *Girl's* models.

# The Model "A" Rovers

## 1912

These were similar to the 1909 Popular models but had minor changes. The *Rover Roadster Model "A"* had Warwick tyres, enamelled saddle-springs, a Rover tool-bag, a forward extension to the front mudguard, and rims with enamelled centres and plated tracks. It cost £6 15s with front brake and coaster hub, £7 17s 6d if fitted with Armstrong-Triplex three-speed with central top-tube control or with three-speed coaster and front rim brake. The *Lady's Rover Model "A"* had dropped the 20" frame and the 26" wheels and had changes similar to those on the gent's model, except that there was no front extension and the rim-enamelling was specified as black. The comparative prices were £6 17s 6d and £8. A Sturmey-Archer three-speed or a Tricoaster hub could be fitted.

## 1913

The prices dropped to £5 17s 6d for the gent's and £6 for the lady's model. With front brake and coaster hub, or with Armstrong-Triplex three-speed, the prices rose to £6 or £6 17s 6d and £6 2s 6d or £7 respectively. Cambridge tyres were fitted, and the lady's had an all-leather gearcase. A Sturmey-Archer three-speed could be fitted to either model if required, and a three-speed coaster hub cost 7s 6d extra on the lady's machine.

## 1914–1915

The *Model "A"* was not listed in the catalogues.

## 1916

The *Rover Roadster Bicycle Model "A"* and the *Lady's Rover Bicycle Model "A"* acquired new and slightly longer names; and a *Rover Road Racer Model "A"* was added to the range. There were few changes to the first two. Edinburgh tyres were fitted and the lady's front mudguard had a forward extension. The frames were bronze-lined. Unfortunately our catalogue does not give prices but as all other models had had their prices increased it seems reasonable to assume that these were up too. The racer was basically the 1909 *Popular Road Racer* but no 26" frame was offered. The saddle-springs were enamelled, only 26" rims (with enamelled centres and plated tracks) were available, and 1½" Edinburgh tyres were fitted. The front mudguard had a forward extension and rim-brakes were fitted. The finish was black enamel lined bronze.

## 1920

After an absence of three years the 1916 models returned. Specifications were unchanged, but prices were: *Rover Roadster Model "A"* £13 13s with Sturmey-Archer or BSA three-speed £1 18s extra; *Lady's Rover Model "A"* £13 17s 6d plus £2 extra for the three-speeds; *Rover Road Racer Model "A"* £13 13s – no mention of extra for speed gears. Note that the word "Bicycle" had been dropped from the official name.

## 1921 and 1922

The catalogue specifications of all models were unchanged from those for 1920, but the prices of gears altered. These are shown in the section on gears.

## 1923

This was the last appearance of this name. In 1924 it was changed to *Meteor*. Cambridge tyres were fitted, but there was otherwise no specification change. Prices were: *Roadster Model "A"* £7 19s 6d with £1 5s extra for Sturmey-Archer or BSA three-speed; the lady's version (the word "Lady's" had again been dropped from the official name) £8 10s with £1 7s extra for a three-speed; *Rover Road Racer Model "A"* £7 19s 6d – still with no mention of extra for speed gears.

# The Chainless Rover

In *The CTC Gazette* for December 1912 F.T. Bidlake reviewed the Olympia Cycle Show. Among his comments were the following on a new Rover model.

"In another departure from standard practice, the New Rover Cycle Co. Ltd has reintroduced a chainless drive in the form of propeller shaft and a bevel drive at each end of the shaft. In the new Rover rendering of this idea there are points which distinguish it from the Acatène, the Columbia and other bevel gear drives, the most noteworthy being that the bevel on the crank axle is mounted centrally in the plane of the frame, between two bearings, and not outside. This variation is an improvement, making a better provision against twist and end thrust. Also it is, no doubt, correct that the machining of the teeth on bevel wheels is more correctly done than was formerly possible, except at prohibitive cost. On the score of weight the nett result is not a gain, for although the absence of chain and chain wheel is claimed as resulting in a substantial reduction, the presence of a propeller shaft enclosed in a stay and the presence of four necessarily substantial bevel wheels more than compensates the reduction, and the bicycle complete is not any lighter than a similarly equipped chain-driven machine. The enclosing of the parts is certainly less bulky than a similar complete enclosure for a chain drive, and there is no risk of entanglement of skirt or need for the use of trousers clips. There is also an improvement in the accessibility of the fit-up by rendering the fork tubes opposite the driving side removable, and the hub has been modernised as a coaster, which has never before been seen in association with chainless work. Again, the price has been levelled down to 10 guineas, so that it stands four-square with the current Imperial or best quality Rovers, but there is a drawback to the use of bevel gears – namely, that they are demonstrated to be not so mechanically efficient as chain drive. Chain efficiency has reached 98 to 99 per cent., there is no room for much greater approach to the absolute and impossible perfection of 100 per cent., and in fact the efficiency of bevel gear has never been found to be as high as that of the chain. Hence it is usually employed when a corner has to be turned and not for such direct transmission as a cycle-drive where the turning of a corner has to be compensated by a second turning of a corner in the opposite direction. It is true, of course, that chain efficiency falls rapidly from perfection when the chain is neglected, and the protected bevel gear maintains the efficiency it possesses at a pretty constant level, but when all is summed and said the selection of a bevel gear, if made, must rather be on collateral advantages than on any plea of efficiency. Fortunately there is the choice offered without the distracting element of differing price . . . "

The magazine editor had added a footnote to Bidlake's comments on the weight: "We were informed that it is rather lighter than a chain machine with a gearcase." He might have added that Bidlake was wrong in saying that a coaster hub had never before been associated with a chainless drive.

The Columbia certainly and the Lloyd Cross-Roller probably had been so equipped.

Here we have another example of a dating problem that crops up all too often, of which the outstanding example is the Coventry Lever tricycle. That was patented in 1876 but was not available until 1877; yet it takes the earlier date by custom, probably wrongly. The patent for the BSA safety was granted in November 1884, yet the BSA is known as an 1885 machine. Pausey's *Pioneer* safety was patented two months before the BSA, and it takes the 1884 date. Bidlake was reviewing cycles that were destined for the 1913 season; should they be dated 1912 or 1913? Perhaps 1912 is safer. They were, after all, on show in that year.

## 1913

The mechanism is shown below in Fig. 132.

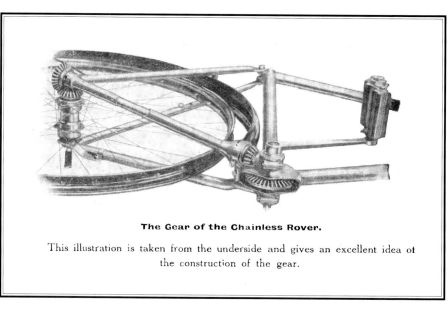

**The Gear of the Chainless Rover.**

This illustration is taken from the underside and gives an excellent idea of the construction of the gear.

*Fig. 132*

# Chainless Lady's Rover.

## Specification.

**Frame**—22-in., 24-in., or 26-in.

**Forks**—Box crown, oval to round sides, 3½-in. curve; lamp bracket.

**Handle-bar**—2½-in. upturned, celluloid handles.

**Saddle**—Brooks' B302L, plated springs

**Tool-bag**—Brooks' No. 9060/1, with cleaning cloth and tools.

**Gear**—63-in.

**Cranks**—" Rover " pattern, 6½-in.

**Pedals**—3½-in. " Rover " Pattern, rubber.

**Wheels**—28-in., black enamelled centres, lined to match frame, plated tracks.

**Tyres**—1½-in. Dunlops

**Guards**—Best steel, with strengthened edges. rear guard laced for the protection of the dress

**Brakes**—Coaster hub and front rim brake.

**Steering.**—Special ball-bearings top and bottom, " Rover " steering-lock.

**Bearings**—All cups, cones, and balls of special steel.

**Finish**—Finest quality black enamel, fine gold lines with centre line green, all bright parts heavily plated on copper.

### Oilcan, Spanners and Pump.

*All parts guaranteed interchangeable and true to gauge.*

See Description on Page 27.

## PRICE.

(For Great Britain and Ireland only).

**Nett Cash** ... ... ... ... ... ... ... ... **£10  10   0**

This bicycle may be finished all black and lined green and gold without extra charge.

*Fig. 133*

# Chainless Rover Roadster.

## Specification.

**Frame**—22-in., 24-in., or 26-in.

**Forks**—Box crown, oval to round sides, 3½-in curve ; lamp-bracket.

**Handle-bar**—1½-in. upturned celluloid handles

**Saddle**—Brooks' B95, plated springs.

**Tool-bag**—Brooks' No. 425, with cleaning cloth and tools.

**Gear**—70-in

**Cranks**—" Rover " pattern, 7-in.

**Pedals**—4-in , " Rover " pattern best quality rubber.

**Wheels**—28-in., black enamelled centres, lined to match frame, plated tracks.

**Tyres**—1½-in. Dunlops

**Guards**—Best steel, with strengthened edges ; extension to front guard.

**Brakes**—Coaster Hub and front rim brake.

**Steering**—Special ball-bearings top and bottom, " Rover " steering lock.

**Bearings**—All cups, cones, and balls of special steel.

**Finish**—Finest quality black enamel, fine gold lines with centre line green, all brightparts heavily plated on copper.

### Oilcan, Spanners and Pump.

*All parts guaranteed interchangeable and true to gauge.*

See Description on Page 27.

## PRICE.

(For Great Britain and Ireland only).

**Nett Cash** ... ... ... ... ... ... ... ... **£10 10 0**

This bicycle may be finished all black, and lined green and gold without extra charge.

*Fig. 134*

# 1914

There was a forward extension to the front mudguard on the gent's version and that was specified on the lady's model (shown here to illustrate the new frame) although it was not depicted.

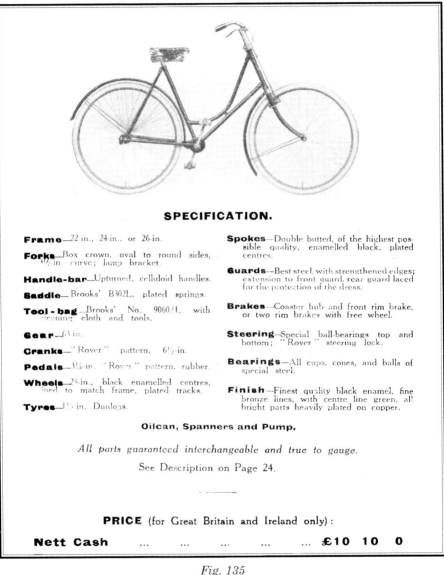

## SPECIFICATION.

**Frame**—22 in., 24 in., or 26-in.

**Forks**—Box crown, oval to round sides, 4½-in. curve; lamp bracket.

**Handle-bar**—Upturned, celluloid handles.

**Saddle**—Brooks' B302L, plated springs.

**Tool - bag**—Brooks' No. 9060/1, with cleaning cloth and tools.

**Gear**—63 in.

**Cranks**—"Rover" pattern, 6½-in.

**Pedals**—3¼-in. "Rover" pattern, rubber.

**Wheels**—28-in., black enamelled centres, laced to match frame, plated tracks.

**Tyres**—1½-in. Dunlops.

**Spokes**—Double butted, of the highest possible quality, enamelled black, plated centres.

**Guards**—Best steel, with strengthened edges; extension to front guard, rear guard laced for the protection of the dress.

**Brakes**—Coaster hub and front rim brake, or two rim brakes with free wheel.

**Steering**—Special ball-bearings top and bottom; "Rover" steering lock.

**Bearings**—All cups, cones, and balls of special steel.

**Finish**—Finest quality black enamel, fine bronze lines, with centre line green, all bright parts heavily plated on copper.

### Oilcan, Spanners and Pump.

*All parts guaranteed interchangeable and true to gauge.*

See Description on Page 24.

**PRICE** (for Great Britain and Ireland only):

**Nett Cash** ... ... ... ... ... **£10 10 0**

*Fig. 135*

# 1915

The roadster was available in 24" and 26" frame-sizes only, the lady's machine in 22" and 24". The latter had either the 1914 frame or the double-curved version. Prices dropped to £8 15s. The *Chainless* did not appear again.

# The Rover Military Bicycle
## 1915

# The Rover Military Bicycle

### Fitted with Rifle Clips.

*As supplied to the War Office.*　　　*Specially strong, but not heavy.*

### SPECIFICATION.

**Frame**— 24-in., 26-in., or 28-in.

**Saddle**— Brooks' B90/3, enamelled springs.

**Tool-bag**— Brooks' No. 8024, with cleaning cloth.

**Cranks**—7-in.

**Pedals**— 4¼-in. square rubber.

**Wheels**— 28-in., black enamelled centres, lined to match frame, plated tracks.

**Tyres**— 1¾-in. Dunlop Magnum.

**Brakes**— Front and back rim, outside levers. Or Coaster hub and front rim brake.

**Finish**— Best black enamel, lined green and bronze, bright parts plated.

### Oilcan, Spanners and Pump.

———

Enamelled black all over if required.

———

**PRICE** (for Great Britain and Ireland only) :

**Nett Cash,** complete with Rifle Clips　**£8　19　6**

With Sturmey-Archer Three-Speed Gear　...　**£9　19　6**

*Fig. 136*

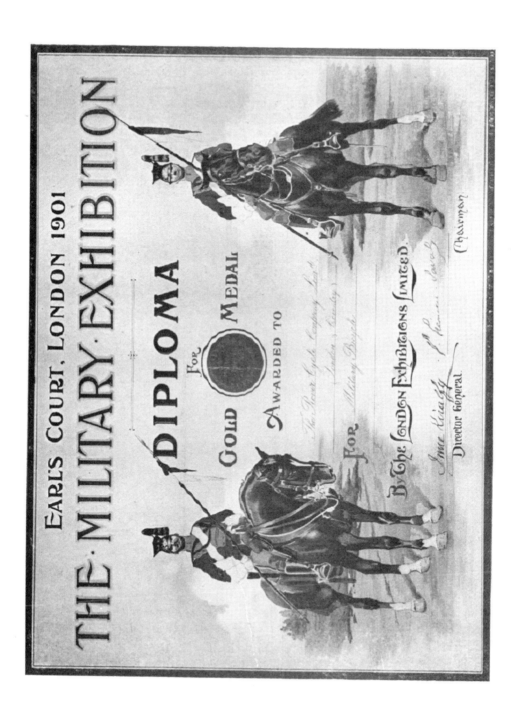

# Achievements and Advertising

When John Foster Fraser, Edward Lunn and F. H. Lowe made their 19,237-mile world tour they used Rover Roadsters. Whether the firm produced them free is not known, but there was clearly some arrangement. On 23 December 1896 Fraser wrote to J. K. Starley from Tehran to ask for a new handlebar and "a new cushion or whatever its name is that fits above the fork and in which the balls run." In addition he asked for "an assortment of balls in case they may be required." In Fraser's *Round the World on a Wheel* there is little mention of the firm, which would suggest that there was no firm commitment to advertise Rovers.

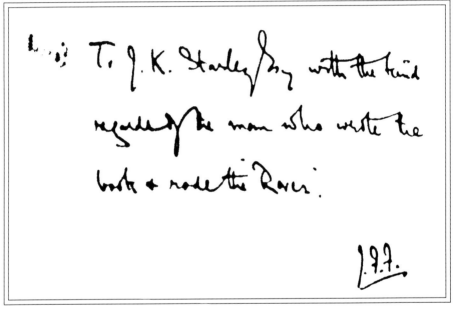

*Facsimile (reduced in size) of Fraser's note accompanying the copy of "Round the World on a Wheel" he sent to Starley.*

An extract from Hampshire Chronicle August 27th 1898:

*Winchester* - The three Commissioners of Travel, Messrs. Fraser, Lunn and Lowe, who have ridden round the world on Rover cycles during the last two years, and have had most thrilling adventures in Persia, India, China, and Japan, have arrived in Southampton by the American line steamship Kensington. They will leave the office of the American line to ride to Winchester at three o'clock this (Saturday) afternoon, and it is hoped that there will be a good attendance of cyclists to welcome them back to Old England and to send them on the last stage of their journey, St Pancaras Church, London, from which they started two years last July 17th.

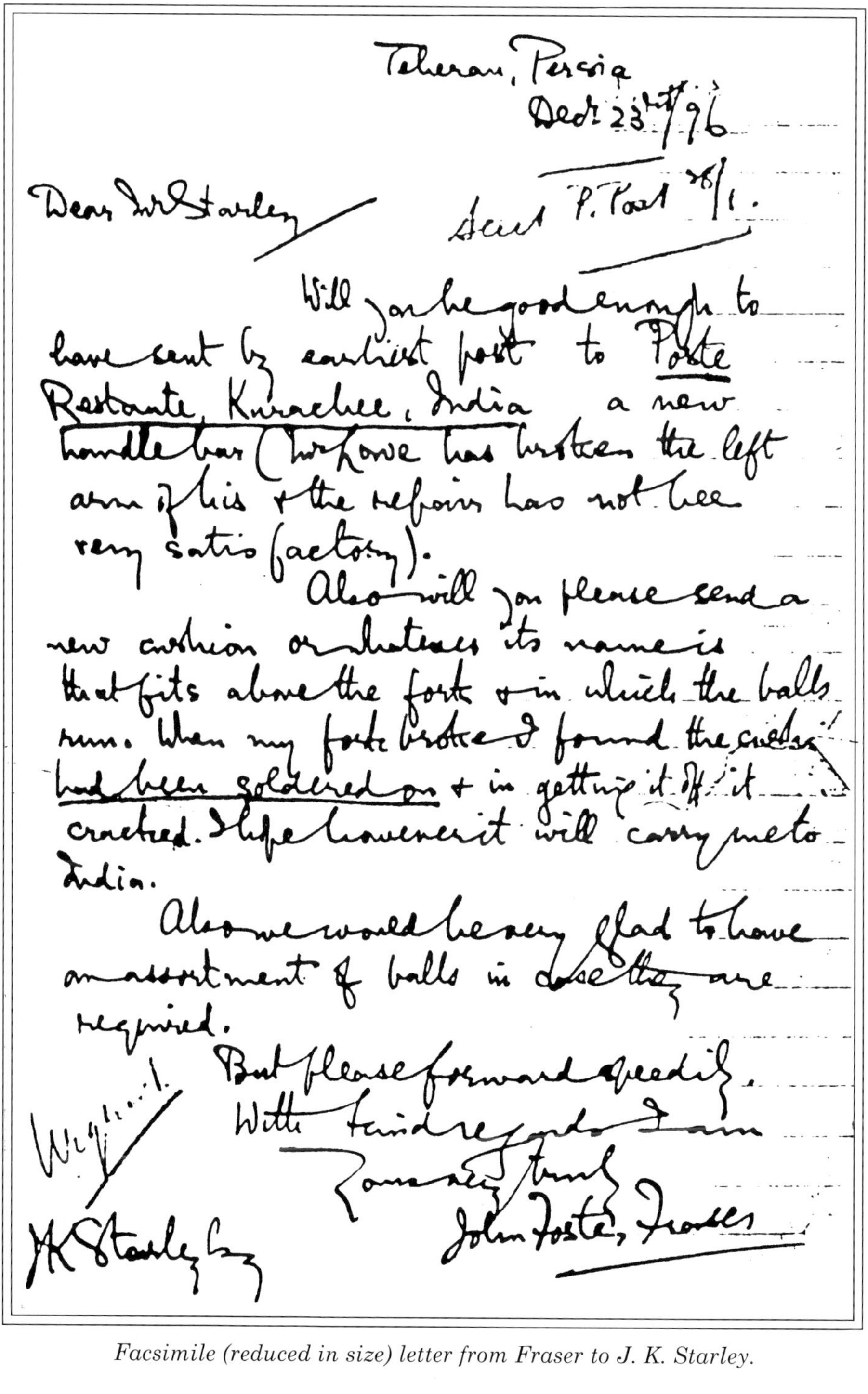

Teheran, Persia
Dec: 23rd/96

Dear Mr Starley        Sent P. Post 25/1.

Will you be good enough to have sent by earliest post to Poste Restante, Kurachee, India a new handle bar (who/one has broken the left arm of his & the repairs has not been very satisfactory).

Also will you please send a new cushion or whatever its name is that fits above the fork & in which the balls run. When my fork broke I found the cushion had been soldered on & in getting it off it cracked. I hope however it will carry me to India.

Also we would be very glad to have an assortment of balls in case they are required.

But please forward speedily.

With kind regards I am

Yours very truly

John Foster, Fraser

*Facsimile (reduced in size) letter from Fraser to J. K. Starley.*

In *The Cyclist Year Book* for 1892 the Rover advertisement published a letter from E. Walton, of Cupar, who enthused over his Rover's 70,000 in six years.

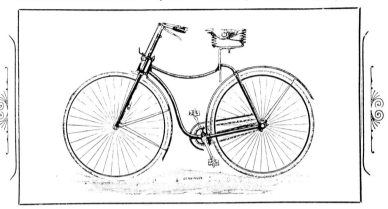

In November 1896 a Rover advertisement mentioned Robert Louis Jefferson's ride across Europe into Russia, and reminded readers of his 1895 trip on his Rover to Moscow and back.

As will have been seen from the preceding pages, Rovers understood the value of advertising and did not confine it to the cycling press. Here is an extract from the issue for 15 May 1897 of *Focus,* a photographic magazine. Photography, like cycling, was largely a pursuit of the better-off in those days, and the cycle enabled the photographer to reach areas of interest and beauty.

From their early days Rovers used racing to promote their bicycles and by the end of the 19$^{th}$ century their riders were capturing local, national and world records. This extract from their 1899 catalogue lists some of them.

The following are a few of the performances accomplished upon "Rovers" during the past season:

# WORLD'S RECORDS –

Quarter-mile paced
Half-mile paced
Threequarter-mile paced        J. Platt-Betts.
One mile paced
Quarter-mile unpaced
Half-mile unpaced
Threequarter-mile unpaced      J. Platt-Betts.
One mile unpaced
One Kilometere, J. Platt-Betts.
Quarter-mile unpaced amateur standing start.
Quarter-mile unpaced amateur flying start.
Half-mile unpaced amateur standing start
One mile amateur, H. W. Payne.

# GENERAL RECORDS –

Half-mile Scotch record
One mile Scotch record      J. Platt-Betts.
One mile standing start track record, Lees, Cordang.
One hour Irish record, distance 30 miles 377 yards, Cordang.
Five miles Northern record, Cordang.
Fifty miles Yorkshire road record
Hundred miles Yorkshire road record    Mark Higham.
Hundred miles Cornish road record, G. Bramble.

# FOREIGN RECORDS –

Ten to hundred kilometres, French records, Cordang.
Seventy-five to two hundred kilometres, German records, Cordang.
Quarter-mile, flying start, Austrialia
Half-mile, flying start, Australia
Threequarter-mile, flying start, Australia    J. Platt-Betts.
One mile, flying start, Australia
One mile, standing start, Australia
Five miles, standing start, Australia    J. Platt-Betts.
Ten miles, standing start, Australia
One mile, West Australia
Five miles, West Australia    J. Platt-Betts.
Twenty-five miles, West Australia, G. F. Best.
Melbourne to Sydney, Australia, E. A. Pearson.
Quarter-mile flying start, South Africa
One mile flying start, South Africa    A. Van Heerden.
Quarter-mile standing start, South Africa
Half-mile standing start, South Africa    A. E. George.
Two miles, South Africa
Three miles, South Africa
Four miles, South Africa    A. E. George.
Five miles, South Africa
Five miles, South Africa (unpaced), F. G. Connock.
One hour, South Africa, disctance 28 miles 1,190 yards, A. Van Heerden.
One mile, Natal, South Africa, H Banman.

The racing successes continued. At the end of the 1908 season they issued *The Racing Supplement to the Rover List*, which contained the following: "One of the most remarkable features of the season [1908] has been the extraordinary success of the Rover Racing Bicycle. At nearly every race meeting the Rover scored heavily, the bulk of the championships – World's, National Cyclists' Union, British Empire and British Centres' – have fallen to Rover riders, while at the Olympic Games it achieved the astounding record of winning every race decided upon single bicycles. Trophies galore have been won, and Records at all distances have been broken, while abroad the Grand Prix of Paris has been accounted for by the Rover.

THE WORLD BEATERS
*The famous Rover Team which beat all comers at the Olympic Games*
*Meredith, Jones, Kingsbury, Pyne.*

1908 *Cycling* show report: The novelty on the Rover Co. stand is the *Cata* bicycle. The ordinary diamond frame is crushed down, as it were, from the seat pillar into a rhomboidal shape and two additional tubes start from the head, supported at the saddle-pin end by a strong spring designed to take up road shocks & to retain the rigidity of the whole frame. The machine will be supplied only to members of the Cycle & Allied Trades Alliance & will retail at £10 10s.

Rovers claimed world-wide sales. In their 1896 catalogue they listed North and South America, Australia, India, Canada, Germany, France, Austria, Italy, Switzerland – indeed the whole of the Continent of Europe – plus China, Japan and South Africa. In 1904 Colonel Younghusband's expedition entered the forbidden city of Lhassa, and one of the surprises it encountered there was a Rover bicycle. However, they did not have New Zealand on the list; perhaps they reasoned that as it was only about 1,000 miles away from Australia it was almost the same place. But while researching this book a single-sheet advertisement was located for a "Specially designed model for the New Zealand market". It bore the 1925 version of the Rover badge and appeared to be a Meteor Light Roadster with sloping top-tube, 28" x 1½" wheels and a coaster brake. It was endorsed in ink "All sent direct 19 3 26" (Fig. 119). Until then we had assumed that Rover Cycle sales had ceased at the end of 1925, but the October 1925 *CTC Gazette* carried a Rover advertisement offering cycles for the 1926 season. So far no other reference to sales for that year has been found.

*Preparing for the Rover Centenary Ride, 1985*
*Dorothy, John and Doug Pinkerton.*
The two day ride from Peterborough to Birmingham via Coventry was close on
100 miles. The Rational Tandem was having its first long distance ride this
century. The event souvenir programme is reproduced in Appendix 2.

*The Rover Centenary Ride 1985.*
*Successful riders, including J. K. Starley IV and younger son, arrived at the*
*Museum of Science and Industry, Birmingham.*

# Variable Gears

Most of the information in this section is available elsewhere but it is repeated here to give a clearer picture of the firm's policy on variable gears. We have earlier commented on some peculiarities in the Rover catalogues; this peculiarity is maintained over gears. Some gears are named, some are not. Sturmey-Archer is in favour one year, Armstrong-Triplex the next. Some years both are offered. As these details have nearly all come from the catalogues it is, as always, possible that the gears listed could have been fitted or available earlier and that unlisted gears could have been supplied to order.

## 1903

Unnamed gears with two or three speeds were listed for the *Imperial* models only. No prices were given.

## 1904

The 1903 offer was extended to *Royal* models, still unpriced.

## 1905

The catalogue says "we have also introduced for the benefit of those who require multiple speeds, the Rover Two-Speed Gear. We are also prepared to supply the Sturmey-Archer three-speed gear." This of course ignores the offers of gears in 1903 and 1904. It is probable that the three-speed gear available then was the Sturmey-Archer, but it is not safe to assume that the two-speed was the Rover. The gears were available on all models except racers. The Sturmey-Archer cost £3 3s extra, the Rover £2 2s. The latter was illustrated and commented on in the *NCU Review and Official Record* (1905, page 77), as follows: "there are many riders who do not think it necessary to have more than two speeds, and this company, in deference to the expressed wishes of such, have put upon the market a two-speed gear built on the sun and planet motion and fitted to the driving wheel, with the usual stop arrangement to govern the gear. As will be seen from the illustration the gear is simple and compact, and resembles in miniature the Monopole gear which was the forerunner, so to speak, of this type of gearing."

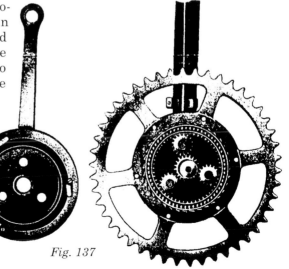

*Fig. 137*

## 1905

CHANGING GEAR

THREE SPEED HUB

## 1906

There was an illustration of the Sturmey-Archer three-speed (available at £3 3s extra) showing the control-wire on the drive side. The ratios, shown in the table below, were those provided in 1905.

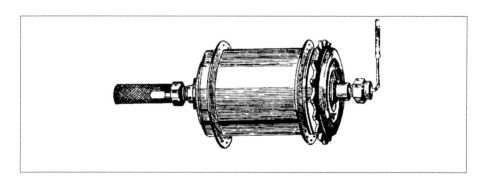

| No. of Teeth on Gear Wheel | Low Gear | Medium or Normal Gear | High Gear |
|---|---|---|---|
| 40 | 49.8 | 62.2 | 77.7 |
| 42 | 52.3 | 65.3 | 81.6 |
| 44 | 54.8 | 68.4 | 85.5 |
| 46 | 57.2 | 71.5 | 89.3 |
| 48 | 59.7 | 74.6 | 93.2 |
| 50 | 62.2 | 77.7 | 97.1 |
| 52 | 64.7 | 80.8 | 101 |

Rover, Griffin or Fagan two-speed gears were available at £2 2s extra, the Griffin being illustrated (fig. 138). All these gears could be provided on all models except racers.

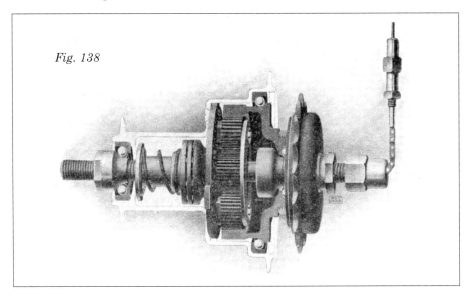

*Fig. 138*

## 1907

The extra cost for the Sturmey-Archer three-speed gear dropped to £2 2s; the new ratios are listed below.

| Teeth on Gear Wheel | Low | Middle | High |
|---|---|---|---|
| 36 | 48.6 | 63.1 | 82.8 |
| 38 | 51.3 | 66.5 | 87.1 |
| 40 | 54 | 70 | 91 |
| 42 | 57.5 | 73.5 | 96.4 |
| 44 | 60 | 77 | 101 |
| 46 | 62.5 | 80.5 | 105.5 |
| 48 | 65 | 86 | 110.2 |
| 50 | 66.3 | 87.1 | 114.3 |
| 52 | 71.0 | 91 | 119.4 |

Only the Griffin (Fig. 139) and the Hub (Fig. 140) two-speeds were offered at £1 10s extra. Note that the Griffin had changed from the one shown in 1906.

Fig. 139

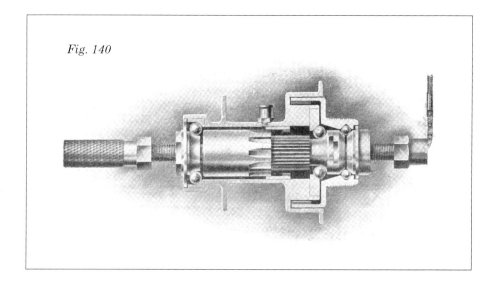

Fig. 140

# 1908

Either the Sturmey-Archer or the Armstrong-Triplex gear was available at £2 2s extra; the latter is shown in Fig. 141. The Hub, the Griffin, "or other standard two-speed gear" was offered at £1 10s extra; there was no hint of what was a non-standard gear.

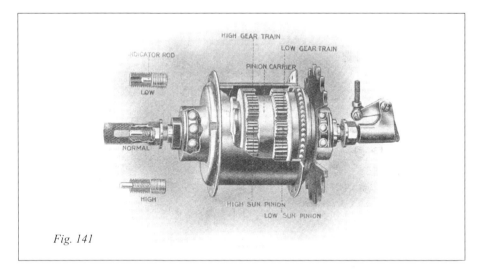

*Fig. 141*

# 1909

The Armstrong-Triplex was the only gear offered, at £1 15s extra. The Three-Speed Special with that gear and the Armstrong central top-tube control cost £8 8s. This control (shown here) was fitted with all the gears.

# 1910

Again only the Armstrong-Triplex was offered, at £1 10s extra. The ratios offered are shown below.

| Teeth on Chain Wheel | Cog | Low | Norm | High | Teeth on Chain Wheel | Cog | Low | Norm | High |
|---|---|---|---|---|---|---|---|---|---|
| 44 | 16 | 59 | 77 | 101 | 50 | 16 | 66 | 87 | 114 |
| 44 | 18 | 52 | 68 | 90 | 50 | 18 | 59 | 78 | 102 |
| 44 | 20 | 47 | 62 | 81 | 50 | 20 | 52 | 70 | 92 |
| 46 | 18 | 54 | 71 | 93 | 52 | 16 | 69 | 91 | 119 |
| 48 | 16 | 64 | 84 | 110 | 52 | 18 | 62 | 81 | 106 |
| 48 | 18 | 57 | 75 | 98 | 52 | 20 | 55 | 73 | 95 |
| 48 | 20 | 51 | 67 | 88 | | | | | |

## 1911

The Armstrong-Triplex gear cost £1 7s 6d extra. In small print below the prices we find "Sturmey-Archer three-speed gears can be fitted if required." No price was quoted and the offer did not apply to the Three-Speed Special.

## 1912

An Armstrong-Triplex gear, or an unnamed Three-Speed Coaster and a rim front brake, cost £1 2s 6d extra. This would have been an Armstrong-Triplex coaster. A Sturmey-Archer gear or a Sturmey-Archer Tricoaster could be fitted but no price was given.

## 1913

The Armstrong-Triplex gear (no coaster) cost £1 extra. The Sturmey-Archer was still in small print and unpriced.

## 1914

Either a Sturmey-Archer or an Armstrong-Triplex gear – in that order – was available at £1 extra.

## 1915

Only a Sturmey-Archer gear was offered, at £1 extra.

## 1916–1917

No variable gears were listed, possibly owing to the war.

## 1918–1919

No catalogues for these years have been found so far.

## 1920

Either a Sturmey-Archer or a BSA three-speed was available at £1 18s for gents and £2 for ladies.

## 1921

The 1920 offer was repeated but prices had risen to £2 10s and £2 17s 6d.

## 1922

No catalogue for this year has been found so far.

## 1923

The 1920 offer was repeated but prices had dropped to £1 5s and £1 7s.

Dutch customers of Rover were offered an EADIE 3-speed hub gear at a similar extra cost to British buyers. From the catalogue illustration it is obviously a BSA with the name over-printed; perhaps the Dutch preferred Eadie to BSA.

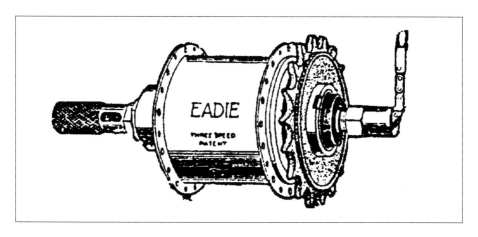

## 1924

The BSA gear was standard on *Imperials* with a 68 normal for gents; Lady's was not stated. On the *Royal*, *Rover* and *Meteors*, prices had dropped to £1 3s and £1 5s. It was not available on the *Meteor Rover Road Racers*, *Boy's* or *Girl's* models

## 1925

The BSA gear was listed before the Sturmey-Archer; both cost £1 3s extra.

There was no production of Rover cycles after 1925.

# Fittings

The 1901 catalogue gave details of the workmanship and fittings on the *Rovers*. The front rim brake had been introduced in 1900 for *Imperial* models except the *Cob*.

---

## Illustrations and Descriptions of the Salient Points in Rover Bicycles for 1901.

Our first illustrations show the front fork, the steering tube and fork sides of which are all tapered - the former from the bottom, where the heaviest strain comes, and is thus greatly strengthened at this point; the upper part is parallel inside, sufficiently far down, to admit of the adjustment of the handle-bar. The fork sides are tapered from the crown to the bottom, so that sufficient strength is obtained at the point where the greatest strain comes upon the fork. It will therefore be seen that the liners formerly used in making up the front forks have been superseded by this special and improved method of strengthening at the most critical points.

The **FOOTRESTS** illustrated are of a new pattern of our own registered design, materially strengthened and improved since last season.

The **STEERING LOCK**, which is generally considered to be the neatest form now in use, is manipulated by turning the small lever, the plunger being held in position by a spring, so that it is impossible for it to come into use accidentally. We have used

this form of steering lock now for many years and it has been found to give entire satisfaction.

**PEDAL FASTENINGS**. - We are continuing to fasten pedals with right and left hand

threads, and believe this to be the best possible form of ensuring a good fit, in addition to which it is exceedingly neat, and as there are no projections, it is impossible for ladies' dresses to catch.

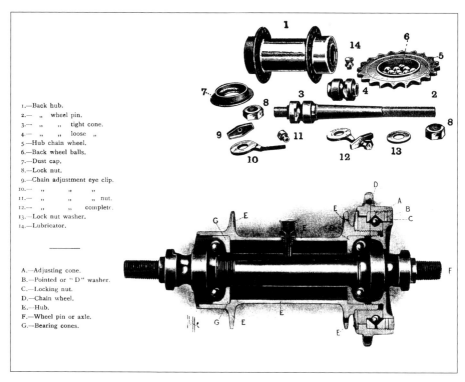

1.—Back hub.
2.— „ wheel pin.
3.— „ „ tight cone.
4.— „ „ loose „
5.—Hub chain wheel.
6.—Back wheel balls.
7.—Dust cap.
8.—Lock nut.
9.—Chain adjustment eye clip.
10.— „ „ „
11.— „ „ „ nut.
12.— „ „ complete.
13.—Lock nut washer.
14.—Lubricator.

A.—Adjusting cone.
B.—Pointed or "D" washer.
C.—Locking nut.
D.—Chain wheel.
E.—Hub.
F.—Wheel pin or axle.
G.—Bearing cones.

The above illustrations show the details of the **BACK HUB** separately, also complete hub in section, from which it will be seen we have made this dustproof, oil-retaining, and very simple to adjust.

The first of these illustrations shows our method of **Fastening the Cones to the Bracket** and of obtaining that adjustment which has been proved by long practice to be very efficient and satisfactory, while the next shows the **Bracket complete**.

The illustration shows our patented **Method of Adjusting the Band Brake**, and its attachment to the frame of the bicycle. The power is communicated by means of a lever at the handle-bar through a Bowden wire. When this brake is used it is not necessary to have a second brake, as is the case where a back-pedalling brake is fitted.

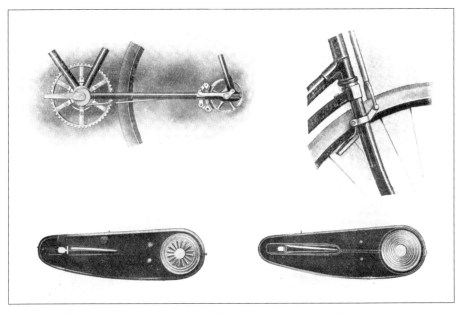

The first illustration above shows our **New Back-pedalling Block Brake**, one of the advantages of which is that it is not possible to lock the wheel when applied with force, and we have no hesitation in recommending it as one of the best forms of back-pedalling brakes it is possible to conceive. The illustration of the **Rim Brake** shows the form which we have adopted. It is simple and effective, and when this class of brake is preferred it will be found very efficient in action and simple in adjustment. The last illustrations show the **"Carter-Rover" Case** supplied on Imperial Ladies' and Roadsters, and the **"Rover" Gear Case** supplied on Ladies' Rovers and Rover Roadsters.

The first illustration shows the front-wheel pull-up rim brake, as fitted to our IMPERIAL and ROVER Cycles, the second shows those used on METEORS in 1902.

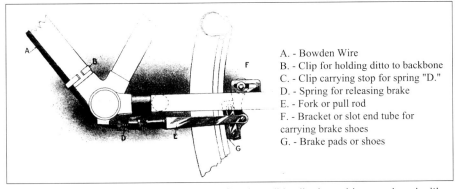

A. - Bowden Wire
B. - Clip for holding ditto to backbone
C. - Clip carrying stop for spring "D."
D. - Spring for releasing brake
E. - Fork or pull rod
F. - Bracket or slot end tube for carrying brake shoes
G. - Brake pads or shoes

Above: ROVER BACK-RIM BRAKE as fitted to all Ladies' machines ordered with free-wheel and two rim brakes.

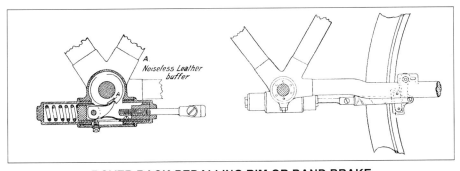

## ROVER BACK-PEDALLING RIM OR BAND BRAKE

The above illustrations show our new one-point (right side) Back-pedalling Brake, from which it will be seen that we mount on the centre of the bottom bracket spindle a cam with one ratchet. A reverse action of the pedals causes contact to be made with the tooth shown underneath, which, when engaging, draws up the brake rod and so applies the brake. It will be noticed that all the mechanism is enclosed, and that the whole of the parts occupy very little space. At the end nearest the front wheel a spring is fitted in the barrel, which keeps the pawl or engaging tooth up to its work, while at the point marked "A" leather buffers are fitted to prevent the pawl making a noise.

# THE
# ROVER BALL-BEARING FRICTIONLESS FREE-WHEEL CLUTCH

Fitted to Imperials.

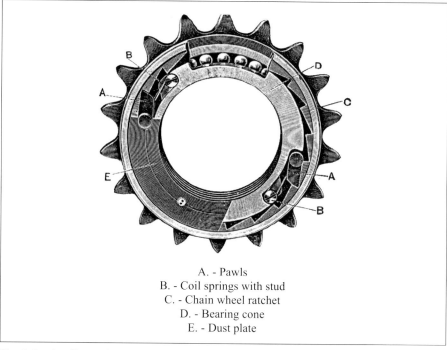

A. - Pawls
B. - Coil springs with stud
C. - Chain wheel ratchet
D. - Bearing cone
E. - Dust plate

The following illustration of our new Free-wheel Clutch, which is on the pawl and ratchet principle, but with some important modifications. There are four rocking pawls, which are so shaped that when the machine is running free they rock over the ratchet noiselessly, and when the pedals are pressed forward, take up the drive quickly. As will be seen from the second figure, the clutch is mounted on a ring of balls, which further conduces to the sweet running of the chain wheel.

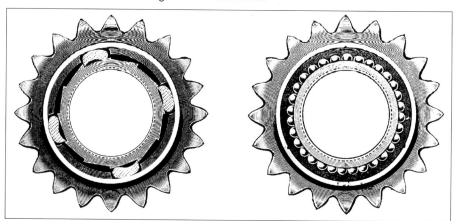

# THE ROVER FREE-WHEEL CLUTCH

The above illustrates our new roller free-wheel clutch which we are fitting to "Rover" and "Meteor" Cycles for 1901. In consequence of the difficulty experienced in keeping the rollers up to their work, we have altered the formation of the grooves entirely, and have substituted twelve for the eight rollers originally used.

This clutch is instantaneous in its action, quite noiseless, and can thoroughly be depended upon as efficient and reliable for its work.

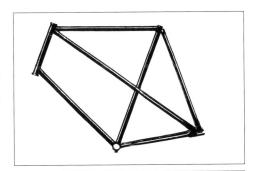

The illustration shows a **Diagonal Stay to Frame**, which is specially recommended for heavy riders, and is fitted to "Imperials" and "Rovers" free, but a charge of £1 is made if fitted to "Meteor Rovers".

## ROVER STANDARD PATTERN HANDLE-BARS.

These illustraions show the Standard Pattern Handle-bars fitted to "Rover" and "Meteor" bicycles. They are described as:

    The full upturned.
    The medium upturned.
    The flat or "rational".
    The full drop or path racing bar.
    The medium drop or road racing bar.

The 1903 catalogue gave details of the brakework.

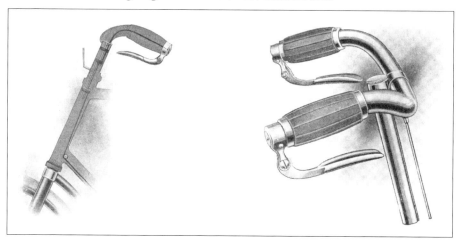

The above illustrations show our new concealed-wire brake, as fitted to the "Imperial Light Roadster" and "Lady's". It will be seen that provision is made in the head of the machine for taking up the slack of the wire and adjustment. This is effected by turning the milled cap at top of the handle, adjusting tube to the right or left, according to whether it is desired to increase or decrease the length of the wire. The drawing on the right-hand side shows the handle-bars, inverted levers and milled cap more clearly.

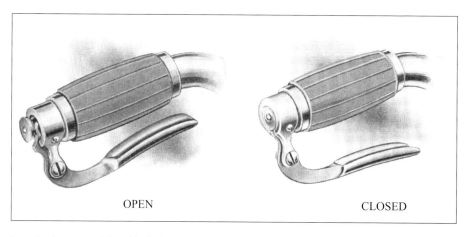

OPEN                                              CLOSED

In order to prevent the rider's hands being pinched by the closing of the inverted grasps, we have introduced a very neat fitment, as illustrated above, and we feel confident that this will be regarded as a great improvement, and one that has long been required.

On all back-wheel brakes, where Bowden Wire is used, we are fitting our Patented Wire Coupling (Patent No. 15,398, of 1902), which will be found most convenient when removing the handle-bar or brake work, which can be done without having to unsolder the wire as formerly. The illustration opposite shows this in three ways, viz.:-

1. Close
2. Hinged washer open and sleeve lowered.
3. Ditto, with coupling detached.

*[Alex Moulton used a cable joint on the 1980's range of AM bicycles and the later ATB and APB bicycles, including the Land Rover model, which are demountable]*

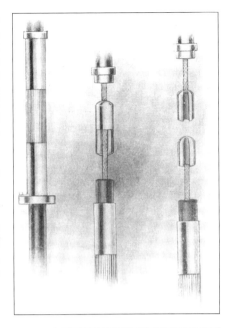

**PEDALS.** - Feeling that the lubricating devices for pedals have always been more or less crude, we have this year made a very big improvement by grooving the pedal-bush and fitting a circular band of steel, as illustrated; and we are quite sure that this simple but useful alteration will be thoroughly appreciated by all classes of cyclists.

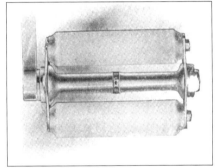

**VALVE-CAP HOLDER.** - Since the introduction of the free-wheel and two rim brakes, it has been found necessary to do away with the chain which formerly held the tyre-valve cap to the spoke, and consequently much irritation and annoyance has been caused by the constant loss of caps and consequent dust, etc., getting into the valves. The illustrations show a neat, simple, but very effective arrangement for preventing the valve cap being lost or mislaid.
*[Sunbeam also used this retainer]*

## ECCENTRIC BRACKET

This ingenious device for facilitating the chain adjustment without interfering with the back brakes and enabling us to fit a much neater gear case than formerly, has been well received by all classes. The illustration shows the internal part of the bracket together with chain wheel and crank, and will be readily understood by the following index: -

A. - Cone or Cup for adjusting bearings.
B. - Bolt and nut for manipulating blocks C. & C1.
C & C1. - Expanding blocks for fastening bracket.
D. - Chain wheel ring.
E. - Spindle.
This device is registered.

## ORDINARY PATTERN BOTTOM BRACKET

This pattern is used on all "Royal Rovers", "Rovers" and "Meteors", and being lighter than the eccentric bracket illustrated above, is used also on the "Imperial Light Roadsters" and "Road Racers". It is probably too well-known to need a detailed description, but for those who are not acquainted with the construction of this bracket we may say that it differs from the Eccentric inasmuch as it is fixed; the slack of the chain having to be taken up at the back forks.

The bolt on the left hand side of the sketch shows the system of tightening the fixed cup, and that on the right the method for adjusting the bearings.

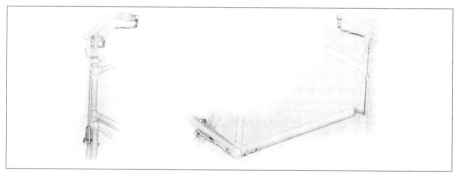

## ROVER BRAKES - INVERTED LEVERS

The first of these illustrations show the "Rover" pull-up Front Rim Brake with inverted lever, and the second illustrates our new Rod and Lever Back Rim Brake, as now fitted to all our "Imperial" and "Royal Rover" bicycles, and which we claim to be the most efficient and reliable brake at present before the public.

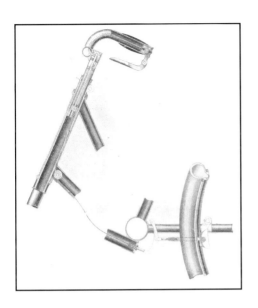

### CONCEALED BRAKES

This form of brake is specially designed for neatness and efficiency in connection with our curved tube "Ladies' Imperial Rover" and has been greatly improved and strengthened for 1904 models. It will be seen from the illustration that the brake is actuated by a stranded wire running through the handlebar for the inverted lever into the adjusting tube, thence from the socket of frame over a pulley in the bottom lug and through the backbone tube to the bracket, where it is connected to a specially designed lever and brake fork.

In 1905 there was an illustration of the *Imperial* gearcase and a eulogy of the Sturmey-Archer three-speed bub. There was also one of the pedals shown in the 1904 catalogue for use on *Imperial Rovers* with a note that it was a new and improved form of pedal specially produced for use on our cycles for season 1905!

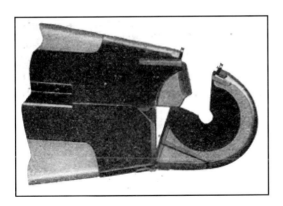

### IMPERIAL ROVER GEAR CASE

The Gear Cases fitted to "Imperial Rover" Cycles are made with a hinged end, as illustrated. In this way, by the removal of a screw, the back wheel can be taken out without disturbing the Gear Case in any way.

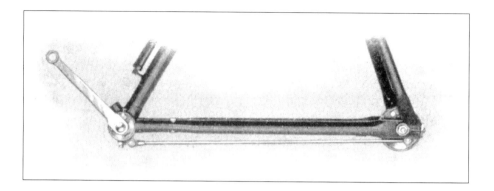

**BACK-PEDAL BRAKE** - We show here our method of fixing a back-pedal Band or Rim Brake, which, although not adopted as a standard pattern, can be supplied to order.

PEDAL. - A new and improved form of Pedal specially produced for use on our "Imperial Rover" cycles for season 1904.
[Fitted to all 1905 Rover Cycles]

METEOR WRENCH. - We are producing this very serviceable little tool in three sizes, as follows:-

| | |
|---|---|
| Cycle wrench | 3/- |
| Motor-Cycle wrench | 7/6 |
| Motor-Car or general engineering wrench, | 12/6 |

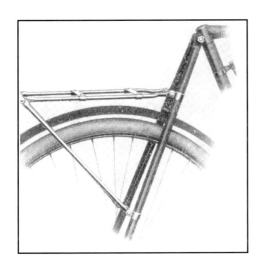

**LUGGAGE CARRIER** - Recognising the scarcity of a really reliable carrier, we have decided to put this on the market at the low price of 7/6 each. The stays and main supports of this are made of tubing. It has been thoroughly tested, having been used by Mr. R. L. Jefferson on his ever-to-be-remembered journeys to Irkustsk, the capital of Siberia, Khiva, &c.

## 1906

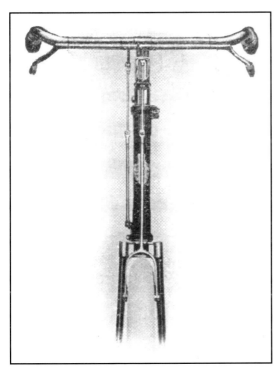

## The Rover Roller Brake

Outside lever brakes were fitted to "Imperial Roadsters" and "Ladies'" models as being "so much more satisfactory than the usual inverted brakes, being neater and having the great advantage of ease to remedy any flaw or breakage".

Outside brake levers fitted to *Imperials* only in 1905 were now used on all models.

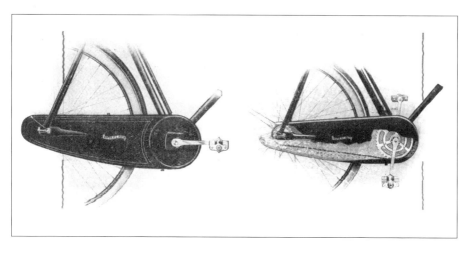

## The "Rover" Oil Bath Case

The "Rover" Oil Bath Case was standard on "Imperials" except "Light Roadster" and "Path Racer". It could also be fitted to "Royal" & "Rover" patterns at a slight extra cost. *[Being soldered to the frame it was following Sunbeam's development of the Carter but needed two fluid ounces of oil where the Sunbeam used only one.]*

*Left: 1911. E. Payne. The Worcester Wonder The best English rider on grass. Holder Talbot Memorial Trophy amd Grangetown Cup.*

*Right: 1911. E. T. Ryan Polytechnic C.C. 1 mile Champion Southern Counties, Middlesex and LASSO 100 Guinea Cup*

In 1908 the full range of Rover handlebars was shown, a range which may surprise many of our readers. Unfortunately no dimensions were given, but it is clear that most riders would have been able to find a bar to suit them whether they were sedately praffling or scorching.

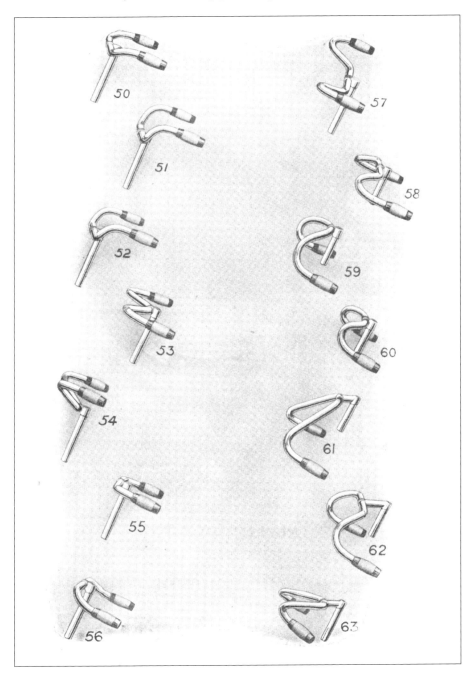

# The Rover Steering Head Tubes

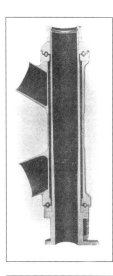

Attention is drawn to the manner in which the main tube of the steering head of Rover cycles is tapered. By the employment of this tapered tube, great strength is given to that part of the head where the stresses are most pronounced. All road shocks are encountered by this reinforcement at the point most requisite. Ease of steering is a sine qua non, and the careful manner in which the adjustments are effected ensures perfect steering without the slightest "play" at the ball races.

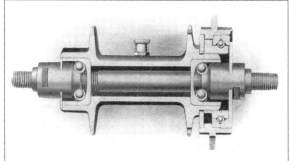

*Back Wheel Bearing and Free-Wheel Clutch*

## The Rover Wheel Bearings.

Extra-large balls ($5/16"$) are employed in the Rover back and front wheel bearings and free-wheel clutch, while cones and cups are specially and most carefully machined and hardened. The fitting and adjustment of all parts is finely accurate, so that while there is no play of the ball races, perfect spinning freedom is secured.

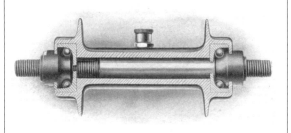

*Front Wheel Hub with Spindle, etc.*

# Rover Brakework

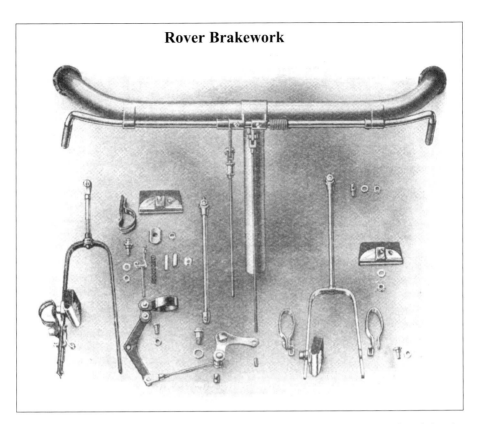

Not only is the brakework of Rover cycles exceptionally neat and well fitted, but its efficiency is beyond all question. On the back brakes attention is called to the ball joint on the top of the main rod, which enables the handle-bar to be swung to any angle without straining the tension of the rod, and also to the facile manner in which the front brake shoes can be removed form the stirrups. The back brake is of more than ordinary merit; by compressing the spring guides, the stirrups disengage instantaneously from the permanent studs, enabling the whole of the brakework to be swung clear of the wheel, which can then be removed if required for any purpose.

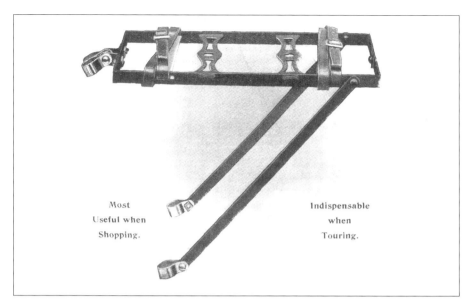

## The Rover Back Carrier

This extra at 3/- (15p) acclaimed the manufacture by British labour using British materials in the Rover Works.

*[This is obviously a knock at cheap imports]*

## 1911

Page seven of the catalogue gives details of "How the 'Rover' is made". The major change illustrated was the front fork with oval section at the top, where the greatest direct strain is, and taper-to-round nearer the fork ends,

A selection of six lamps were illustrated, three oil, the rest gas-powered by calcium carbide and water. Although listed as "Rover Lamps" it is doubtful that they were actually manufactured by them.

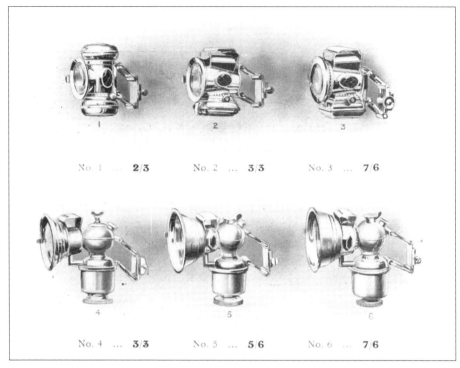

| No. 1 ... **2/3** | No. 2 ... **3/3** | No. 3 ... **7/6** |
| No. 4 ... **3/3** | No. 5 ... **5/6** | No. 6 ... **7/6** |

**1912 Rover Specialities**

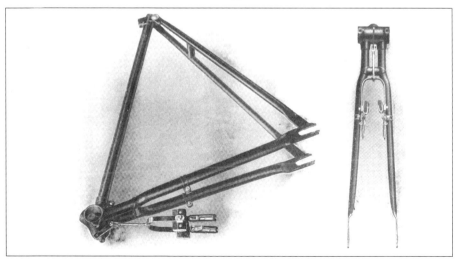

These views illustrate the strong but neat design of the Rover back brake; easily cleaned or adjusted, and quickly detached should it be necessary to remove the back wheel for tyre troubles.

# Rover Handle-bars.

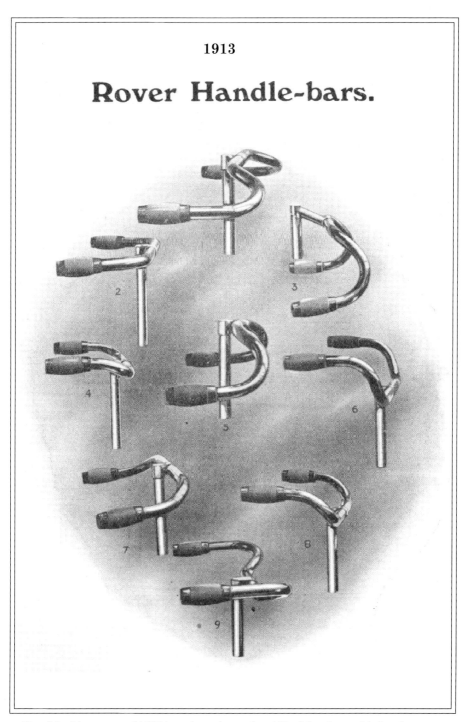

*Six of the 14 patterns of 1908 have been dropped and No. 9 has been added to the range.*

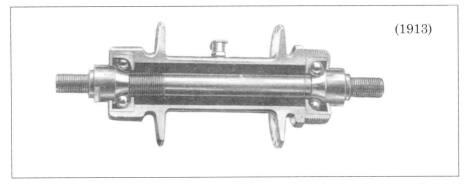

(1913)

The Rover hubs, made in one piece of solid metal, illustrated above, showing the bearings of finest possible steel, thoroughly protected from dirt and wet.

*[Comparison with the 1910 versions shows distinctive annular grooves next to the flanges, another useful dating feature]*

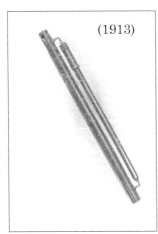

(1913)

Left: The Rover Pump Clips and Pump, the clips being brazed to the frame; a very sound and serviceable fitment.

**1915**

Right: Boxed fork crown with Domed Top.

(1915)

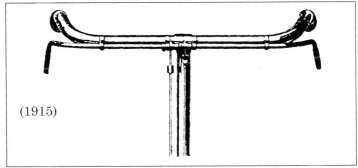

(1915)

Notice the clean design and neat appearance with brake lugs brazed to the handlebar.

*Six Rovers and Riders ready for action.*
*Hawick, c1889*

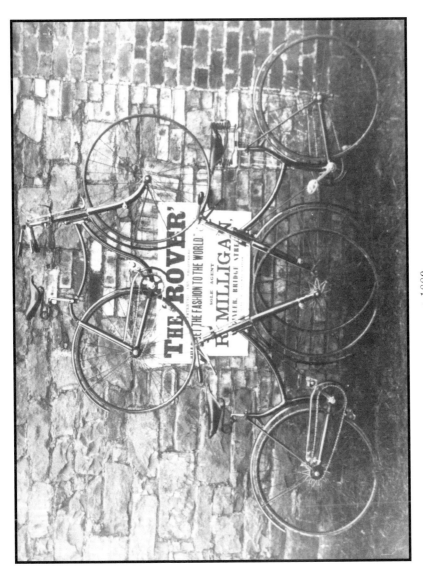

Popular (semi-diamond)

c 1889
"New Light Rover"

Popular (semi-diamond)

*Above: c1887 Three Rovers. The Rover No. 1 without footrests.*
*Below: c1893 A Rover No. 1 of 1887 with footrests and a Psycho Racer.*

*Above: Three Campbelltown ladies. A c1899 Lady's Rover on the right.*

*Below: A proud ten year old Keith Marfell with his brand new Rover Youth's bicycle outside his father's shop in Moorland Road, Weston-Super-Mare c1920.*

# PART 5 - OTHER CYCLES, 1885 ONWARDS

After the success of the Rover Safety bicycle the company continued experimenting with other designs, probably in the hope that they might find another trend-setter. Here are some of these machines.

---

# The "Roamer" Tricycle.

1888 PATTERN.

(Patented and Registered.)

"I am a roamer bold and gay,
Who thro' the world have danced my way,
From Poland to the Irish Sea
Do I know all and all know me."—OLD SONG.

THE " Roamer " is our very latest and most improved Tricycle. It is fitted with four bearings to the axle and also a *stay rod* running across below the axle, which is connected to, and supported by, the centre bearings ; this prevents any deflection of the axle or any opening of the gearing box, and is a most essential point, as any tube bent to a bridge-like shape on being pressed down at the centre opens at the ends, thus causing a great strain upon the bearings. This Machine is also fitted with Starley's new Patent Spring Connection, which absorbs all vibration. Such advantages are not found in any other tricycle. This Machine is steered by a handle-bar similar to the " Rover " Bicycle, thus giving the direct pull-action, which is most essential for mounting hills with the least possible amount of exertion. The position is a great improvement over that of the ordinary small front-wheel steerers, being easy and natural, and with the non-vibrating springs, forms the best tricycle at present before the public.

SPECIFICATION.—A central-geared non-vibrating front-steering tricycle ; 36in. side and 26in. front wheels, geared to 54in. (unless otherwise ordered) ; tyres, ⅞in. ; patent double-driving balance gear ; adjustable ball bearings to all running parts ; four bearings to axle ; Starley's patent detachable cranks ; band brake ; adjustable handles ; vertical seat-pillar adjustment ; finished in best black enamel, or painted in three colours, and all bright parts plated.

## Price £25.

### New Pattern for 1889, with Ball-bearing Links, £26 10s.

EXTRAS.—Ball pedals, 15/- Crates, 4/-, not returnable.

See Spring Frame *re* New Link Connection.

---

*1887/8 tricycle version of the 'Special Rover' favoured by Rt. Hon. Viscount Bury, President of NCU (see fig. 25).*

# THE "METEOR" TANDEM

This Machine is made to meet the demand for a good, sound, strong, safe Tandem, suitable for touring purposes; is easily mounted and dismounted from behind, and can be pushed up hills, with the front rider seated, without a stoppage. It is also a most convenient Machine for carrying luggage.

Fitted with ball bearings to all wheels, plated hubs, handles, seat rods, etc. Enamelled and lined in two colours. Powerful band brake, which can be applied by both riders. 42in. or 46in. wheels. 1in. best rubber tyres. Roller pedals. Plain case-hardened bearings to crank-shaft.

### PRICE .... .... .... .... £30.

EXTRAS. - Arab springs, 5/- each. Ball bearing pedals, £1 each crank.
Ball bearing crank-shaft, 15/- each shaft.
Fitted with the Crypto two-speed gear, price £7 7s.

*Another attempt to utilise the Coventry Chair (see fig. 17), but this time the passenger also pedalled (1887).*

# THE "METEOR" CONVERTIBLE TANDEM.

The rapidity with which the popular "Rover" Safety Bicycle has come to the front during the past twelve months has induced us to put on the market an entirely new Tandem, with "Rover" steering and large front wheel. The demand for a first-class Convertible Tandem, which, while possessing all the stability of a single tricycle, can yet be confidently used in its double form without any fear of collapse, is a continually increasing one, and in the present machine we think we have succeeded in attaining the desired end without sacrificing either lightness of weight or thorough strength throughout in the construction of the machine.

**Price** ... ... ... **£35 : 0 : 0**

SPECIFICATION.—Driving Wheels, 40in.; Steering Wheel, 30in.; concentrically adjustable Ball Bearings to Main Axle, Crank Axles and Front Wheel; Tubing—best weldless steel throughout; Starley's patent detachable Cranks; best moulded Tyres; patent Springs, adjustable Handles and Seats; patent suspension Saddles; butt-ended Spokes; rat-trap or rubber Pedals Painted in two colours; Plated Hubs, Handles, Seat-rods, Pedals, Lamp Bracket, Bearings and Bolts.

*Ball Pedals £2 extra. If desired, an attachment to enable both riders to steer can be fitted for 15s. extra.*

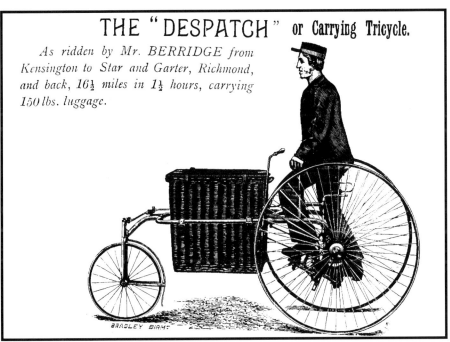

THE "DESPATCH" or Carrying Tricycle.

*As ridden by Mr. BERRIDGE from Kensington to Star and Garter, Richmond, and back, 16½ miles in 1½ hours, carrying 150 lbs. luggage.*

1887

*1888. Singers seem to have produced the first manumotive tricycle for the handicapped cyclist but Rovers were not long in providing a similar machine.*

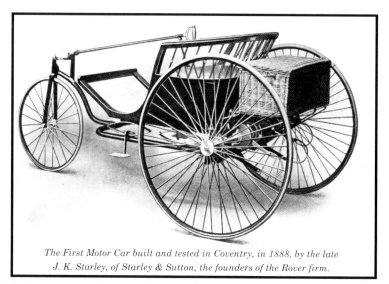

*The First Motor Car built and tested in Coventry, in 1888, by the late*
*J. K. Starley, of Starley & Sutton, the founders of the Rover firm.*

*In 1888 the Coventry Chair, which had been converted into a Despatch carrier, was fitted with an electric motor and storage battery. This was probably the first British motorcar. As British law prohibited the use of motorised vehicles the tricycle was taken to Boulogne for trials. As it was not put into production it may be assumed that those trials were unsuccessful. The year 1998 saw the 50th anniversary of the Land Rover, as well as the 110th of Rover's first car.*

*1889. The* Despatch *has "double-driving balance gear" and a riding position enabling the rider to push the machine clear of the pedals etc.*

266

# THE "ROVER" SOCIABLE.

## SUITABLE FOR LADY AND GENTLEMAN OR TWO LADIES.

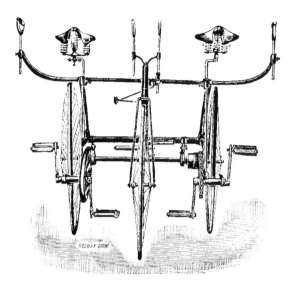

**SPECIFICATION.**—26in. front steering wheel, ¾in. tire; 28in. driving wheels, ⅞in. tires, geared to 53in.; Starley's patent double-driving gear; adjustable ball bearings to all running parts; Starley's patent detachable cranks; powerful band brake; independent handle and vertical seat-pillar adjustment; ball pedals; finished black enamel, and lined two colours; plated parts.

## PRICE £35.

**Extras.**—Hollow rims, **30/-**  ⅞in. tires to front wheel, **7/6**   Gold lining, £.1   Crates, **15/-** each, not returnable.   Also fitted with the outside handles removable, so as to reduce the width, for storing.

*This appeared in the catalogues from 1889 to 1891*

This model has not been found illustrated in any catalogue or other cycling publication, but the head badge shows that it must have been made in 1895 or 1896. It was found in the stables of a large house in Holland. A 1930 Cycle Tax plate indicated its last year of use before restoration and participation in the 1985 Rover Centenary.

269

*An Unknown Rover*

*This drawing is a copy of an old photograph of what is clearly a Rover bicycle of the late 1880s, but no such machine was ever listed in a Rover catalogue, and there was no mention of it in the publications of that period. Unfortunately, no information on it is available; the photograph bears no date and the background is unidentifiable. But if anyone ever asks whether a lever-driven Rover was made the truthful answer is yes. Whether it was made by J. K. Starley & Co. or by an enthusiastic amateur is not so easy to say; but the odds seem to be on the amateur.*

*This is a photograph which was among some letters from H W Bartleet to J. K. Starley II concerning an article Bartleet was intending to write for the cycling press. Although there is no mention of this machine, it has many Rover features, notably the rear forks and chain-adjusters.*

*Above: Alie Gerrits with the tandem shown on pages 268-269*

*Above and Right: Another tandem still undergoing restoration. No head badge, but all the features of post 1898 Rovers. No catalogue or Cycling Press references have been found.*

# PART 6 - ROVER'S RETURN

## By Tony Hadland

## Moulton and Rover

As we have seen, the Rover motor company began with bicycle manufacture. Conversely engineer Alex Moulton's career started with power-driven vehicles. His interest in cycle design arose only in early middle age.

There is a strong symbiotic relationship between Rover and Moulton. For the last four decades millions of Moulton-designed suspension units have been fitted to cars produced by what is now the Rover group. These range from the classic Mini (still in production after nearly 40 years) to the MGF sports car of the 1990s. It is therefore fitting that Rover returned to its roots via a Moulton bicycle.

## The Key Players

This process involved a number of people in both the USA and UK. Key among them were Matt Dekker, John Thomas and Adrian Williams. Each realised the analogies between the design functionality and market position of:

- the fully suspended separable spaceframe Moulton ATB/APB among bicycles, and

- the Range Rover among cars.

## 1992 - Matt Dekker and the Germ of an Idea

In spring 1988 the Alex Moulton All Terrain Bicycle (AM ATB) was launched in the USA[1]. This followed much development work in the Seattle area of Washington State involving Angle Lake Cyclery, then the USA's premier Moulton dealer. At the time Matthew L. Dekker, now the US distributor for Moulton bicycles, was a product manager at Angle Lake.

Over several years Matt Dekker noticed that a number of owners of Alex Moulton bicycles also owned Range Rovers. In 1992 he therefore proposed a joint marketing plan with Range Rover North America. This involved Range Rover introducing their clients to Moulton ATBs and referring leads back to Angle Lake Cyclery.

Accordingly on the afternoon of 5 August 1992 Matt telephoned Bill Baker at Range Rover. At Bill Baker's suggestion Matt sent details of the proposal to Bill's colleague Bob Rolland. However, the idea was not taken up by Range Rover, which shortly afterwards changed its name to Land Rover North America, Inc.

# John J. Thomas - Great Minds Think Alike

A few months later long-time Moulton enthusiast John J. Thomas stopped at Angle Lake for a repair to the rear suspension pivot of his AM ATB. John is a Briton who has lived in the USA since 1980. His home is in Orange County, California, a 20 mile cycle ride from the Land Rover office in Aliso Viejo.

At the time of his visit to Angle Lake, John Thomas was a field engineer and trainer. He had heard that Land Rover was looking for a bike to form part of their range of branded merchandise. An active member of the British-based Veteran-Cycle Club, John thought it would be good to launch a Rover-branded bicycle in 1995, to coincide with the original company's 110th anniversary.

John considered the Moulton ATB to be a good fit for this purpose. In his view it was analogous to the Range Rover, being a unique British design with great suspension and commanding a premium price. He mentioned the idea to Matt Dekker who, as we have seen, had already been thinking along these lines. Matt recognised that he now had a useful contact inside Land Rover who was also a Moulton enthusiast.

# 1993 - Interbike

In summer 1993 Matt Dekker realised that things were changing at Angle Lake Cyclery. In particular his speciality, Moulton sales, were in decline due to "inadvertent de-emphasis". As career insurance he therefore decided to travel at his own expense to the Interbike trade show at Las Vegas, Nevada that September. His aim was to maintain industry contacts and perhaps make some new ones. Matt's decision to attend Interbike '93 proved seminal in two respects. It was there he first encountered:

- Adrian Williams, managing director of W. R .Pashley Limited of Stratford-upon-Avon. He was promoting the Moulton APB (All Purpose Bicycle) derived from the Moulton ATB and built under licence by Pashley on jigs designed and made by Moulton.

- The Sachs 3x7 hub, a three-speed epicyclic hub gear matched to a seven-speed derailleur sprocket cluster.

Matt Dekker acquired one of the Sachs 3x7 hubs and tested its durability. He did this by recruiting Tom Tuling, a Seattle area Moulton ATB owner and hard core cycle commuter. After a month of very tough daily use, Tom reported that the hub performed flawlessly.

The 3x7 test coincided with the news that Angle Lake Cyclery was being put up for sale. In Matt's own words, "Since the AM business had been falling off at Angle Lake, and I liked what I saw with the APB14 and the other Pashley product at that '93 Interbike show, I decided to start Dekker Service to import and distribute APBs and make AMs, parts and accessories available to all dealers."

# Support from Alex Moulton and Adrian Williams

As a way of expanding Moulton visibility and business for Dekker Service, Matt Dekker sought the views of Alex Moulton and Adrian Williams on the idea of a Land Rover badged Moulton APB. Both were enthusiastic and offered their support.

At about this time Matt learned of the deal between German car maker BMW and the US folding bicycle company Montague. Shortly afterwards BMW bought Rover. John Thomas advised Matt that this was unlikely to affect the Land Rover APB proposal, as Rover would probably want to maintain a separate brand identity.

# 1994 - The Theme Develops

Matt Dekker took part in the Anaheim Interbike show in September 1994. After this he began experimenting with Land Rover badging of an APB. Taking the blue APB14 Shimano Plus that he had exhibited at the show, he stripped off the decals and replaced them with gold Land Rover decals on the front fork and seat tube. A Land Rover head badge was created from a cover plate logo normally used on the Safari Cage (roll cage) of the North American specification Land Rover Defender 90. John Thomas assisted considerably by providing not only support and contacts, but also the camera-ready logos and type for making decals.

In October 1994 John Thomas took the blue APB to Land Rover North America's corporate headquarters in Lanham, Maryland. He left the machine with Rob Myers, the company's merchandise and sales development manager.

After several months of use and evaluation, Rob Myers returned it with his views. Although he found the bicycle interesting, it was not a "real" mountain bike. It was insufficiently macho yet more expensive than Land Rover's target price point of $1,000. And it was up to Land Rover's Solihull-based English headquarters to determine which cycle, if any, would bear the Land Rover badge.

Undeterred, Matt continued to work on a target specification for the Land Rover APB. In December 1994 he submitted a component schedule to Adrian Williams at Pashley. The production version of the Land Rover APB uses very similar componentry to that originally proposed by Matt Dekker.

From Rob Myers at Land Rover North America, Matt obtained the names of contacts at Design Rights International (DRI), the company newly responsible for licensing the Land Rover name for use on products other than motor vehicles and parts. Matt forwarded this information to Adrian Williams.

# Adrian Williams and "New" Pashley

Adrian Williams joined W.R.Pashley Limited in 1993. Initially he lodged at a bed & breakfast run by J. K. Starley IV, whose ancestor John Kemp Starley had invented the Rover safety bicycle. This historical connection had already led Adrian to think it would be a good commercial idea to remake a link between Rover and bicycles. One possibility he considered was a replica of the original Rover bicycle.

He was also aware of the more recent link between Moulton and Rover. As Pashley was already building the Moulton APB under licence, Adrian started looking for contacts with whom to develop ideas.

In December 1994 Adrian Williams was involved in a management buy-out of the Pashley company. The DRI contact information from Matt Dekker therefore arrived at a very opportune time. Better yet, soon after this DRI themselves contacted Adrian, as they were keen to find a cycle for Land Rover to market.

# 1995 - Negotiations with DRI

DRI expressed interest in the Moulton APB but were also considering the possibility of Pashley supplying a conventional mountain bike. Land Rover themselves strongly favoured the mountain bike approach but Adrian Williams questioned this. He pointed out that other car manufacturers were likely to offer mountain bikes, as seen subsequently with the Volvo/Cannondale collaboration, and that Land Rover should lead rather than follow. Also, Pashley were not interested in a product group in decline..

Adrian therefore suggested doing something different. The Moulton APB was the most versatile option, combining sport and utility themes. He argued that, regardless of the preferences of Land Rover staff, it is the lifestyles and tastes of Land Rover owners that are most relevant. Therefore demographics must be carefully considered. These indicated that most Land Rover owners do not drive off-road to any great extent. (The popular jibe about 4x4s whose most arduous duty involves trips to the hypermarket contains more than a grain of truth). Adrian therefore reinforced the views of Matt Dekker and John Thomas that the APB was eminently suitable for adoption by Land Rover.

Adrian Williams persuaded DRI to let him mock-up a product before they made a recommendation to Land Rover. The mock-up was based largely on Matt Dekker's specification, supplemented by input and review by others. Among these was Hilary Stone, a consultant to Pashley and then also Technical Editor of *Cycling Plus* magazine.

Adrian also started developing ideas around the graphics. At first he intended to use only the Land Rover house colours (British Racing Green and ivory - one frame colour version based on each, with lettering reversed out). However, the ivory proved too tame. Adrian recalled the vivid golden yellow of one version of the original Moulton ATB and decided to try that instead of ivory. He had been struck by its visual impact when he saw a Moulton-ATB being ridden along the Bristol-Bath cycleway.

DRI were happy with this proposal. To reinforce the case, Adrian Williams mapped the Land Rover marque values, as set out in an in-house manual, against the proposed Land Rover APB.

## Support from the Land Rover Marketing Director

The next step involved Adrian Williams making a presentation of the mock-up bike to the then Land Rover brand marketing director. He was Russell Turnham, an Australian who made his name with the Land Rover Experience showroom concept in the USA.

Russell Turnham repeated that a number of people at Land Rover really wanted a conventional mountain bike. However, Adrian again argued the need for Land Rover to differentiate its bicycle from the offerings of other car manufacturers. This was a little ahead of the 1995 Frankfurt Motor Show at which Adrian rightly suspected that a number of car manufacturers would be marketing mountain bikes. Russell Turnham finally agreed with Adrian's proposal, despite the internal opposition at Land Rover.

DRI therefore signed up formally to the Land Rover (Moulton) APB concept. This led to feverish work by Pashley for the Frankfurt Motor Show in September 1995.

Meanwhile a yellow Land Rover APB without decals was delivered to Matt Dekker just in time for the 1995 Interbike Expo at Anaheim, California. It was there that Matt Dekker learned from Adrian Williams that Land Rover had finally approved the design. Adrian had to leave Anaheim before the end of the show to join Hilary Stone in England and then travel on to Frankfurt for the motor show.

## Marketing and Distribution

Pashley proposed that the Land Rover APB should be distributed first and foremost via cycle dealers, and only secondarily through Land Rover franchisees. In the latter case there had to be a linkage with a cycle dealer for technical support. Otherwise, there could be major problems, as had been highlighted by the BMW/Montague partnership. The bike must be properly set up and serviced before customer use.

Adrian Williams devised a special display stand for the Land Rover bike, involving camouflage netting to give a rugged outdoor look and keep the bike off the floor and at eye level. After discussing the merits of the bike, it could be removed from the stand and would immediately show the ease of frame separability. Other incentives were devised, such as giving a free Land Rover watch with each bike.

*Above: The Land Rover APB*

*Left and below: Front and rear suspension details*

The Land Rover APB was one of the first Land Rover products to evolve with DRI involvement. Accessories and complementary products had hitherto been developed and marketed via the Land Rover parts department.

Moulton distributors in Germany and Japan took up the product very swiftly. To the surprise of many observers, it soon became the best-selling model in the APB range, despite initially being the dearest. At the time of writing (February 1998) sales in the southern hemisphere are coming on stream, particularly South Africa and Australia. This minimises seasonal production variations.

Suggestions that the Moulton-based Land Rover APB was "not macho enough" were countered by demonstrations. One of the most impressive was at the 1996 Interbike Expo at Anaheim. A prelude to the main show comprised a "Dirt Demo Day". This allowed dealers and their staff to try various cycles in a rented county park. Adrian Williams, Matt Dekker and others were there among all the major big-wheeled cycle makers, such as Trek and Specialized. Matt Dekker recalls:

"While I was a bit apprehensive about showing the 20" wheeled APB among 'serious' mountain bikes, virtually every test rider was amazed that the APB did as well as it did in the serious off road trails. Most commented that it was more than capable on the trails and quite suitable for what most people would use a mountain bike for."

Alex Moulton's attitude to the Land Rover APB development was very supportive throughout the process. He was delighted by the idea, building as it did on his old connections with the car industry, and specifically the Rover group. His main stipulation was that the AM head badge should be retained.

The Land Rover APB is offered in golden yellow or British racing green. At the time of writing it retails in the UK at a recommended price of £899.

## The Range Expands

After the launch of the Land Rover APB, DRI were still under pressure from Land Rover for a big-wheeled machine. The North American Land Rover operation also wanted a mountain bike. Meanwhile mountain bike suppliers were beating a path to Land Rover offering their products.

Product range extension had been envisaged since Adrian Williams' first meeting with DRI. Therefore, Pashley supported the idea that, whilst the Moulton APB with its unique separable spaceframe and dual suspension would remain the definitive Land Rover bike, others could now be developed.

Accordingly Pashley attended a committee meeting of Land Rover brand management people and received an undeveloped request for a "mountain bike". Pashley's product design team already had a prototype full suspension

MTB in the latter stages of development. For the time it was both radical and novel. Indeed similar designs have since been seen from manufacturers such as X-Lite and Rotec. Pashley , however, made a policy decision to shelve the project and not enter the MTB scene, principally because it was felt that the market was in decline. Also, even if the machine were fitted with the best components and was "Best in Class", it would be out of style in the market place in six months and difficult to market.

Pashley were keen that, as in the case of the Land Rover APB, the product they developed would "lead rather than follow".

## 1996 - Development of the Land Rover XCB

Demographics identified people in the Land Rover market profile (40-50 years of age) investing substantial sums in dual-suspension bikes, yet finding them highly unsatisfactory on the road. In particular, it was apparent that ride comfort was becoming increasingly important to customers.

During 1994/95 Pashley had developed their range of Tube Rider/ Paramount range of bicycles. These have a non-folding frame inspired by the BSA military folding cycles of World War 2 . By this time Pashley also had on the workforce a number of keen mountain bike riders from whom to seek input. The company therefore took the Tube Rider frame style and developed it. They thus evolved a product that initially looked like a mountain bike but which had a number of distinguishing features apparent on closer inspection. Within a month a working prototype was created, thanks to good co-operation from component suppliers such as the British specialist firm USE.

Pashley went to the next Land Rover brand meeting without saying that they had created the prototype. They wheeled it in and dramatically placed it on the table, emphasising as Adrian Williams puts it, the machine's "wow factor". It was finished again in golden yellow and with blue-green Michelin tyres. The committee was suitably impressed. Adrian then took them through the brand values, mapping out why this was a potential Land Rover product.

He pointed out that the first reaction of the consumer is "mountain bike ... no it's different" and they liked the different style. This encourages closer inspection of the technical features and a test ride confirms the ride comfort and control. "This is the business!". In this way Pashley tried to emulate in bicycle terms the consumer appraisal of the vehicle it represented. The result is a consumer friendly MTB but with interesting technical features, such as disc brakes. It also has a something of the speedway image, which is both different and "retro". It rides well on the road but is also good for cross-country. It is a good all round leisure bike.

At this time no other manufacturer was producing such machines, which were rather like a cross-country cruiser. The committee agreed to the Pashley proposal and also that a child's version should be produced. (The latter, together with another machine for adults, was being tested when this book was being printed.)

## Launch of the Land Rover XCB

The resulting Land Rover XCB (Cross Country Bicycle) was first shown at the National Cycle Show in February 1997 at the National Exhibition Centre, Birmingham. It was released in summer 1997 and was fully online by late summer. The machine was somewhat ahead of the market. Subsequently several other manufacturers introduced cross-country cruisers.

Like the Moulton Land Rover APB, the XCB uses a Sachs 3x7 transmission. However, instead of dual wheel suspension it uses an air-damped telescopic front fork and elastomer-sprung seat pillar, both by USE. Braking is via Sachs disc brakes. The frame neither folds nor separates. Hence, unlike the Moulton, the XCB cannot as readily be stowed in the Land Rover's luggage bay. Frame colours are as for the Land Rover APB but the price, at £1499, is considerably higher.

## Conclusion

The return of the Rover brand to the world of cycling via a Moulton design was most appropriate. This was not only because of Alex Moulton's long involvement with Rover cars, but also because of the analogies between the Moulton APB and the Land Rover in their respective markets.

How the Moulton came to be the first and primary Land Rover bicycle owes much to the involvement and enthusiasm of Matt Dekker, Adrian Williams and John Thomas. Without their combination of brand awareness, inventiveness and sustained enthusiasm Land Rover would still have marketed a bicycle. But it would have been some run of the mill mountain bike that by now would probably have been deleted from the range. This would have given the message that Land Rover were merely climbing on a fashionable bandwagon, rather than emphasising brand values such as originality, versatility, fitness for purpose and British origin.

While additions are now being made to the Land Rover bicycle range, the Moulton Land Rover APB remains the core product. Thereby Rover have a link with cycle development from the early safety bicycle to an evolutionary stage significantly beyond it.

---

[1] *For the design history of the AM ATB and the inception of the Moulton APB, see chapters 7 and 8 of* The Spaceframe Moultons *by Tony Hadland, published in 1994 by Tony Hadland.*

[2] *For details of the BSA military cycle, see pages 26-28 of the book* It's In The Bag! *by Tony Hadland and John Pinkerton, published in 1996 by Dorothy Pinkerton.*

# APPENDIX 1
# ROVER CYCLES 1900 - 1925: A LIST OF MODELS AND THEIR PRICES

We have listed and whenever possible illustrated every detail of the production of Rover cycles, with most of the information coming from the firm's catalogues. As we have already noted, what appeared in them may not always have been what was on sale, but the general picture is an accurate one.

For the benefit of owners of Rovers made from 1900 to 1925 we have listed all the catalogued models and their prices. A study of these will show how the cycle industry was affected by the end of the Society Boom of the late 1890s, the 1914-18 Great War and the Boom and Bust cycle of the 1920s which, together with the popularisation of the motorcar, led to the end of production and sales of Rover cycles. We have done our best to be accurate, but should any readers find errors or omissions we should be pleased to hear from them.

Prices in the following list are quoted in pounds sterling, shillings and pence, in some cases guineas (g) = £1 1s.

| | 1900 | 1901 | 1902 | 1903 | 1904 | 1905 | 1906 | 1907 | 1908 |
|---|---|---|---|---|---|---|---|---|---|
| **IMPERIAL** | | | | | | | | | |
| **L & G** Roadster | 20 | 20 | C | 18g | 18g | 15g | 16g | 14g | 14g |
| Light Rdtr | 20 | 20 | A | 18g | 18g | 15g | 16g | 14g | 14g |
| Road Racer | 19 | 19 | T | 18g | 12g | to | order | | to order |
| Path Racer | - | 19 | A | 18g | 12g | 12g | 12g | 12g | 12g |
| Cob | 20 | 20 | L | - | - | - | - | - | - |
| **ROVER** | | | O | | | | | | |
| **L & G** Light Rdtr | 16g | 15g | U | 15g | 12g | 10g | 10g | 8g | 8g |
| Roadster | - | - | E | 15g | 12g | 10g | 10g | 8g | 8g |
| Ladies | | | | | | | | | |
| Light Roadster Special | | - | N | 15g | - | - | - | - | - |
| Road Racer | 15g | 14g | O | - | - | - Sloping Top Tube | | | 8g |
| Path Racer | 15g | - | T | - | - | - | - | - | - |
| **METEOR** | | | P | | **NO.1 METEOR ROVER** | | | | |
| **L & G** Light Rdtr | 12g | 12g | R | 12g | 10g | 8g | - | - | - |
| Cob | 12g | 12g | I | Rdstr. | 10g | 8g | 8 15 | - | - |
| Road Racer | 11g | 12g | C | 12g | - | - | 8 15 | - | - |
| Path/Road Racer | - | - | E | - | - | 7.15 | - | - | - |
| | | | D | | | | | | |
| **METEOR No.2** | | | | | | | | | |
| **L & G** Light Rdtr | 10g | 10g | " | 10g | - | - | - | - | - |
| Road Racer | 10g | 10g | " | 10g | - | - | - | - | - |
| **ROYAL** | | | | | | | | | |
| **L & G** Roadster | - | - | - | - | 15g | 12g | 12g | 10g | 10g |
| Light Rdtr | - | - | - | - | 15g | 12g | 12g | 10g | 10g |
| Road Racer | - | - | - | - | - | - | - | - | - |
| **JUVENILE** | | | | | | | | | |
| Boys | - | - | - | - | - | - | - | - | 5 |
| Girls | - | - | - | - | - | - | - | - | 5g |
| **SIX GUINEA** | | | | | | | | | |
| Roadster, Ladys & Road Racer. | - | - | - | - | - | - | - | - | 6g |
| **POPULAR** | | | | | | | | | |
| Roadster, Ladys & Road Racer. | - | - | - | - | - | - | - | - | - |
| Special Road Racer. | - | - | - | - | - | - | - | - | - |
| **MODEL "A"** | | | | | | | | | |
| Gents | - | - | - | - | - | - | - | - | - |
| Ladys | - | - | - | - | - | - | - | - | - |
| **R. I. C.** | | | | | | | | | |
| Gents. only | - | - | - | - | - | - | - | - | - |
| **THREE SPEED** | | | | | | | | | |
| Roadster | - | - | - | - | - | - | - | - | - |
| Ladys | - | - | - | - | - | - | - | - | - |
| **TRADESMAN** | | | | | | | | | |
| Gents only | - | - | - | - | - | - | - | - | - |
| **ALL WEATHER** | | | | | | | | | |
| Gents | - | - | - | - | - | - | - | - | - |
| Ladys | - | - | - | - | - | - | - | - | - |
| **CHAINLESS** | | | | | | | | | |
| Ladys & gents | - | - | - | - | - | - | - | - | - |
| **MILITARY** | | | | | | | | | |
| Gents only | - | - | - | - | - | - | - | - | - |

| | | 1909 | 1910 | 1911 | 1912 | 1913 | 1914 | 1915 | 1916 | 1917 |
|---|---|---|---|---|---|---|---|---|---|---|
| **IMPERIAL** | | | | | | | | | | |
| **L & G** | Roadster | 14 | 11 15 | 14 | 14 | 10g | 10g | 10g | 12g | 14 5 |
| | Light Rdtr | 14 | 11 15 | 13 *Imperial Rover Special | | | - | - | - | - |
| | Road Racer | - | 11 5 | 12 | 12 | - | - | - | - | - |
| | Path Racer | 8g | 8 10 | 9 10 | 9 10 | 8 5 | 8 5 | 7 10 | 7 10 | - |
| | Cob | - | - | - | - | - | - | - | - | - |
| **ROVER** | | | | | | | | | | |
| **L & G** | Light Rdtr | 8g | - | - | - | - | - | - | - | - |
| | Roadster | 8g | 6 10 | 8 10 | 8 10 | 6 17 6 | 6 10 | 6 15 | 8g | 10g |
| | Ladies | | 6 10 | 8 10 | 8 10 | 6 17 6 | 6 15 | 6 19 6 | 8 12 6 | 10 15 |
| | Light Roadster | - | - | - | - | - | - | - | - | - |
| | Road Racer | 8g | 6 10 | 7 10 | 7 10 | 5 15 | 5.19.6 | 5.19.6 | 7 10 | - |
| | Special Road Racer | - | 7 10 | 7 10 | 7 10 | 5 19 6 | 5 19 6 | 5 19 6 | 7 10 | - |
| **METEOR** | | | | | | | | | | |
| **L & G** | Light Rdtr | - | - | - | - | - | - | - | - | - |
| | Cob | - | - | - | - | - | - | - | - | - |
| | Road Racer | - | - | - | - | - | - | - | - | - |
| | Path-Road | - | - | - | - | - | - | - | - | - |
| **METEOR No.2** | | | | | | | | | | |
| **L & G** | Light Rdtr | - | - | - | - | - | - | - | - | - |
| | Road Racer | - | - | - | - | - | - | - | - | - |
| **ROYAL** | | | | | | | | | | |
| **L & G** | Roadster | 10g | 8.15 | 10g | 10g | 8 10 | 8 10 | 8 10 | 10g | 12 10 |
| | Light Rdtr | 10g | - | - | - | - | Ladys | 8 15 | 10 15 | 12 15 |
| | Road Racer | 10g | - | - | - | - | - | - | - | - |
| **JUVENILE** | | | | | | | | | | |
| | Boys | 5g | 5 10 | 6 10 | 6 10 | 5g | 5g | 5g | 5 15 | 8 10 |
| | Girls | 5g | 5 10 | 6 15 | 6 15 | 5 10 | 5 10 | 5 10 | 6 | 8 15 |
| **SIX GUINEA** | | | | | | | | | | |
| | Roadster, Ladys & Road Racer- | | | - | - | - | - | - | - | - |
| **POPULAR** | | | | | | | | | | |
| | Rster, Ladys & RR | 6 10 | - | - | - | - | - | - | - | - |
| | Special Road Racer | 7g | - | - | - | - | - | - | - | - |
| **MODEL "A"** | | | | | | | | | | |
| | Gents | - | - | - | 6 15 | 5 17 6 | - | - | n p | - |
| | Ladys | - | - | - | 6 17 6 | 6 | - | - | n p | - |
| **R. I. C.** | | | | | | | | | | |
| | Gents. only | 8g | 8 15 | 10g | 9 10 | 8 15 | 8.15 | 8.15 | 10g | - |
| **THREE SPEED** | | | | | | | | | | |
| | Roadster | 8g | 8 10 | 10g | 10g | - | - | 7.15 | - | - |
| | Ladys | 8g | 8 15 | 10g | 10g | - | - | 7 19 6 | - | - |
| **TRADESMAN** | | | | | | | | | | |
| | Gents only | - | 8 10 | 10g | - | - | - | 7.17.6 | 8g | - |
| **ALL WEATHER** | | | | | | | | | | |
| | Gents | - | - | 12 | 12 | 8 10 | 8 10 | 8 10 | 10 10 | 13 |
| | Ladys | - | - | - | - | 8 15 | 8 15 | 8 15 | 10 15 | 13 5 |
| **CHAINLESS** | | | | | | | | | | |
| | Ladys & Gents | - | - | - | - | 10g | 10g | 8 15 | - | - |
| **MILITARY** | | | | | | | | | | |
| | Gents only | - | - | - | - | - | - | 8 15 | - | - |

| | | 1918 | 1919 | 1920 | 1921 | 1922 | 1923 | 1924 | 1925 |
|---|---|---|---|---|---|---|---|---|---|
| **IMPERIAL** | | | | | | | | | |
| **L & G** | Roadster | ? | 20 10 | 20 10 | 20 10 | n p | 14g | 15g | 15g |
| | Light Rdtr | ? | - | - | - | - | - | - | - |
| | Road Racer | ? | 15 | - | - | - | - | - | - |
| | Path Racer | ? | 15 | 15 | 15 | n p | 10 17 6 | - | 9 10 |
| | Cob | ? | - | - | - | - | - | - | - |
| | | | | | | | | | |
| **ROVER** | | | | | | | | | |
| **L & G** | Light Rdtr | - | - | - | - | - | - | - | - |
| | Roadster | ? | ? | 16 | 16 | n c | 9 10 | 9 | - |
| | Ladies | ? | ? | 16 15 | 16 15 | n c | 9 19 6 | 9 5 | - |
| | Light Roadster | - | - | - | - | - | - | - | - |
| | Road racer | ? | ? | - | - | n c | 10 5 | - | - |
| | Path Racer | ? | ? | - | - | - | - | - | - |
| | | | | | | | | | |
| **METEOR** | | | | | | | | | |
| **ALL BLACK** | Gents | ? | ? | 16 | 16 | - | - | 7 10 | 7 10 |
| | Ladies | ? | ? | 16.15 | 16.15 | - | - | 7 15 | 7 15 |
| | Road Racer | - | - | - | - | - | - | 7 10 | 7 10 |
| | Path-Road | - | - | - | - | - | - | - | - |
| | | | | | | | | | |
| **METEOR No.2** | | | | | | | | | |
| **L & G** | Light Rdtr | - | - | - | - | - | - | - | - |
| | Road Racer | - | - | - | - | - | - | - | - |
| | | | | | | | | | |
| **ROYAL** | | | | | | | | | |
| **L & G** | Roadster | ? | ? | 18 15 | 18.15 | n c | 12g | 10g | 10g |
| | Light Rdtr | ? | ? | 19 | 19 | n c | 12g | 10g | 10g |
| | Road Racer | - | - | - | - | - | - | - | - |
| | | | | | | | | | |
| **JUVENILE** | | | | | | | | | |
| | Boys | ? | ? | 13 | 13 | n c | 7 10 | 6 10 | 6 10 |
| | Girls | ? | ? | 13 10 | 13 10 | n c | 7 19 6 | 6 17 6 | 6 17 6 |
| | | | | | | | | | |
| **SIX GUINEA** | | | | | | | | | |
| | Roadster, Ladys & Road Racer | - | | - | - | - | - | - | - |
| | | | | | | | | | |
| **POPULAR** | | | | | | | | | |
| | Roadster, Ladys & Road Racer | - | | - | - | - | - | - | - |
| | Special Road Racer | - | - | - | - | - | - | - | - |
| | | | | | | | | | |
| **MODEL "A"** | | | | | | | | | |
| | Gents | - | - | 13g | 13g | ? | 7 19 6 | - | - |
| | Ladys | - | - | 13 17 6 | 13.17.6 | ? | 8 10 | - | - |
| | | Road | Racer | 13g | 13g | - | - | - | - |
| **R. I. C.** | | | | | | | | | |
| | Gents. only | - | - | - | 19 5 | - | - | - | - |
| | | | | | | | | | |
| **THREE SPEED** | | | | | | | | | |
| | Roadster | - | - | - | - | - | - | - | - |
| | Ladys | - | - | - | - | - | - | - | - |
| | | | | | | | | | |
| **TRADESMAN** | | | | | | | | | |
| | Gents only | - | - | - | - | - | - | - | - |
| | | | | | | | | | |
| **ALL WEATHER** | | | | | | | | | |
| | Gents | ? | ? | 20 10 | 20 10 | 20 10 | - | - | - |
| | Ladys | ? | ? | 20 10 | 20 10 | 20 10 | - | - | - |
| | | | | | | | | | |
| **CHAINLESS** | | | | | | | | | |
| | Ladys & Gents | - | - | - | - | - | - | - | - |
| | | | | | | | | | |
| **MILITARY** | | | | | | | | | |
| | Gents only | - | - | - | - | - | - | - | - |

EXTRACTS FROM THE SOUVENIR PROGRAMME OF
THE ROVER CENTENARY RIDE
28TH & 29TH SEPTEMBER 1985

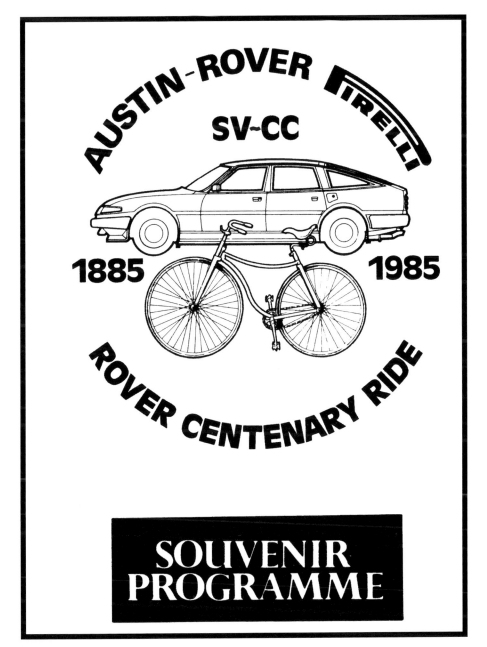

# THE ROVER CENTENARY RIDE
## 28th & 29th September, 1985

John Kemp Starley launched The Rover bicycle at the Stanley Show in January 1885, and also at the Bingley Hall Exhibition in Birmingham the following month. The market must have been just right because The Rover attracted orders from the four corners of the world.

By the Autumn of that year certain alterations and improvements had been made and to prove its worth the Rover 100 Mile race was organised; not from London to Brighton and Shoreham as announced in The Cyclist, but from Norman Cross, on the Great North Road just south of Peterborough, to Twyford; this was to fool the police who took a dim view of cycle racing on the road. The resultant records for 50 and 100 miles established the Rover for all time. The Editor of The Cyclist suitably summed it up in his phrase:- *"The Rover has set the fashion to the World"*, and this was used by Starley in his catalogues and advertising for many years.

Rover safety bicycle: 1885

Despite the fact that there had been Safetys before this date The Rover was the one which altered the path of cycle history. The high wheeled Ordinary with its rider precariously perched five foot or so above the ground may have looked graceful but many a rider took a header, cropper or imperial crowner which often left him injured and unable to ride for a considerable time. The Rover however with its seat much closer to the ground and rear wheel drive was not so easily upset. The chain drive offered the rider a choice of gearing which was predetermined on the Ordinary by the riders leg length. A greater distance was travelled with one rotation of the pedals on The Rover than even the tallest of riders could have achieved with the direct drive Ordinary.

The Rover continued to develop and the company's name was eventually changed to the Rover Cycle Co. Ltd. This had to be changed yet again when the Company had established its place in the motor cycle and car industry. Regretfully the post World War I depression caused both cycle and motorcycle to be dropped in favour of the motor car production. Today the name still lives on and as with the first Rover its products are sold in all four corners of the world.

To celebrate this Centenary, members of The Southern Veteran-Cycle Club (note the hyphen, it is the cycles that are veteran and not necessarily the members) and The Rover Sports Register are riding Rover cycles and solid tyred machines with rear chain drive from Peterborough to Birmingham. An overnight stop will be made in Rugby and visits to The Museum of British Road Transport, The National Motorcyle Museum, Bickenhill and The Museum of Science & Industry, Birmingham, these museums all having direct links with Rover cycle history.

Our thanks are extended to the Civic Dignitaries who have helped the riders on their way, the support team who have fed and watered the riders, the mechanical backup and the baggage carriers who have all made life a little more pleasant for the riders.

The sponsors Austin-Rover and Pirelli receive our special thanks because without their support it would not have been possible to organise this event. And last but not least YOU the general public for your support and interest in this event.

# WORLD FASHIONS

In the mid 1880s cyclists had two choices, the Ordinary bicycle which had developed from the heavy wooden wheeled boneshaker to a lightweight machine with front wheel size between 48" and 60" according to the riders leg length, and the Tricycle which was in some cases slower and certainly took up more room both on the road and to store.

The Ordinary (now sometimes called pennyfarthing which was a derogatory name given to it by street urchins after it had become obsolete in the early 1890s) was undoubtably a most graceful and attractive machine to behold. However the rider was often upset from his precarious perch five foot or so from the ground; the result may have been amusing to some but certainly not to the rider.

Cycle makers looked for alternatives, the Singer Xtraordinary Challenge with its lever drive offered some safety from the header over the bars but still needed some acrobatic skill to reach the saddle. Lawson & Likemans Bicyclette of 1879 had all the advantages of the Safety with rear chain drive and front wheel steering through raked forks. However invention isn't enough: the market must be right and unfortunately it wasn't right, in 1879, for a change. Cyclists were in a minority and not welcomed by the other road users with their horses or horsedrawn vehicles, so it does not seem unreasonable that the cyclists didn't want to be divided even further than they already were between bicyclists and tricyclists.

The Facile and Kangaroo achieved some success; had the Rover not come along, probably even more.

John Kemp Starley was nephew to the Father of the Cycle Industry, James Starley and on occasions these two have been mixed up. James had the beard and John the sideboards. The two had worked together and James' inventive mind in constant search for new ideas had rubbed off on John. In 1878 John set up a cycle making business with William Sutton; the latter was the account/office manager while John managed the works, the company was Starley & Sutton. In 1878 J.K.and J.M. Starley jointly patented a chaindrive to a wheel on

a single leg fork. The single fork idea had been used by James on boneshakers when he first became involved with cycle manufacture in 1868/9. The chaindrive was intended for the front drive to a tricycle and enjoyed some success but didn't start any fashion.

During the ensuing years J.K. undoubtedly tried many ideas, none of which made any great impact but by 1884 Starley & Sutton at their Meteor Works, West Orchard Coventry were well established offering five solo tricycles a sociable and four Ordinary bicycles including the Meteor Racers and Boys'

machines. Prices ranged from £22 for the best tricycle to £8 for a 36" front wheeled Boys' bicycle. But J.K. wasn't satisfied and during 1884 he worked away in his spare time building a Safety Bicycle. The front end was very much the same as an Ordinary but the backbone turned horizontal just below front wheel centre height, supported a crank and chainwheel, similar to the 1878 patent, then divided and formed the rear fork. The saddle and remote steering were somewhat flimsy affairs.

According to H.W. Bartleet, and he was seldom wrong in these matters, Stephen Golder a Coventry Pressman suggested that the forks be raked in much the same way that Likeman & Lawson had arranged their machines steering.

By September the Rover had been tidied-up even more and was produced in racing trim. Weight of 33½ lb. and geared to 60" were the general specifications but Golder had gearing of 66". On Saturday, September the 26th 1885 at 8.30am fourteen riders mounted on both roadster and racing Rovers started in The 100 miles road ride for "ROVER" Safety Bicycles. A last minute change of start and finish point was to prevent the police from interfering with the illegal road race. The actual start was at Norman Cross on The Great North Road, a favourite for sporting cyclists then and now, the finish was at Twyford.

Rover safety bicycle: 1885

## "ROVER" SAFETY BICYCLE 100 MILES ROAD RIDE, SATURDAY, SEPT. 26, 1885.

Course—London to Brighton and Shoreham and back
(subject to alteration).

Entrance fee, 2s. 6d. Amateurs only.

These points were many miles away from the advertised location of the race as can be seen in the accompanying notice from "The Cyclist" as late as 23rd September. So effective was this move to hoodwink the police, who took a dim view of road racing, that the race itself had virtually no spectators at all.

Stephen Golder was the favourite, but a broken saddle spring and a nasty fall caused him to fall behind. G. Smith of the Stoke Newington Harriers came up from third place at the fifty mile point to finish in 7 hrs. 17 mins. 3 secs. Hale who had been second at the halfway had fallen and spent 15 mins. at a blacksmiths having his machine repaired. So the Rover was well and truly established. To quote The Cyclist: - "The Rover has set the fashion to the world" and so it had. Within five years the G.O.O. (Grand Old Ordinary) was relegated to the back of cycle catalogues and by the early '90s was obsolete.

Although Rover continued to use curved tubes in their frames for many years the arrangement of steering, wheels, cranks etc. was copied by most manufacturers. Hillman, Herbert & Cooper offered an alternative in 1886 with their Cross Frame. This also was copied by most makers. By the early 1890s the bicycle design had settled down to the diamond pattern developed by Starley.

Since that time little has changed and with the exception of Dursley Pedersen and Moulton, frame design has remained much the same, only materials and equipment have been affected by fashion.

Regretfully, William Sutton didn't live to enjoy the success of their company, he was killed in a horse and trap accident shortly after the 100 mile race. In 1888 the company name was changed to J.K. Starley & Co., in 1896 to The Rover Cycle Co. Ltd., on 25th October 1905 to The Rover Co. Ltd., and after a decision at the June AGM of 1912 to The New Rover Cycle Co. Ltd. In December 1923 it reverted to The Rover Co. Ltd. Cycle production continued until 1925 when the AGM accepted a motion to discontinue cycle and motorcycle production to concentrate on cars.

Forty years of development had brought out many different models to suit all tastes and most pockets. The £30 Imperial with enclosed chain, hollow rims, dust-proof pedals, double-butted spokes, steering lock, bearings of special diamond cast steel, finished with heavy nickel plate on copper and best black enamel lined in two colours must have been the envy of all cyclists but beyond the reach of most people.

IMPERIAL ROVER ROADSTER

In the 1908 catalogue the fashion of a very basic and inexpensive machine was offered at only Six Guineas, this model is easily identified with its BLUE lining and leather (?) chaincase. The World War and subsequent inflation coupled with mass unemployment left its casualties amongst cycle makers and Rover was one of them. Fortunately their place in the motor industry was fairly well established and so the name was carried on.

In 1888 Starley tried his first motorised machine. He used the layout of the Coventry Chair, which had been introduced to their range in 1884. The human power was replaced by an electric motor driven by batteries and the steering was moved from the rear to the driver who was seated at the front.

Tests had to be carried out in France because of British controls; however the machine wasn't developed further. Had it been, it might have set another fashion to the world. No further attempts were made to enter the motorised field while J.K. was still alive.

However soon after his death, a Rover motorcycle was launched in 1903.

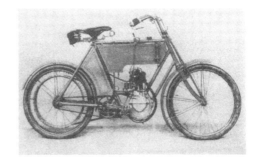

Further developments continued with a tri-car in 1905 and a T.T. car in 1906.

The shield shaped badge which had decorated the bicycles was built into the design of the radiator. The name Meteor which had been with the company from the very early days was used on the less expensive models (no Rover could be referred to as cheap) then dropped from the cycle range to be used later on the better Rover motorcars.

The Rover Company continued to produce motorcars but dropped the production of cycles and motorcycles in 1926. Various models of their range have continued to set Fashions, as in 1885 Rovers are to be found all over the world and are the foremost in the all terrain vehicle and luxury four wheel drive class.

Although Rovers no longer produce bicycles there are still designers in this country with new ideas. The Windcheetah from Burrows Engineering could well be the machine that will '*Set the Fashion to the World*' from 1985 onwards.

# THE ROUTE

**Saturday, 28th September**

**Start Marshalls, Peterborough. 9.00 a.m.**

**Norman Cross** Token stop to remember the Rovers in the 1885 Race.

**Glapthorn,** North of Oundle Coffee break.

**Sunday School Buildings, Rothwell Market Square**. Luncheon.

**Cold Ashby** Tea break.

**Dunchurch Lodge**, College of Management, Dunchurch. Overnight stop.

**Sunday, 29th September**

**Start Dunchurch Lodge. 9.00 a.m.**

**Museum of British Road Transport,** Coventry. Coffee break.

**National Motorcycle Museum**, Bickenhill. Luncheon.

**Museum of Science and Industry**, Newhall Street, Birmingham. Finish and tea.

## MACHINES AND RIDERS
## ROVER MACHINES WITH SOLID TYRES

1. 1885/6 Third Pattern similar to the Racing machine.    *Bob Jones*
2. 1886 Fourth pattern which lasted until the '90s    *Bill Haylor*
3. 1889 Ladies Dwarf Roadster. Loaned by Museum of Science and Industry, Birmingham.    *Bill Brookes*
4. 1890 Universal. Gents/Ladies. Loaned by British Motor Industry Heritage    *John Kemp Starley IV*
5. 1891 Ladies Model. Loaned by Bill Bush    *Dot Pinkerton*
6. 1891 Rational Tandem.  Ordinary front and chain driven rear. Loaned by Museum of Science & Industry Birmingham.    *Doug and John Pinkerton*
7. 1891 New Diamond.    *James Peatling*
8. 1891 New Diamond pattern.    *Hilary Stone*

## ROVER MACHINES WITH PNEUMATIC TYRES

9. 1893 Rover pattern.    *Vic Smith*
10. 1894 Giraffe.  Loaned by Museum of British Road Transport.    *Frank Turner*
11. 1896 Tandem.  Lady-front with coupled steering. Especially brought over from Holland.    *Martin Gerrits & Passenger*
12. 1900 Gentlemans model.    *James Kyrle-Pope*
13. 1900 Ladies Imperial double curved tube model. Loaned M.B.R.T.    *Val Elsden*
14. 1901 Ladies Meteor. Loaned SV-CC.    *Andrew Heaps*
15. 1902 Tandem Double Gents.    *Peter Keatley & Sue Couldry*
16. 1903 Imperial Path Racer.  Possibly used by T. Johnson in record breaking rides.    *R.M. Starley. Fifth generation*
17. 1905 Meteor No. 2.    *Martin Gee*
18. 1905 Imperial gents model.    *Tony Huntington*
19. 1906 Meteor Ladies model.    *Elsie Huntington*
20. 1910 Rover Ladies model. Loaned Brian March.    *Miss Suzie Huntington*
21. 1908 Ladies model. Loaned B.M.I.H.    *Pat Collins*
22. 1909 Gents model. Loaned by Peter Shirtcliffe.    *John Coleman-Smith*
23. 1909 Rover Gents model.  Loaned by B.M.I.H.    *Paul Evans*
24. 1910 Special Three Speed model.  Loaned by M.B R.T.    *Andrew Millward*
25. 1910 Special Three Speed Ladies model.    *Alison Millward*
26. 1910 Meteor.    *John Barrett*
27. 1910 Rover.Loaned by M.B. R.T.    *Simon Antill*
28. 1912 Royal Irish Constabulary model. 30" frame. The first year this strengthened frame was offered.    *Mike Knight*
29. 1912 Rover Racing machine. Loaned by M.B.R.T.    *Malcolm Young*
30. 1914 Rover model.    *Keith Hannan*

| 31. 1914 Rover Gents model. | Mike Couldry |
| 32. 1915 Imperial with the new domed front forks. | John Hill |
| 33. 1915 Rover Gents model. | Gerry G. Gibbons |
| 34. 1916 Imperial Ladies model. | Hilary Brown |

## SOLID TYRED SAFETYS

**Diamond Frames.** These followed the Rover pattern.

35. 1887 Premier by Hillman Herbert & Cooper.
Loaned A. Twycross. *Brian March*
36. 1888 Singer Appollo. *Graham Garfield*
37. 1890 Diamond Frame. *Les Bowerman*
38. 1890 Diamond Frame of unknown origin. *Tony Colegrave*
39. 1890 Diamond Frame. Similar to Dad's but unknown make.
*Andrew Colegrave*
40. 1890 Rudge Tandem Quadricycle. Lady front rear steered.
Loaned C.T.C. *Derek & Sue Duxbury*
41. 1893 Hercules. Cushion tyred. *John Elsden*
42. 1895 Vinco of Peterborough. *Colin Hilliam*

**Cross Frames.** The alternative to the Rover pattern.

43. 1890 Hillman Herbert & Cooper. The designers of this type.
*Lesley Calder*
44. 1888 F.G. model S.T.S. probably French. *John D. Ivins*
45. 1889 Singer Semi-diamond frame. *Alex Brown*
46. 1890 Baylis Thomas. *Loren Hufstetler*
47. 1890 Juvenile cross-frame. *Miss Melanie Colegrave*
48.to52. Machines of unknown make.
*Margaret Smith, Mike Christy, Pam Colegrave,*
*Tony Lane & Tony Whitehead*

## THE BICYCLE OF THE FUTURE ???

Will this set the fashion to the world as the Rover did 100 years ago???

53. 1985 Windcheetah. Carbonfibre Monocoque. *Mike Burrows*

## ROVER MOTORCYCLES

54. 1913 Rover Racing machine. *Eric Lunn*

## ROVER MOTORCARS

55. 1912 Clegg Van. In constant use until 1962.
Carrying the riders' overnight baggage. *Geoff & Vivienne Ryder*
56. 1937 Rover 16 Sports Saloon. Our backup/mechanical
aid vehicle. *Bernard Gee*

# SOUTHERN VETERAN-CYCLE CLUB

(Founded 25th June 1955)

Organisers of the first annual veteran-cycle run.

Publishers of the first veteran-cycle magazine.

The club caters for all those interested in rescuing, restoring and riding old cycles and also for those who prefer reading, researching and recording information about cycles and cycle history.

This special Commemorative Ride has been organised by the Midland Section of the S.V.-C.C. which organises a varied programme throughout the year to suit anyone interested in historic cycles. This includes a monthly social meeting and regular cycling events, ranging from short runs to the more strenuous 50 mile ride.

*The word "Southern" was dropped from the club's name in 1987 to more accurately represent this International Club which has members world-wide, produces ten publications each year and has a very extensive reference library.*

For further information about the club contact

G. Pain, 31 Yorke Road, Croxley Green, Rickmansworth WD3 3DW.

# TRADE MARKS REGISTERED

Besides the cycle hea- badges that we illustrated earlier, J K Starley, Starley and Sutton and The Rover Cycle Company registered at least six other Trade Marks between 26th January 1881 and August 1898, most of which do not appear to have been used to any extent.

*John Kemp Starley, of and on behalf of the Firm of Starley and Sutton, Meteor Works, Coventry, Warwickshire; Bicycle and Tricycle Manufacturers.*
*Tricycle Application number 25,584, 26th Jan. 1881*

**REMORA**

*John Kemp Starley, The Meteor Works, Coventry, Warwickshire; Machinist.*
*Rubber Cement. No. 53,591, 8th Mar. 1886.*

*Starley and Sutton, Meteor Works, Coventry; Velocipede and Carriage Manufacturers.*
*Velocipeds generally, and Wheeled Carriages. No. 77,782, 27th July 1888.*

*J. K. Starley and Company, Meteor Works, Coventry; Velocipede Manufacturer. Velocipedes, i.e., Bicycles and tricycles. No 80,663, 27th Sept. 1888.*

# BUNI

*John Kemp Starley, The Meteor Works, Coventry, Warwickshire; Manufacturer. Velocipedes. No 156,954, 11th June 1891.*

# THE METEOR

*The Rover Cycle Company, Limited, Cycle Works, West orchard, Coventry; Cycle Manufacturers. No. 209,737, 2nd December 1897.*

*The Rover Cycle Company, Limited, Cycle Works, West Orchard, Coventry; Cycle Manufacturers. Cycles. No. 216,247, 11th August 1898.*

*Right: Rover Cycles. An Everest Product.*
*This sign was manufactured by Sun Enamel, no*
*origins,*

*Above: Crest detail from the sign.*
*We have no knowledge of Everest in connection*
*with Rover Cycles. Any information would be*
*most welcome.*

# APPENDIX 4
# THE FAMILY TREE OF JOHN KEMP STARLEY

### John Kemp Starley
Rover Tricycle 1884 and cycles 1885 onwards.

|

### J. K. Starley II
Rover sales. Recognised need for economical ligh-car to compete with Ford Company. When the Company did not agree, he resigned and set up an insurance company.

|

### J. K. Starley III
Rover car until father left. Continued in motor trade in nearby Leamington Spa.

|

### J. K. Starley IV
Royal Navy career. Set up as electrical/mechanical engineering designer.

|

### J. K. Starley V
Computer aided design consultant.
Like his great-grandfather, is at the cutting edge of this field.

|

### J. K. Starley VI
Born January 1985, 100 years after Rover safety bicycle. Makes radio controlled cars.

# ACKNOWLEDGEMENTS

Gillian Bardsley
Les Bowerman
Alex Brown (Scotland)
Anders Clausager
Mike Couldry
Alister Dodds (Scotland)
Ian Elliot
Bob French
Martin Gerrits (Holland)
Tony Hadland
Andrew Heaps (France)
Hawick Museum
Harry Hilgerdenaar (The Netherlands)
Elsie Huntington
'J D' Ivins
Bob Jones
Mike Knight
Arnold C Lamb
John Liffen
John Malseed
Mark Hall Museum, Harlow
Museum of British Road Transport, Coventry
Museum of Irish Transport, Killarney (Ireland)

Museum of Science and Industry, Birmingham
Geoff Kent
Ron Miller (Canada)
Andrew Millward, PhD
Peter Mitchell, OBE
Nicholas Oddy (Scotland)
F Parkinson-Bates
Rod Safe
Lesley Sayers
Denis Shone
Margaret and Vic Smith
John Spong (Wales)
J K Starley IV
J K Starley V
Hilary Stone
Catherine Strung (Aurora, Ontario, Canada)
David Thirlby (VSCC)
John Thomas, (California)
Ron Thompson (South Africa)
Jiri Uhlia (Czech Republic)
Colin Wagner (Australia)
Dave Westwood

## Photographs and other material

British Motor Industry Heritage Trust Gaydon for use of original material from their Archive

Page 9 upper ©1998 The Trustees of the National Museums of Scotland.

Pages 9 lower, 260 and 261 upper The McGrory Collection © Argyll & Bute Libraries and Trustees of the National Museums of Scotland.

Inside front cover, pages 258 and 259, Courtesy of Hawick Museum Archive Collection.

Other photos not specifically credited by Sue Couldrey, Martin Gerrits, Mike Hessey, Bob Jones, Ron Miller and John Wood